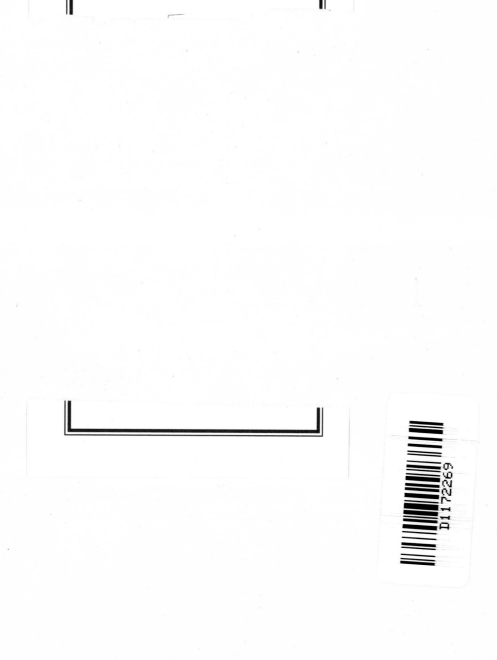

# NEOCLASSICISM IN POLAND

History of Art in Poland

Stanisław Lorentz, Andrzej Rottermund

# NEOCLASSICISM IN POLAND

Arkady · Warsaw

Original title:
"Klasycyzm w Polsce"

Translated by Jerzy Bałdyga

Graphic design
Henryk Białoskórski

Editor
Aleksandra Czeszunist-Cicha

Editor of English version
Monika Krajewska

Technical editors
Magdalena Kosewska, Zbigniew Weiss

# Contents

# Introduction

The term "classical" is used to denote works of art from a variety of periods and styles. Harmony, symmetry and rhythm, so strongly interrelated that they evoke an impression of order, balance, calm and dignity, are given as the characteristic features of classical art. Classical art is understood to be an art which is static, clear and lucid; which is linear rather than painterly; which operates with simple forms; and which is modest in decoration. Classical art is said to follow rules and instructions; to be full of rationalism, moderation and on a human scale. In different periods, to a greater or lesser extent, classical revivals have been inspired by the art of ancient Greece and Rome. Those who have supported classical art have thought it perfect.

The theory of classicism was formulated in the second half of the 17th century by the Roman connoisseur of antiquity Bellori, a representative of St. Luke's Academy. His cult of Raphael and his conviction that after a period of decline the Carracci had reinstated respect for the rules of art and its strict order, were taken over by the later theoreticians and supporters of classicism. In the last third of the 18th century the aesthetic theory of the arts shared and advocated the view that there was only one art, that some of its forms were perfect, that the forms were absolute and eternal: that Nature had given patterns and Reason could find in them immutable rules. Since the declaration of Johann Joachim Winckelmann in the middle of the 18th century it is above all Greek art, characterized by its "noble simplicity and sedate grandeur", that has been considered classical. This view was expressed in the aesthetic writings in the second half of the 18th century and the first half of the 19th century, which claimed that Greek art was Nature intensified to an ideal, that to follow Nature meant almost the same as to follow the Greeks, and that to follow the Greeks meant to create as they had, rather than to imitate.

In different periods classical and neoclassical art took on a great variety of forms. The 5th century B.C. was regarded as the classical period in the art of Greece; classical art was sometimes understood to have covered both Greek and Roman art. Renaissance art, and specifically the art of the first quarter of the 16th century, was defined as classical. The classical trend in baroque architecture in the 17th and 18th century was introduced by the Italian architect Andrea Palladio, who worked from 1540 to 1580, and hence it was called Palladianism. For the French, the classical period in their art was that in the second half of the 17th century.

In the middle of the 18th century a new neoclassical movement began to form. It gradually spread to the culturally leading countries of Europe and to North America. Changes in political, social, economic and intellectual life, and above all the French rationalism and the development of physical and natural sciences and humanities, affected the formation and development of this new trend. There was an increase in interest in the art of ancient Rome, manifested by, among other things, archaeological excavations, most notably those in Herculaneum and Pompeii. In time, this interest spread to include Greece. Art theory and history developed, mainly due to the works of Winckelmann, who laid the foundations for modern research on ancient art. There was a distinct turn to the art of the Renaissance, particularly to the painting of Raphael, and the Palladian style became widespread in architecture.

The arts reflected the Enlightenment philosophy, which set itself practical aims, endeavoured to improve thought and life, and advocated the gaining of knowledge for the enlightenment of minds and liberation from superstitions, ignorance and belief in the supernatural. The

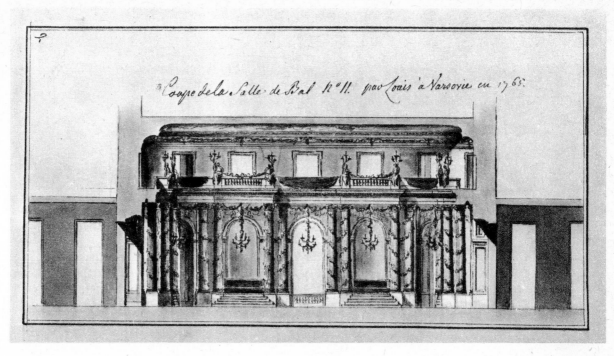

Warsaw, Royal Castle, draft design of the Ballroom, V. Louis, 1765

"enlightened" free-thinking philosopher, who verified everything with his reason, supported social reforms and universal education. Secular architecture now developed to a greater extent than ecclesiastical as a result of new needs, novel types of buildings arose to serve the needs of the economy, rapidly developing towns, science and education. The didactic and educational tasks required of painting and graphic arts caused particular attention to be paid to the themes and contents of paintings, drawings and engravings. This favoured the development of allegoric, history and genre painting.

In the second half of the 18th century, Italy began to attract artists and admirers of art as a centre of studies on ancient culture and art carried out by archaeologists, and as the scene of excavations and the country of Palladio. But only the sculptor Antonio Canova achieved world fame in the arts.

France was then the main centre of European art. The trip to Italy in 1749–1751 made by the Marquis de Marigny, the director of Royal Buildings, accompanied by Cochin and Soufflot, constituted a turning point towards neoclassicism. In the period of early neoclassicism, 1750–1760, Jacques Ange Gabriel was the leading architect. Soufflot, the author of St. Genevieve's Church in Paris, which was later transformed into the Pantheon, is considered the most outstanding representative of mature neoclassicism. In the last years of the 18th century, the avant-garde style was represented by Claude Nicolas Ledoux. Jacques Louis David, whose paintings (e.g. the "Oath of the Horatii" of 1784) exerted a great influence on the development of artistic culture at the turn of the 18th and 19th centuries, was the most outstanding personality in painting. Jean Antoine Houdon was the most famous sculptor. The impact of France on the development of neoclassical art and the artistic culture of the Enlightenment was so strong that the name "French Europe" has been adopted for this period. The French neoclassicism of the second half of the 18th century has been called the style of Louis XVI, although it also covered the second half of the reign of Louis XV.

In Great Britain, neoclassical art developed in a different manner. The century or so between 1714 and 1820 is treated as one period, called Georgian, from the names of the three kings: George I, George II and George III, who reigned at that time. In the second part of the 18th century, there arose a different version of neoclassicism, created by two brothers, architects

Warsaw, Royal Castle, draft design for reconstruction, J. Fontana, 1772

named Adam, and hence called the Adams' style. Great Britain contributed greatly to the development of neoclassicism, and its effect on the artistic culture of Europe in the last thirty years of the 18th century included not only architecture and architectural decoration, but also painting, garden architecture, artistic gardening and fashion in dress.

In Russia, the neoclassical trend in the arts began in the middle of the 18th century and developed mainly in St. Petersburg and Moscow and the surrounding areas, reaching in the first half of the 19th century a great monumentalism of design in planning, architecture and gardening. In Sweden, the individuality of its own version of neoclassicism was expressed in the name of the style: Gustaviansk, after the King. In the United States of America, the neoclassical style, called Colonial (since the style was formed still under the British colonial rule), spread very widely and was considered the national style, as a result of the fact that the first public buildings were executed in it.

In the second half of the 18th century neoclassicism spread as a style to almost the whole of Europe. Although it derived from the same sources and was based on the same theoretical premises, it took different forms in different countries.

In Poland, neoclassical art developed between about 1760 and 1830 – these time limits have most frequently been accepted. Over that long period of 70 years, Poland went through fundamental political, social, economic and cultural changes, while the arts underwent continuous evolution. The art which developed under the Polish state before the loss of independence after the third partition of Poland in 1795, and was linked with the Polish Enlightenment, has been distinguished as the first period. The next period covered the art between 1795 and 1807, when there was no centre of Polish rule, nor state patronage in the arts. The beginnings of a new cultural policy can be discerned in the period of the Duchy of Warsaw, in 1807–1815. Neoclassical art was expressed in new forms at the time of the Kingdom of Poland, between 1815 and 1831, when state patronage was active on a large scale.

8

The most important years in the history of Polish neoclassicism came in the periods of the Enlightenment and the Kingdom of Poland (1815–1831).

In the art of the Polish Enlightenment two periods can be discerned: one between 1760 and 1780 and the other between 1780 and 1795. Another division has also been proposed: namely, 1760–1775, 1775–1789 and 1789–1795. The last period has been distinguished because of the themes of independence, patriotism and revolution at the time of the Four-Year Parliament and the Kościuszko Insurrection. It has also been proposed that the year 1800 should be taken as the final date, in view of the traditions of the intellectual and artistic trends of the Enlightenment, which were also continued after the loss of independence. This view does not seem to be justified, since the loss of independence was doubtless of extreme significance. A successful development of culture in a great number of fundamental fields, including planning and public architecture, was broken. There was no longer court patronage, which had gradually been taking on the features of state patronage. Warsaw, the main centre of political and intellectual life in the Enlightenment, was degraded to the rank of a provincial town. Certainly, the cultural traditions of the Enlightenment persisted, not only until 1800, however, but much longer, as in some fields they extended as late as the time of the Kingdom of Poland. This connection was consolidated by artists who were educated and created in the 18th century and who were active until the twenties of the 19th century.

Over the last decades there has been frequent reference to the Enlightenment art. This term is, however, not equivalent to the "neoclassicism of the Age of Enlightenment", since the term "Enlightenment art" covers all art productions, a variety of trends and not only neoclassicism. Of these trends, a few can be distinguished. The intellectual life of the Enlightenment had room for rationalism, sentimentalism and romanticism; in the arts, apart from the decadent baroque and rococo forms, there were parallel developments in the various versions of the neoclassical trend, in the sentimental trend, and in the romanticist one, in which exotic and neo-gothic currents could be distinguished. Neoclassicism was the leading trend, particularly in architecture; it had baroque and rococo versions; it could be Palladian, antiquating and also avant-garde. In turn, in the art of gardening, which in 1770–1831 played such an important role in the artistic culture of the country, the leading trend was related to landscape, so-called English, gardening, with sentimental and romanticist overtones. In the architecture of the first thirty years of the 19th century, neoclassical trends also dominated; monumental forms arose, particularly in some versions of public building. In those years the pseudo-classical trend was accompanied by the increasingly strong pseudo-gothic current.

The present book is concerned with neoclassical art, but this does not signify that an attempt is made here to distinguish it artificially from the whole of the artistic events of the epoch. It is impossible to separate the landscape garden, with its numerous neoclassical pavilions, from the neoclassical palace. It is impossible to distinguish with complete accuracy between that which in painting and sculpture is neoclassical and that which is an echo of the baroque or rococo, or that which is so conventional that it is sometimes called academic. Therefore, the title of this book should be understood more broadly, as referring to both neoclassicism proper and related developments.

Warsaw, Solec Garden, draft design of an artificial ruin and wooden mill, S.B. Zug, c. 1772

# The Sources, Beginnings and Main Trends of the Art of the Polish Enlightenment

New trends in the art of the mid-18th century reached Poland by various routes. It seems that they first came from France, brought by magnate patrons, who had even earlier maintained direct contacts with France. The great Polish magnates, such as Czartoryski or Branicki, brought from Paris not only architectural designs, but also specially ordered panelling, furniture, textiles and products of artistic industry. The contacts with France were of a permanent nature and, since Paris was the main centre of the thought and art of the Enlightenment, it influenced Poland directly. The more forward-thinking magnates, who were greatly interested in the philosophy and writings of the Enlightenment, were well versed in the theoretical considerations which gave shape to new aesthetic views. But essential influence on the development of the arts was not exerted by aesthetic theory, but rather by aesthetic practice, particularly by discussions and commentaries contained in engraved publications devoted to ancient monuments, architecture, great collections, outstanding artists and works of art.

There is reliable evidence that new neoclassical trends began to occur in Poland about 1760, before Stanislas Augustus Poniatowski came to the throne. This evidence includes designs of the French architect Charles Pierre Coustou, who stayed in Poland from 1760 to 1762, probably at the invitation of Izabela Lubomirska, née Czartoryska. His design of the small palace at Jordanowice near Grodzisk in the area of Warsaw, which is dated at 1761, was an example of early French neoclassical architecture, of the version called the Gabriel style. The close contacts between the owner of Jordanowice, Andrzej Mokronowski, and the Branicki family from Białystok permit the supposition that the latter showed an early interest in the new trends in the arts; this is all the more probable as the commander-in-chief of the army, Branicki, had personal political ties with France.

In the same years distinct signs of the new trends could be seen in the work of the Warsaw architect Efraim Szreger, particularly in his design, from the turn of 1761 and 1762, of the façade of the Church of Discalced Carmelites in Krakowskie Przedmieście Street in Warsaw. It was an interesting, individual work, which combined in an original way baroque and neoclassical elements. It can also be assumed from other works of Szreger that he used in design various engraved French publications, including *Architecture française* by N.F. Blondel and *Recueil d'architecture* by J.F. Neufforge. In the façade of the Carmelites' Church there could be discerned some reverberations of the Gabriel style in the palaces in the

Place de la Concorde in Paris; as a whole, however, it was a creative and outstanding design, perhaps the most interesting example of how the neoclassical style took shape in Poland at the beginning of the Age of Enlightenment.

In 1761, Szreger began the reconstruction of Gniezno Cathedral, following a great fire. This reconstruction was expected to include the plastering of the façade and towers, "reforming" of the cornices and the most beautiful decoration of the façade and towers, "to the taste of the contemporary age". In 1766 work was finished on the construction of the great altar, designed by Szreger, with marbled columnar architecture, which was distinctly neoclassical. In the early sixties, Szreger gave neoclassical features to still another building, the palace at Skierniewice, which was rebuilt, at the order of Primate Łubieński, between 1761–1765.

The designs of Coustou and Szreger mentioned above indicate that it would be wrong to identify the beginnings of neoclassicism in Poland, as some scholars have done, with the accession to the throne of King Stanislas Augustus Poniatowski, despite his enormous role in the formation of Polish neoclassical art.

Everything that in 1760–1780 showed symptoms of a new taste in the arts, constituting a new stage in artistic evolution, all that indicated interest in the new views and arose under royal, magnate, gentry, burgher or ecclesiastic patronage, should justly be included in the artistic culture of the Age of Enlightenment in Poland, and – whether it showed signs of the antiquating, Palladian or neoclassical trends from the Renaissance, the 17th or 18th centuries – be called early neoclassical art. These trends of the Enlightenment art came about 1760–1780.

The interest in ancient art and artistic culture, which was so important a factor in the process of the formation of neoclassical trends in European arts from the middle of the 18th century, became distinct in Poland about 1760. It was first manifested in archaeological interests, which in time extended to collecting. At that time there were imports of 17th- and 18th-century engraved publications, which illustrated Roman antiquities, particularly the excavations at Herculaneum and Pompeii. Many libraries had large sets of Giambattista

Warsaw, Royal Castle, draft design for reconstruction and novel shaping of the Castle square, E. Szreger, 1777

Piranesi's engravings and the royal library had some dozens of volumes of them. Perhaps, it was the *Vedute di Roma* by Piranesi contained in the King's collection that Canaletto used in 1769 to paint for the King fourteen views of ancient and papal Rome, where most of the ancient motifs were derived from the above publication. The libraries of Polish patrons included *Athenian Antiquities* by Stuart-Revett as well as *The Ruins of Baalbek* and *The Ruins of Palmyra* by Wood.

In Rome, in the circles of admirers of antiquity, great popularity was enjoyed by Franciszek Smuglewicz, who, over his twenty-year stay there, made a large number of water colours and drawings of ancient monuments. We can mention at least ten Polish architects who studied the buildings of ancient Rome and their decoration on the spot. In the late seventies, Stanisław Kostka Potocki, the first Polish archaeologist, who was the precursor of Polish studies on ancient art, began work on classical art, and later excavations. His activity in this field was crowned with his four-volume work *The Ancient Art, that is Polish Winckelmann*, published in 1815. The popularity in Poland of antiquating, arabesque-grotesque interior decoration was affected by the decoration of the Golden House of Nero in Rome, engraved by Smuglewicz and published in 1776 in the well-known publication, erroneously called *Titus' Hot-Baths*, and by the magnificent water colour reconstructions of the villa of Pliny the Younger, made under the supervision of Stanisław Kostka Potocki. In the last quarter of the 18th century in Poland antiquating arabesque-grotesque ornamentation decorated tens, or perhaps hundreds, of interiors. There were many versions, including sometimes motifs from Raphael's Logge and the decoration of the Wedgwood ceramics from England.

Palace interiors were sometimes decorated with elements such as antique, so-called Etruscan, vases and their imitations, ancient sculptures and goldsmith's works, and also their copies and imitations. A special gallery of the Łańcut Castle provided the most magnificent housing for the collection of ancient sculpture owned by the Marshal's wife, Izabela Lubomirska. A large collection of ancient sculptures, collected by Helena Radziwiłł, was in the Arkadia at Nieborów.

Monumental architecture has been justly said to have included as the most outstanding specimens of the antiquating trend the façade of Vilna Cathedral and the façade of the Vilna Town Hall, designed and built by Wawrzyniec Gucewicz. In Warsaw, the best example of this trend was the Evangelical Church designed by Szymon Bogumił Zug; the idea, derived from the Roman Pantheon, was creatively transposed by this Warsaw architect. The trend in question included the designs of the Temple of Divine Providence, which had clear links with ancient architecture. (Certainly, one should not suppose that such architecture was deemed best to satisfy the needs of religious worship; since it was the architects and patrons, and not the church authorities, that decided). An outstanding work of the antiquating trend was the amphitheatre in the Łazienki Park, in addition to which it is necessary to mention a building which provided a symbolic closure to the Age of Enlightenment in Poland: the Sybil's Temple at Puławy, a museum in the nature of a mausoleum of national remembrance, patterned after the Sybil's Temple at Tivoli.

In the Polish art of the Age of Enlightenment the antiquating trend found expression in different forms, not only in architecture, but also in painting, sculpture and the decorative arts, in park pavilions and artificial ruins, in sarcophagi and a variety of other park motifs. It came to Poland directly from Italy, brought over by patrons and artists, also by way of Palladio's architecture and English architecture.

The late Renaissance architecture of Palladio, with elements and motifs defined as mannerist, exerted important influence on the formation of English neoclassicism in the 18th century, inspired architects in various countries and had such a major effect in Poland that one of the trends in the architecture of the last quarter of the 18th century is called here Palladian. And since some ideas of Palladio had been derived from the Vitruvius treatise, it can be assumed that it was by this route that ancient architecture affected the process of the development of neoclassical architecture in the 18th century; this would be parallel to the role of Raphael and his contemporaries in the field of decorative painting.

The Palladian trend in Poland was most fully represented by Stanisław Kostka Potocki and the architect Piotr Aigner. Their joint work was a church façade, unique in Poland, designed on the basis of Venetian church façades, above all San Giorgio Maggiore. This was the façade of the Bernardine church of St. Anne in Krakowskie Przedmieście Street in Warsaw, built between 1786 and 1788.

Palladio's famous Villa Rotonda, a central domed palace with pillared porticoes, inspired a few unbuilt designs, including one by Zug. This villa, as a distant stereotype, can be related to two buildings in Poland: the palace designed by Domenico Merlini at Królikarnia in Warsaw (1786–1789) and that by Stanisław Zawadzki at Lubostroń (1800).

These are single examples. Palladianism in Polish neoclassical architecture brings to mind above all those palace designs where the main part of the palace was linked to its wings with galleries, most frequently semi-circular, elliptic at times, the shape of a horseshoe, refracted at right angles and even straight lines. Palladio's galleries had been pillared, in Poland some would be arcaded, taking the character of a refracted palace wing or, in the most modest executions, reduced to a refracted wall.

This type of Palladian palace design occurred in Poland in the seventies and achieved great popularity, soon spreading all over the territory of the former Commonwealth, from Great Poland to Volhynia and Podolia. We know more than forty such palace complexes dating from the last quarter of the 18th century, and most certainly there were more. The Palladian type thus became characteristic of the architecture of the mature Polish neoclassicism of the Age of Enlightenment. To this may have contributed the representational, monumentalised appearance of the residences, corresponding to magnate and noblemen's ambitions, but utilitarian reasons were also of some significance. As in England, there was here convenient communication with annexes, where kitchens and other service rooms were located, where clerks and poor relations would live and where guests would stay.

Warsaw, Royal Castle, draft design for reconstruction and expansion, D. Merlini, 1773

Apart from England, where most of these palace designs appeared, one should mention Poland, then Russia, and to a lesser extent Bohemia, Germany and Italy. Refraining from any analysis of the properties of the various Palladian types of palace design, the most outstanding examples of it can be given here; namely, in the seventies, the Primate's Palace in Warsaw, the palaces at Kock and Siedlce; in the eighties, the palaces at Tulczyn, Rogalin, Mała Wieś and Walewice, and, in the nineties, the palaces at Białaczów and Śmiełów. The Palladian principles were followed by various architects. Most of them were executed in the eastern territory of the previous Commonwealth.

In the late seventies, in the work of two architects, Szreger and Zug, there could be discerned trends which are now called avant-garde. In Poland, they were equivalent to a trend in French architecture which has also been called revolutionary, whose leading representative was the architect Ledoux. The avant-garde trend in 18th-century neoclassical architecture indicated a new, creative attitude of architects. The conception of buildings was based on a juxtaposition of basic geometrical solids, either interpenetrating or combined. This was the fundamental feature of the 18th-century avant-garde architecture. It was accompanied by other features, but these were already common to the avant-garde and antiquating architecture in its later stage. These features were the austerity of harmonious compositions, the reduction of decoration to a minimum, the rustication of surfaces and a predilection for the Doric order, most frequently in its Tuscan variety. All these features were characteristic of the later stage of antiquating neoclassicism and were concurrent with the avant-garde trend. What was essential in the avant-garde trend was experimentation, expressed above all in the juxtaposition of the simplest geometrical solids.

In the seventies, Zug was a true avant-garde architect. This was indicated by his designs of garden pavilions, composed of cubes and cylinders, striking with the expression of their geometrical structure and by his truly magnificent work, the Evangelical Church in Warsaw, where, while making reference to the ancient building type, so many novel solutions were introduced. In Zug's work certain avant-garde features could also be discerned in the shaping of some public buildings. An outstanding avant-garde work was the church at Skierniewice designed by Szreger: a domed rotunda with ring-shaped horizontal divisions – among multilateral blocs; the whole structure being contained between the façade and the tower. And in the eighties, avant-garde tendencies became distinct in the work of yet another architect – Jan Chrystian Kamsetzer – in the design of the sepulchral chapel of the Poniatowski family, 1784, and in the façade of the church at Petrykozy, 1791, composed of geometrical blocks.

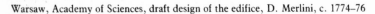

Warsaw, Academy of Sciences, draft design of the edifice, D. Merlini, c. 1774–76

Warsaw, draft design of the National Theatre, S.B. Zug, c. 1776

# The Stanislas Augustus Style and His Cultural Patronage

King Stanislas Augustus Poniatowski played an outstanding role in the history of Polish culture in the second half of the 18th century. A typical man of the Enlightenment, highly educated, a supporter of French culture, but at the same time of the English political system, an admirer of Voltaire and Shakespeare, promotor of political and social reforms, he supported the development of sciences and created around him a court of artists. He imported foreign artists and used the services of those who had settled in Poland, also those passing through, but nevertheless he consciously worked towards the formation of Polish art and contributed to the education of artists of Polish nationality. He gathered large valuable art collections, as he was a true admirer of art, but he also thought that these collections should be open to the public.

The significance of the presence in Warsaw of the King's court of artists in the years when the independence of Poland was threatened may be realized by referring to the previous state. Under the reign of the two Saxon kings, Dresden was the true cultural capital of the governing dynasts and Warsaw was regarded as a residence of secondary importance. It was in Dresden that the most outstanding artists who worked for the King and the magnates related to the court gathered, and it was as if on tour that they came to Warsaw. In Poland, there were many outstanding and minor Dresden artists and builders, while Warsaw and the whole of Poland was overrun by Saxon craftsmen: stucco workers, stone cutters, painters, carpenters, tinsmiths and glaziers. If French or Italian artists – as earlier Zacharias Longuelune and Louis

Głosków, draft design of a villa for Piotr Tepper Sr., S.B. Zug, c. 1775–80

Silvestre the Younger or later Francesco Placidi and Marcello Bacciarelli – came they usually arrived via Dresden, in passing, or when Saxony was at war. In Dresden, magnificent works of art were collected and the famous painting gallery established.

When Stanislas Augustus came to the throne the royal court became again one of the centres of Polish culture, indeed undoubtedly the main one. The cultural patronage of Stanislas Augustus was supposed to satisfy the personal needs of the ruler and of the royal court, but it also had broader significance. This patronage had an enormously larger range than that of the magnates; it covered planning, architecture, sculpture, painting, applied arts and art collection, at the heart of which was the great painting gallery. The royal sponsorship had the features of state patronage. This could be seen above all in the care for the development of national art, involving attempts to create a group of Polish artists and to improve their skills. From the early years of his rule the King granted fellowships to Polish artists abroad and encouraged their visits to European centres of culture. Such a fellowship was given to Franciszek Smuglewicz, who spent 20 years in Rome; some royal assistance was granted to Szreger when he left for Italy and France in 1766–1767; Aleksander Kucharski and Anna Rajecka were on a fellowship in France. In turn, Kamsetzer was sent east to Turkey, i.e. to the old Greek territory, and later to Italy and France.

At home, artists were to be educated at the Academy of Fine Arts. As early as 1766, Marcello Bacciarelli was the first to draft a project of the Academy and in subsequent years new plans were proposed by Michał Jerzy Mniszech and August Moszyński. Like many other useful ideas of the King, this was never put into effect. To some extent, the role of an educational centre was played by Bacciarelli's painting studio and the sculpture studios at the Castle. The idea of establishing the Academy of Fine Arts was not an isolated enterprise. In 1773–1775 it was proposed that an Academy of Sciences should be formed in Warsaw; in 1775 Mniszech published his project for the Museum Polonicum which would have served scientific purposes, and the idea of founding scientific institutions, both central and local, gained more and more supporters. All these proposals doubtless involved the conviction that sciences and arts could be of assistance in sustaining the national identity. To a large degree, this also

16

caused the problem of the Polish language to recur as one of the major issues in the Polish Enlightenment, as expressed in the words: "While there is the (Polish) language, there is the name of Poland".

Władysław Tatarkiewicz was the first to discern the singular nature of the art sponsored by Stanislas Augustus, proposing in 1916 in a booklet on the Łazienki Palace and Park, that the notion of a Stanislas Augustus style should be introduced. Whereas similar terms, particularly the "style of Louis XVI", do not signify any more than the duration of the individual reign, since the latter king never affected the shape of artistic events, nor the development of the arts, the term "the Stanislas Augustus style" has a different meaning. It defines the art to which the King made not only a financial but also a personal and most direct contribution. This art therefore did not include all that was created in the arts in 1764–1795, but only what was produced for the King, at his request or under the influence of the court arts. The meaning of "the Stanislas Augustus style" can be further restricted by defining it as only that art sponsored by the King which had its own style, one that had not been borrowed and was not to be seen elsewhere. In his later studies, Tatarkiewicz formulated precisely which art, in his view, could be covered by the royal name. Thus, this term would exclude the earlier period, even the White Pavilion and Myślewice within the Łazienki Park, and also the work performed at the Royal Castle in the seventies. "This Stanislas Augustus art strictissimo sensu – Tatarkiewicz wrote – did not begin until 1783: with the Assembly Hall at the Castle and the southern façade of the Łazienki Palace". It was only in those years, according to Tatarkiewicz, that the specific Stanislas Augustus art, his own style, arose.

This view does not seem to be correct. It is possible to agree that the Stanislas Augustus style should only include those phenomena which were neoclassical. The Chinese paintings of Pillement at the Royal Castle and the early interiors by Szreger at Ujazdów Castle were certainly rococo echoes in the arts of the early period of the King's reign. But all the designs of Fontana and Louis, as early as 1765 and subsequently, doubtless represented a new classical revival in the arts. And the interest of Stanislas Augustus in ancient art dated from before his accession to the throne. It is possible to define very precisely the beginnings of the formation of the style which can justly be given the name of Stanislas Augustus. They came at a time when he was certain to come to the throne and when he had made his first attempts to reconstruct the Royal Castle which was to be his residence. The Stanislas Augustus style evolved continuously and the present author does not think that strict periods can be distinguished within it, since this art developed in a rather fluid fashion. If one, however, tried to discern some stages of it, there would perhaps be three. The first would include the years 1764–1773, when Jakub Fontana was the chief architect and Victor Louis played a very important role. In those years Stanislas Augustus created his court of artists. Some of the artists who came to Warsaw left it after a short stay, others – like Bacciarelli, Canaletto and Le Brun – remained forever. The sensitivity of the King to the different versions occurring in French neoclassicism at that time was indicated by his interest in the trend called *goût grecque.*

The second stage would cover approximately the ten years between 1774 and 1783: the activity of Merlini at the Castle, the complex of new interiors at the Łazienki Park – the White Pavilion. The third, in turn, would consist of the last ten years of Stanislas Augustus' reign, including the Throne Room and the Knights' Hall at the Castle, the great historical paintings of Bacciarelli; at Łazienki, the alterations of 1784, 1788 and the subsequent years. At this stage, Kamsetzer was working together with Merlini.

The Stanislas Augustus style was one of the versions of neoclassicism; it drew on many sources, but was mainly inspired by French art. The King's taste was rather moderate, very typical of the 18th century and indifferent to avant-garde tendencies. Over the 30 years, the

17

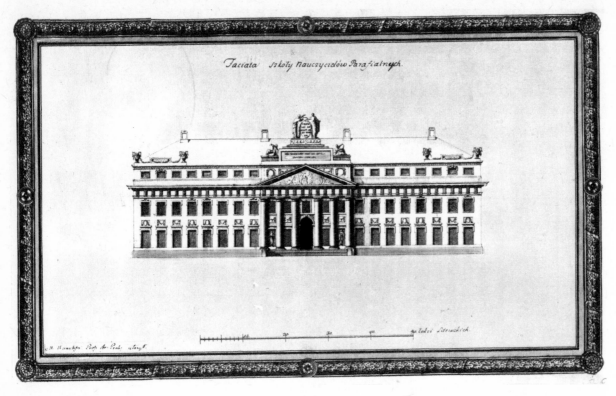

Vilna, draft design of a parish teachers' training college, M. Knakfus, 1776

Stanislas Augustus art did not go through any violent revolutions, but developed regularly; therefore, despite the changes that occurred in it in time, this art can be considered a continuous phenomenon, distinct within the art of the Polish Enlightenment. The Stanislas Augustus style was expressed not only in architecture but also in the painter's and sculptor's decoration of architectural interiors, in painting, sculpture and decorative arts. The term is only fully justified when it is applied to complexes consisting of different complementary fields of art, since the King, conscious of their mutual relationships, saw to all of them. This specific trend of Polish neoclassicism which has been called the Stanislas Augustus style was most fully expressed at the Royal Castle and Łazienki.

The reconstruction of the Castle, performed under the two Saxon Kings and including both the external architecture and the interiors, was left unfinished. An inspection made soon after the death of Augustus III, in October 1763, showed that the Castle "had few rooms of the main story, was somewhat better in the part closest to the Vistula River and barely good for incidental residence; in the other wings there were only passageways and ordinary dwellings, partly in ruin, also on the second floor; whereas the ground floor only held stores, apart from some used as offices and archives [...] the sordidness of the remaining rooms was indicated by the dwellers as only the lower servants lived there then." It was insignificant for the royal court at that time. Augustus II and Augustus III had resided not only in Warsaw, but also in Dresden, whereas in Warsaw they had kept their own residence in the Saski (Saxon) Palace. Now, the question of preparing residential apartments at the Castle for the King and suitable reception halls became very urgent. Therefore the Convocation Seym (Parliament) passed a resolution ordering the reconstruction of the Castle and an enlargement of the Castle area. Jakub Fontana was asked to implement the building demands by a rapid adaptation and decoration of the most necessary interiors, and also to design the reconstruction and modernisation of the Castle.

As early as March 1764, it was certain that Stanislas Augustus Poniatowski would gain the throne. The future King sent the Warsaw merchant Kazimierz Czempiński to Paris, to carry

18

out purchases and orders. The interest in the appearance and artistic level of the decoration of the Castle was the first sign of Poniatowski's cultural patronage; his artistic taste was closest to France. As early as 1753, in Paris, he had met the most outstanding representatives of French culture and became a very close friend of Madame Geoffrin, in whose salon the best scholars and artists gathered. Imports of French artistic works began in 1764. Slightly later, Stanislas Augustus invited to his court three outstanding French artists. Jean Pillement arrived in the spring of 1765; an excellent painter-decorator, who decorated the palace interiors in the "Chinese taste", he has already been mentioned above; in the summer of the same year, the eminent architect Victor Louis arrived for a short stay; and in 1768 the King sent for the sculptor André Le Brun, who stayed in Poland until his death. From 1766 Marcello Bacciarelli, who had known the Poniatowski family since 1756, when he came to Warsaw from Dresden, worked most closely with the King on the Castle, and later on Łazienki.

It was recognized that the royal apartments on the first floor in the wing closest to the Vistula River should be the first to be finished. It was for those apartments that in 1764 Czempiński bought in Paris and Lyon wall hangings, clocks, mantlepiece vases, gueridons (candlestands), desks, escritoires, mirrors, chandeliers, etc. Although the interior decoration in the early part of the reign of Stanislas Augustus still contained rococo designs and motifs, in his letters to the King Czempiński emphasized, clearly in accordance with the King's intentions, that he had tried in his purchases to include above all goods in the ancient spirit, in a definitely Greek taste, buying among other things, for the throne, a galloon "à la Gréc", which may have signified meander decoration.

The planned transformation of the Castle was from the very start aimed in three directions. Firstly, it was important to create a complex of Parliament halls, including the imposing Senatorial and Deputies' Halls. Secondly, rooms were to be built – corresponding to the ideas of the Age of Enlightenment – to satisfy the needs of royal cultural patronage, i.e. a Theatrical Hall, Gallery, Library, and the rooms of the Academy of Fine Arts. Thirdly, attention was paid to ways of creating a spacious area in the place of the Front Courtyard, i.e. between the Old Town and Krakowskie Przedmieście, and of the layout of the area between the castle escarpment and the bank of the Vistula River.

From 1764 to 1773, Fontana was the general director of the works. However, the King wanted to give his residence as magnificent, modern appearance as possible. With this intention, he brought over Victor Louis, although not in order to keep him in Warsaw forever. Louis was supposed to see the edifice, make preliminary designs in Warsaw and then later, in Paris, finish a project of the reconstruction of the Castle and serve the King in purchases and orders from France. Louis came to Warsaw in the middle of 1765, made here a series of water colour sketches, which he later discussed with the King, and subsequently, in Paris, in 1766 worked out very beautiful water colour designs. The architectural conceptions of Louis were complemented with the designs of works of decorative arts for the castle interiors. Most of these sketches and designs have been preserved in the Cabinet of Drawings at Warsaw University Library.

In later years, Louis's designs were used in shaping the interiors of the royal apartments and reception halls. A great many of the decorative elements and furnishings in the interiors were made in Paris under the supervision of Louis and sent over to Poland. However, his architectural and planning conceptions, bold and of high artistic value, were not implemented. Over the first few years, the residential apartment of the King and some reception halls adjacent to it were constructed to Louis's design. But very soon, in just ten years, they underwent complete change.

The fire which broke out on December 15th, 1767 in the southern wings of the Castle, on the side of the road to the Vistula River, forced an acceleration of the construction work. In the burnt-down wing, just by the Grodzka Gate, as early as 1768, Fontana built the main staircase which gave access to the Mirowska (Mier) Guard Hall and farther on, to the King's apartments. The neoclassical staircase and the Guard Hall, with Ionic pilasters and decoration of white stucco, represented the early stage in the development of the Stanislas Augustus style. In 1768–1771, Fontana reconstructed the baroque Marble Chamber, which had survived until the time of Stanislas Augustus in the form it had been given under the Vasas, but was in a state of complete ruin. Under the Vasas the Marble Chamber had housed a gallery of the portraits of Polish kings. This intention was maintained. Into the walls of multicoloured marble were set twenty two oval and rectangular portraits of the monarch predecessors of Stanislas Augustus, painted by Bacciarelli. A full-size portrait of Stanislas Augustus in coronation dress was placed over the marble fireplace, as the main accent of the room. The ceiling painting with an allegorical figure of Fame was also painted by Bacciarelli. The conceptual and artistic intention of the chamber was further expressed in allegorical figures and cartouches. The sculptures were the work of Le Brun. In terms of architectural decoration, the Marble Chamber, with its colourful and decorative furnishings of the interior, retained a good deal of the atmosphere of baroque interiors, despite the many neoclassical motifs, of which the table "in the Greek taste" was a reflection of a contemporary short-lived Paris fashion. The baroque echoes can here be explained with the traditions of the Marble Chamber from the times of King Ladislas IV.

The Marble Chamber began a historicising trend in the arts, which in terms of the themes of the Castle interiors was already distinct in Louis's design and was later so emphatically present in the paintings in the Knights' Hall and in the painted and sculpted portraits of great Poles.

Following Fontana's death in 1773, Domenico Merlini, the architect of the King and the Commonwealth, took over as the director of the works. Both he and other architects devised plans for the enlargement of the Castle. One of the most interesting designs, though impossible to implement, was proposed by the Warsaw architect Efraim Szreger. His project envisaged the demolition of the Krakowska Gate and the buildings in the Front Courtyard and some houses in Krakowskie Przedmieście. In a new Castle Square, the column of John III Sobieski was to stand by the column of Sigismund III Vasa and through a triumphal arch

Warsaw, draft design of the palace of the Sanguszko family, S.B. Zug, c. 1778

there would be a view of an equestrian monument to Stanislas Augustus. The square was to be contained between two monumental columnar façades, the design of which was inspired by the famous 17th-century columnar façade of the Louvre by Perrault and the well-known columnar façades built in the middle of the 18th century by Gabriel in the Place de la Concorde in Paris, characteristic of that version of early French neoclassicism which is called the Gabriel style.

The bold and interesting designs of Fontana, Louis, Szreger and Merlini were not implemented. But their designs, kept in the Cabinet of Drawings at Warsaw University Library, remain evidence of creative thought in Enlightenment architecture in Poland.

In 1774–1777, Merlini designed and built a complex of reception halls and royal apartments, which constituted the second stage of the reconstruction of the castle interiors under King Stanislas Augustus. They were the Canaletto Hall, the Chapel and the Reception Chamber, the Bedchamber, the Dressing Room and the King's Study. The architectural decoration of the Canaletto Hall was modest, since it was supposed to serve only as the background for paintings. Here, closely spaced, were *vedute* of Warsaw and environs, and "The Election of Stanislas Augustus". By the Canaletto Hall, in the Grodzka Tower, there was the King's Chapel, consisting of a small, rectangular nave and a rotunda-shaped chancel with light Corinthian columns of greenish stucco with gilt capitals, and a small dome with coffers. The walls and window recesses were made of red stucco. The chapel was one of the best interiors in the early period of the Stanislas style.

Over almost 10 years the Reception Chamber served as the Throne Room. In the middle of the ceiling, over a round painting, Bacciarelli represented "The Flourishing of Arts, Sciences, Agriculture and Commerce under the Reign of Peace". On the frontons, also painted by Bacciarelli, there were the allegorical figures of Valour, Wisdom, Religion and Justice. The new Royal Bedchamber, with an alcove recess, had walls panelled with yew timber and decorated with gilt laurel wreaths. Bacciarelli's frontons represented Biblical scenes. This room was also an interesting work of Polish neoclassicism in the seventies.

In 1777–1781, only one hall in the reception suite of the royal apartments was decorated: the greatest of the castle interiors, the Ballroom, called the Assembly Hall, where social meetings, concerts, and balls took place. This two-storey room in the central projection on the side of the Vistula River, its shape close to an oval, was built in 1741–1746, but its interior was then neither elaborated architecturally, nor artistically decorated. Intending to give the Hall a particularly imposing nature, the King invited in 1777 to a competition for its design the most outstanding Warsaw architects: Merlini, Szreger, Zug, Plersch and Zawadzki. They all proposed that the Hall should have columns, single or in pairs, lining the walls. In turn, there were various compositions of the divisions in the Hall and its decoration. These designs were not used. Only in 1779, Stanislas Augustus asked Merlini and Kamsetzer to produce a new design, which was the basis for creating the architectural interior of the Hall over the next two years. Pairs of columns, set along the walls, were distinct against the background of white stuccoed walls. Arcaded recesses with mirrors in the opposite wall corresponded to the large arcaded walls in the façade. On the axis of the room there was the large niche of the main doorway, over which there was a medallion bust of the King, sculpted in white marble, among winged figures symbolizing Justice and Peace, also done in white marble. At the sides, between the columns there was a white marble statue of Stanislas Augustus imaged as Apollo, in the type of the Belvedere Apollo, and a white marble statue of Minerve, with the features of Catherine II. These sculptures were the work of André Le Brun and his workshop. The great ceiling painting by Bacciarelli represented "Jove Bringing the World out of Chaos".

In 1780–1784, Merlini rebuilt the library wing, and in 1781–1786, another two reception rooms, the Knights' Hall and the New Throne Room with the Conference Closet were

Warsaw, draft design of a triumphal arch at the Zamkowy (Castle) Square, J. Kubicki, 1781

decorated. There had been an earlier design for the Knights' Hall in the drawings of Fontana and Louis – thus the King had conceived of such a room very early in his reign. In 1781, Merlini began to design the Knights' Hall, and the final draft approved for building was made in 1784. In 1786, the Hall, complete in terms of subject matter, was ready in its harmonious composition of architectural, sculptural and painting elements. The King intended this Hall to inspire a patriotic spirit, showing the great events and the worthy men in the history of Poland. The contents of the paintings were inspired by Stanislas Augustus himself, who personally took part in discussions concerning the implementation of the work, in cooperation with Adam Naruszewicz. It was a specific crowning of the ideological programme of the renewal of the Commonwealth in terms of enlightened monarchy and national consciousness. The walls of the Knights' Hall were covered by six historical works by Bacciarelli, on the fronton were placed in rich stucco decoration ten oval portraits of great men, also painted by Bacciarelli. This gallery of outstanding chiefs, knights, statesmen and scholars was complemented with twenty two bronze busts, sculpted by Le Brun and Monaldi. On the axis of the Hall stood great statues of white marble: "Fame" by Le Brun and "Chronos" by Monaldi. In 1783–1786 Merlini furnished the Throne Room, i.e. the New Reception Chamber. The walls were lined with red damask, framed with richly sculpted gilded battens. Plinths, frontons and the facet of the ceiling painting were decked with gilded white-background arabesque ornamentation. In 1784, the walls of the octohedral Conference Closet were covered by Jan Bogumił Plersch with golden-background arabesque work, creating a uniform whole with the portraits of the seven European monarchs who ruled at the same time as King Stanislas Augustus.

The process of shaping the complex of the reception suite at the Castle broke in 1786. The circumstances no longer permitted a new shaping of the rooms beyond the Assembly Hall (Ballroom): the large Dining Chamber, called the Council Chamber, and the so-called Saxon Chapel in the northern projection of the Castle wing on the side of the Vistula. Both of those rooms, which were part of the sequence of reception halls, would have closed the Grand Suite and have been counterparts of the Knights' Hall and the Throne Room on the other side of the Assembly Hall, the latter set on the axis. Nevertheless, the work, from the earliest interiors by Fontana in the sixties, through the apartments from 1774–1781, to the last ones after 1786, was a great artistic achievement of high contemporary significance – evidence of the Stanislas Augustus style and its development over the twenty years.

A basic reconstruction and expansion of the shape of an edifice and its external architecture –

22

which, despite a large number of projects, had not been brought about at the Royal Castle – were carried out in another castle: at Ujazdów near Warsaw, which was the private property of Stanislas Augustus, since he had purchased it from the Lubomirski family when he came to the throne. The reconstruction of the Ujazdów Castle, begun in 1766, was stopped in 1772. In 1784, the King gave away the castle building for barracks purposes to the Old Warsaw township, and it was rebuilt by the architect Stanisław Zawadzki. In 1766–1771, when Fontana furnished the first interiors at the Royal Castle in a new style, Domenico Merlini created the only great, monumental architectural composition which, not only in design but also in reality, in its finished construction, indicated the idea of architecture satisfying Stanislas Augustus' intentions in the first years of his rule. This architecture was neoclassical, which was seen for example in the eight-column portico annexed to the eastern elevation of the Ujazdów Castle, on the side of the Vistula escarpment, and still more specifically in the lateral out-buildings, which were neoclassical in their simplicity of line and their selection of classical decorative motifs. In the same early years of Stanislas Augustus' rule, between 1766 and 1771, there arose a large planning design called the Stanislas axis, designed perhaps by Szreger. Based on the Ujazdowskie Avenue, from the central point of the Ujazdów Circus, later called Na Rozdrożu, a system of intersecting avenues was designed, with a large circus (today's Plac Zbawiciela – Saviour's Circus) and four smaller circuses, constituting a system contained in the hexagon of the outer avenues. From southwest, the whole was closed by the line of the so-called Lubomirski trenches of 1771. One of the exits from the town, which was semi-circular in shape, was later rebuilt into Mokotowska Circus (now Plac Unii Lubelskiej – Lublin Union Circus). The momentum to be seen in the neoclassical expansion of the Ujazdów Castle and large planning design at Ujazdów suggests the ways in which work at the Royal Castle would have developed had the circumstances been favourable. Ujazdów also confirms that the King was a firm neoclassicist in his taste from the time he came to the throne, which is indicated by the neoclassical external architecture of the Ujazdów Castle, designed by Merlini, and the neoclassical architecture of Fontana's interiors at the Royal Castle.

The setting in order of the area of the Ujazdów Zwierzyniec (closed hunting grounds), simultaneously with the reconstruction of the castle, and the plans made then indicate that from the very beginning the King included the whole area in his project of the utilization of the Ujazdów complex. The King, who was, however, also concerned with work on both the Royal and Ujazdów Castles, initially neglected two pavilions built as early as the end of the 18th century by Marshal Stanisław Herakliusz Lubomirski, Łazienka (Bath-house) and Ermitaż (Hermitage). Intensified work in the garden in 1773 suggests that the King had made up his mind then as to the park complex, intending that his summer residence should be there. This is confirmed by the major repair and the partial reconstruction carried out in 1773 at Łazienka, where a bedchamber, an octohedral room on the ground floor and a study on the first floor were furnished for the King, all in new, neoclassical architectural decoration. In 1777, the eastern and western parts of the first floor were added to Łazienka, and the building thus remained until the changes in 1784.

The Łazienka pavilion, even following the expansion, was obviously not sufficient for the needs of the King, his family, guests and court, and therefore, in 1774 and 1775, two new dwelling pavilions, the White Pavilion and Myślewice, and some service buildings were built. The two pavilions were set on a square plan, both in the early neoclassical style, with interiors mainly decorated with paintings; each, however, different and decorated in an individual way. The frescoes were the work of Jan Bogumił Plersch, apart from Pillement the most outstanding painter in this field at the court of Stanislas Augustus. From 1777 to the end of the King's rule, he was active at Łazienki, executing murals and ceiling paintings of varied

 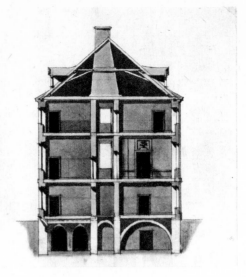

Warsaw, draft design of the "White Eagle" Hotel, S.B. Zug, 80s of the 18th century

character. In the large dining-chamber of the White Pavilion the walls were covered with arabesque-grotesque paintings, derived from Raphael's decoration of Logge at the Vatican, which were very popular in Renaissance art and later on extremely common in the period of neoclassicism.

The rich, colourful and harmoniously composed decoration of Plersch was the first, or one of the first, neoclassical arabesque-grotesque decorations to be met in the eighties and later in a great many palace interiors in Poland. It was the best example of this type of painting decoration, which evolved in his art. In the eighties he painted golden-background arabesque work in the Conference Closet at the Royal Castle and later on in the Solomon Hall at the Łazienki Palace. It seems necessary to credit the King's taste for this version, fulfilling whose wish Kamsetzer designed in 1784 golden-background arabesque work in the King's study on the first floor of Łazienki. The paintings made in 1783 for the Ballroom, although also inspired by Raphael's decoration of the Logge, were different. In these compositions human figures dominated; the four central panneaux represented the elements, while the extreme four ones showed the passage of time and human life.

Another type of wall decoration by Plersch was related to the exotic trend in the architecture of the Łazienki pavilions. In 1777, in the White Pavilion, in a room decorated with Chinese wall paper, he painted a view of Canton, and in the King's study at the Palace on the Island, a view of Peking. Still another kind was provided by landscapes of this type, like those painted by Norblin for Powązki. The decoration of the octohedral study at the White Pavilion, treated as a garden bower, can serve as an example.

The White Pavilion, a low villa with a balustraded attic and a belvedere, has never been rebuilt, preserving its original shape to the present day. Myślewice, however, was enlarged twice in its first ten years, transforming a tall three-story villa with a large doorway into a small palace, first one-storied and later with double-storey quarter-circular wings. The original shape of the building and the baroque motifs, along with neoclassical ones, indicate in its decoration the individual way in which the new style formed in the earlier period.

A turning point for the Łazienki Palace came in 1784, when a new façade was built on the south side. From that time to the present day the view of the palace from that side, with an elevation with a recessed four-column doorway between two lateral projections, with a balustraded attic and a belvedere crowned with sculptures, has been the most typical motif in the entire design of the park. It was a very characteristic feature of the artistic ideas in the sphere of royal patronage that the decoration of the doorway included earlier baroque

24

elements, surviving from the times of Lubomirski and the architect Tylman of Gameren, and some new distinctly neoclassical elements – all combined to give the impression of a uniform whole. The conception of a recessed doorway, so well executed by Merlini and Kamsetzer in the Łazienki Palace, was frequently repeated in neoclassical Polish architecture in the 18th and 19th centuries.

The expansion of the palace on the south side involved changes in the internal arrangement, including the essentially significant enlargement of the Dining Chamber and a complete change in the stucco work of its walls. The hall was lengthened to the south, which damaged its proportions. Therefore Merlini divided off its new part by two pairs of Ionic columns of red stucco, the colour of which corresponded to new red wall marbling on a white background. In the previous years Merlini had followed this idea in the large, elongated Library at the Royal Castle, which he had divided by four pairs of columns.

At the end of 1784, when the expansion of the palace was finished on the south side, the King decided to expand also the northern part. These years saw very intensive construction work, for at that time, in 1784, when the Łazienki began to be developed, the work at the Castle was going ahead at full pace in the Throne Room with the Conference Closet and the Knights' Hall. Perhaps for this reason it was not until 1787 that reconstruction potential was first found for Łazienki, and the northern façade of the palace was built in 1788. As early as 1784, Kamsetzer must be mentioned, apart from Merlini, as the fellow-creator of the style developing at that time, called the Stanislas Augustus style. In time, Kamsetzer's contribution to the King's enterprises steadily increased, and perhaps he should be credited with both the northern façade and the interior decoration in the final stages of the expansion of the Łazienki Palace. The new façade, with a new, projecting doorway, crowned with a triangular tympanum, was a further stage in the development of Stanislas Augustus neoclassicism; the projecting doorway, in turn, became so widespread in Polish architecture that it has come to be considered a peculiar feature of Polish neoclassicism.

In 1789–1795 the palace was enlarged with three new interiors which represented the final stage of the Stanislas Augustus style. Since nothing significant was built at the Royal Castle after 1786, these rooms were the last link in the history of the King's artistic patronage.

The old octohedral salon now became the Solomon Hall, with much gilt in the architectural decoration, and Plersch's paintings. The rich furnishings of the Hall may suggest that

Warsaw, draft design of the Ballroom at the so-called "Four Winds" Palace of P. Fergusson Tepper, S.B. Zug, c. 1784

25

a transition to the Empire style had already begun. A set of Bacciarelli's paintings on the ceiling and on two side walls was a continuation of the ideas implemented in the Knights' Hall at the Royal Castle – in terms of interior composition those paintings constituted a very significant element, expressing thoughts which the King wished to preserve and transmit to his contemporaries and future generations. In the Knights' Hall, by means of Bacciarelli's paintings, the King indicated what should be considered worthy, referring to examples from the history of Poland, alluding to contemporary times. At Łazienki, paintings devoted to the Biblical story of Solomon, conceived by the King, combined to form an organic whole, which was permeated with a common idea of a social-philosophical nature. The idea of this set of paintings took shape exactly in those years when the Four-Year Parliament sat in session, and was related to the person of the King himself, the features of whose face could be discerned very distinctly in the image of the Biblical King in a painting representing "Solomon's Offering". Depicted on the ceiling was God showing himself to Solomon in a dream and giving him, apart from wisdom for which he had asked, also riches and fame. These three gifts were shown in the scenes painted on the facet of the Hall. Two large paintings on the walls contained explicit allusions to Stanislas Augustus. "The Consecration of the Temple in Jerusalem" gave evidence to the wisdom and merits of the King; "Solomon's Offering" referred to his old age. In the painted decoration of the Hall, in the reflections of Stanislas Augustus on his own life and on the stance of an ideal ruler, there also recurred the motifs of freemasonry which was linked with the King's membership of the Masonic order and the role which it played in Europe and Poland in the Age of Enlightenment.

The spacious, well-lighted Ballroom, annexed from the west in 1793, was characterized by simplicity of architectural divisions and predominantly sculptural features of the interior decoration. Plersch's arabesque painting was of secondary importance here. Over fireplaces with architectural encasings were set copies of famous ancient sculptures brought from Rome: the Belvedere Apollo and Farnese Hercules. Le Brun's reliefs over the frontons of the fireplaces represented taking-off eagles, referring to an ancient motif, whereas those on a side wall, showed Hercules and Deianira, Apollo and Daphne.

The Ballroom, doubtless designed by Kamsetzer, represented late Stanislavian neoclassicism, different from that of the Solomon Hall. The direction of its development could be seen in the last of the halls, the Rotunda, finished in 1795. Although the walls of the Rotunda were covered with yellow, golden stucco, recalling the gilded Conference Closet at the Castle and the Solomon Hall, sculpted decoration dominated here. In four niches were set statues of great Polish kings: Casimir the Great, Sigismund the Old, Stephen Báthory and John III Sobieski, and over its four doors the busts of renowned Roman emperors. The sculptures were the work of Le Burn, Monaldi and Pinck. The hardly visible four tondoes in the dome, painted by Bacciarelli, represented personified virtues: Courage, Justice, Prudence and Goodness. The final work, the Rotunda, was thus a Pantheon, as it were, crowning all that which the King had expressed over his entire reign – in the Marble Chamber, the Knight's Hall and the Solomon Hall. A room which used to be a grotto with a fountain in a garden pavilion became, together with the Solomon Hall, a hoard of subject matter which the King intended to preserve in his summer palace.

At a time when the northern expansion of the palace, begun in 1788, was still under way, the King conceived of a further enlargement of his summer residence. The Palace on the Island was to be kept intact and new parts were to be designed beyond the canals. They were to communicate with the palace by small bridges with Ionic colonnades. Meanwhile, in 1792–1793, small lateral pavilions and bridges with colonnades were built to Kamsetzer's design, who also built in 1753 a new small guardhouse, with a wide, recessed doorway of Tuscan columns.

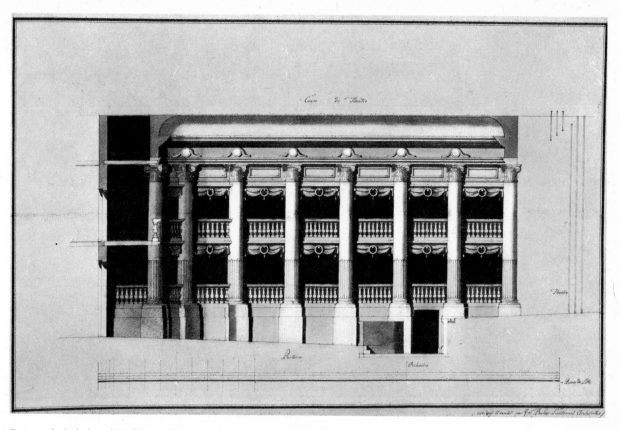

Różana, draft design of the Theatre Room at the palace of the Sapieha family, J.S. Becker, c. 1784

In each of the columnar galleries over the bridges at the palace were four busts of Roman emperors, made by Righi. They complemented the copies of classical works and their imitations which in the late eighties and nineties occupied more and more space in the Stanislavian architecture and the park. Certainly the park was not only decorated by sculptures of classical character; there also stood copies of Étienne Maurice Falconet's sculptures and works by the King's artists. At any rate, the most important sculpted element of the Łazienki Park, the monument to John III Sobieski, was baroque and not neoclassical. It should be noted that it would be erroneous to interpret this monument, set in 1788, as an expression of Stanislas Augustus' taste. At Wilanów there was a plaster model for a monument made after the death of John III Sobieski; moreover, a roughly dressed stone block meant for this monument had for a long time been lying in a quarry. Thus, only an old idea was followed through, which was an easier and less time-consuming thing to do. If the monument had been designed anew, its shape would doubtless have been different.

In 1790–1791, an amphitheatre with a stage on an island was built in the park, so placed on the lake that it could well be seen from the palace terrace. Kamsetzer drew the pattern for the amphitheatre from Herculaneum, and for the ruins which formed a permanent background decoration on the stage, from Baalbek in Lebanon. In his design he used engravings, which he did not copy, however, but freely interpreted the patterns.

In its first stage the Stanislas Augustus style took form at the Royal Castle, where Fontana and Louis contributed as architects, and at Ujazdów, where Merlini was the main designer. In the second stage, from 1774 to 1781, the area of his activity included the Royal Castle and Łazienki, with Merlini as the main architect and Bacciarelli at the Castle and Plersch at Łazienki as painters. In the third stage, from 1781 to 1785, Kamsetzer played an important role in architecture as well as Merlini; in painting Bacciarelli, the author of ceiling paintings and large murals, dominated both at the Royal Castle and at Łazienki. Le Brun played the

Raszyn, draft design of an inn, S.B. Zug, c. 1784–90

most important role in sculpture. The directions which the further development of the royal trend in Polish neoclassical art would have taken are indicated by what was designed and built at Łazienki in 1788–1795, when there were no futher major undertakings at the Royal Castle.

# The New Architectural Landscape

In the middle seventies the great changes that occurred in economic and intellectual life began to be reflected in architecture. Individual expression was gained by the beginnings of the capitalist system, by attempts at reforms of the state and economy, by tendencies towards a strengthening of the defensive power of the country, by intellectual life, science, education and culture.

An extremely telling, and at the same time one of the earliest, example of the reverberation of these phenomena in architecture was the house of the banker Piotr Fergusson Tepper, also called a palace, in Miodowa Street in Warsaw, which was built to a design of Szreger's from 1774. This house had distinctly defined functions: its purpose was to be at the same time a banker's and a commercial house and also a modern tenement house. Thus, it can be considered as a symbol of the changes which it augured. Emphasis is due not only to the thematic programme, but also to the conception of functional value, which accounted for the purpose of the edifice and the variety of functions which it was supposed to fulfill. This deserves particular attention, since the problem of architectural theme and utilitarian functions of buildings was, in terms of the architecture of the Age of Enlightenment, an issue of major significance and also found expression in the shaping of architecture and decoration. This was also the case with bank and commercial houses, including, for example, the Tepper house mentioned above and the large, modern commercial house of Roeslers and Hurtig built in 1784 in Krakowskie Przedmieście Street; the latter house was designed by Zug. It was the case with public buildings, such as town halls, barracks, theatres, buildings for education and scholarship and for transport and finally with small architectural forms, e.g. municipal wells and springs.

All of these buildings were designed and built in the neoclassical style. Initially, their design drew its inspiration from early neoclassical French architecture, but in a different version from that characteristic of Louis's work. Patterns were provided, among other things, by the widely distributed publication of Jean François Neufforge, its 900 engravings representing a variety of building types.

Using the conceptions and motifs formed in France, but widespread all over Europe, eminent Warsaw architects – Szreger and Zug – who played a major role in the field of public building, created designs of buildings satisfying Polish needs, which displayed the Polish taste and their own creative fancy. That which arose in new fields of building, which were so greatly related to the intellectual revolution in Poland in the second half of the 18th century, had a different architectural expression, constituting the Polish chapter in the art of the Age of Enlightenment in Europe. If it is correct to speak of the Stanislas Augustus style in reference to the art created within the royal court, it accordingly is necessary to attempt to distinguish the name of this parallel trend. An essential role was played by burghers' patronage, but it would be excessive to propose the term "burghers' neoclassicism". The artistic expression of this trend was to a large extent the work of architects, particularly of those mentioned above, Szreger and Zug, who should be considered the most creative, apart from Merlini, Aigner and Kamsetzer. Hitherto, this trend has not been given a name, but evidently this version of neoclassicism in the Age of Enlightenment in Poland should be distinguished as an important one, which arose here, in Poland, and reflected its own process of historical development.

The two buildings from 1774–1784, mentioned above and related to banking and commerce, indicated that the beginnings of the capitalist system were reflected in architecture as early as those years. One can mention typical buildings that could be found in other domains of life. It was to satisfy the needs of scholarship that Merlini designed the imposing edifice of the Academy of Sciences and constructed the library wing of the Royal Castle. Marcin Knakfus designed the Astronomical Observatory of the Vilna Academy; Feliks Radwański, the Observatory of the Cracow Academy; Zug designed the reconstruction of the Załuski Library. For educational purposes the Kazimierzowski Palace was converted into the Knights' School, for which a large, modern building was intended. In reference to the postulates of the Commission for National Education, Knakfus designed a school for parish teachers. That attention was drawn to the architectural decoration expressing new, ideological themes was indicated by, among other things, the example of the Collegium Nobilium in Warsaw. The rococo edifice of the Collegium, designed by Jakub Fontana in 1743, was rebuilt in the neoclassical style in 1786 by Stanisław Zawadzki. Among buildings serving culture, Stanisław Kostka Potocki designed a building for the Museum, and on the King's initiative not only were theatre halls designed for Royal Castle and built in Łazienki but also the edifice of the National Theatre was erected. An important field was that of military construction, particularly barracks – an expression of the care for the national security. This domain was a particular speciality of the architect Stanisław Zawadzki.

Reforms in urban development necessitated the construction and reconstruction of town halls. A great number of them were built, in large and small towns. In the design and construction of these buildings a major role was played by Zug. The town hall at Vilna, designed in 1786 by Wawrzyniec Gucewicz, was the most monumental. The "White Eagle" Hotel at Tłomackie in Warsaw, designed by Zug in the eighties reflected new needs auguring 19th-century hotels. Zug's well at Tłomackie, called "Fat Kate", can serve as an example of buildings and pavilions related to hygiene and the urban supply of good water.

The seventies of the 18th century saw the shaping of a type of palace and mansion construction which is commonly considered to be particularly characteristic of Polish architecture, defined as the Polish palace and Polish mansion. This type of building, most often one- or two-storied, with a columned portico or a columned porch, became extremely widespread and connected with Polish landscape. Important elements of the decoration of the interiors of palaces, town and country mansions, large or small, were portraits hung on walls. They were painted by painters in transit, such as Lampi and Grassi, and deeply Polish painters, such as Faworski, and other numerous settled and itinerant portraitists, who continued what was termed the Sarmatian type of portrait-painting.

Over the whole Polish territory there were a great many "Polish" palaces and mansions. For Polish society they have become established as particularly characteristic of the Polish taste. Descriptions of country residences and small town mansions in the novels of the 19th and early 20th centuries have contributed to the popularity of this opinion. As examples, it is possible to mention such "Polish" palaces as the palace of Mrs. Jabłonowska at Kock, one of the many in Mazovia, rebuilt by Zug in 1779, and the palaces constructed by Hilary Szpilowski at Walewice and Mała Wieś, both in 1783, and in Great Poland the most important of all, the palace at Sierniki designed by Kamsetzer in 1786. They showed both the Palladian tradition and inspirations drawn from English architecture, related to the traditions of French architecture which were popular in Poland – despite this, there arose such representative architecture in the Polish style that for a long time it inspired a great number of architects and builders. In those "Polish" palaces and mansions a variety of versions can be distinguished, e.g. the projection in the façade on the side of the garden, usually with a round salon, as at Jabłonna and Sierniki, and numerous palaces and mansions from the last quarter of the 18th century. Their interior decoration was the most expressive, e.g. the palace at Pakosław in Great Poland, owned by Ignacy Zakrzewski. Its rotunda room was decorated with four reliefs, which showed scenes from the history of Poland and were made in imitation of the 1791 engravings of Antoni Smuglewicz.

The development of neoclassical architecture was accompanied, from the early years, by the shaping of theory and artistic practice related to the English landscape park. This new,

Vilna, draft design of the town hall, W. Gucewicz, 1785–86

Warsaw, draft design for the reconstruction of the Piarist college, S. Zawadzki and S.K. Potocki, 1786

creative trend in the art of gardening was not only not based on neoclassical theory, but was even contradictory to it, since it advocated in garden planning irregular, asymmetrical arrangements imitative of Nature and was opposed to symmetrical arrangements against Nature. The landscape park was to imitate Nature in all its beautiful irregularities and to be picturesque, as opposed to linear. Thus, trees were not to be planted in a line, or trimmed, as was the case with the neoclassical gardens of Le Nôtre, the most outstanding example of which was the park at Versailles. It was recognized, however, that man should organize Nature, which was to be seen in garden planning. In landscape parks there were distinguished serene landscapes – which represented the beautiful in Nature; melancholy ones – which showed wild Nature, and surprising landscapes – which caused surprising impressions. It was recognized that parks should be so composed as to give a variety of sensations – impressions of grandeur, awe, or dignity and nobility. The park should be decorated with inscriptions of patriotic and humanist content, devoted to people and events. It should not be enclosed by a wall, but by a ditch instead, so that it would not be separated optically from the environment.

While in the architecture of the Age of Enlightenment the neoclassical stylistic trends with linear arrangements were predominant, in the art of gardening painterly spatial visions referred to the beauty of the natural landscape. Not reason but feeling ruled here; thus landscape parks were related to sentimental and pre-romanticist trends in philosophy, literature and artistic culture.

Sentimentalism coexisted with neoclassicism, not only within the epoch, but also in the works of particular writers and artists, and in the tastes of patrons. There was the parallel development of a universalist-rationalist trend and of the complementary countercurrent, which referred to feeling and Nature, which praised simplicity, tenderness and the idyllic life, as a reaction to the rule of cool reason. Motifs and themes which belonged to the repertory of sentimentalism occured in literature, music, painting and garden architecture, and in particular were expressed in the parks by means of inscriptions and symbolic names. Rationalism and sentimentalism were concurrent but separate intellectual movements of the Age of Enlightenment, which cannot be broken apart, since they were strictly connected, both in men and works of art. The neoclassical park and the landscape park were one whole and they should not be considered two different random elements.

The year 1774 saw the first Polish treatise on English gardening by August Moszyński. From his dedication to Stanislas Augustus, dated from January 17th, 1774, it can be believed that this treatise was written by Moszyński with Łazienki in mind, when, after the 1772 reconstruction of the Ujazdów Castle had been stopped, the King initiated work towards turning the Ujazdów hunting grounds called Zwierzyniec into his summer residence. The influence of this treatise on the development of decorative gardening in Poland was decisive. The author doubtless intended it for publication and therefore he treated it not only as a token homage to the King and an encouragement for new gardening design principles to be used at Łazienki. In his introduction, he expressed his conviction that his views on English gardening might bring about some improvement in this field in Poland.

Moszyński's treatise, which was based on the 1771 French edition of the very popular English book by Thomas Whately on landscape gardens published a year before, is of importance for us not only because it was the first Polish treatise on landscape parks, but also because it was an adaptation of the English text to Polish needs, and thus established a pattern for the Polish version of the English garden. Thus, Moszyński: " ... those who want to give grace to a garden by arranging it in the English taste in the natural style, should seek an intermediate kind, which to some extent could connect the ideas of the English, which are unwarrantedly evaluated as very definite in their irregularity, with the limitations which custom, or necessity, has introduced into our gardens".

Moszyński's treatise began with a reference to specific Polish garden designs. Thus, he wrote that the Warsaw region was not the most suitable for landscape parks to be established, since it was flat and monotonous. Only the owners of the properties situated on the Vistula escarpment had at their disposal areas for the establishment of gardens in the English style. In view of this, and also because on the Warsaw escarpment there were numerous palace residences, Moszyński worked out a typical design for an area, part of which was on an elevation and the remaining part below, and to which it was easy to bring streams.

The King did not respond to the ideas of Moszyński's treatise, but it seems that he was

Sierniki, draft design of the palace of K. Radolińska, J.Ch. Kamsetzer, 1786–88

cognizant of changes occurring in English gardening. During his stay in England in 1753, he visited the park at Stowe, which was the best known, and over a few decades was the site of changes illustrating the development of new ideas in gardening. The Łazienki Park was given a traditional form since it had been taken over by the King, and did not change in the period of intensive work in 1774. It was not until 1775–1779 that new motifs occurred with Kamsetzer's designs and later, when bridges, a gate and small Chinese galleries were introduced in a version which was then popular in Europe, based on the illustrated publications of William Chambers. At Łazienki there were dwelling and amusement pavilions, service and out-buildings. There were no artificial ruins, gloriettes, bowers, ancient temples, peasants' cottages with luxurious interiors or sentimental monuments. With the passage of time Łazienki began to take on the properties of an English park. Trees were more widely scattered over the lawns, picturesque views created, asymmetrical layouts introduced, and ponds of irregular shape designed and dug. The year 1784, when a considerable reconstruction was started on the Palace on the Island, was a turning point. At that time the park began to undergo greater changes. It was then that the "Partie à l'anglaise", i.e. a part of the garden in the English style, was designed. In the following years the entire park took on this character. Gardening work was in those years supervised by Jan Chrystian Schuch, who, after studies in Dresden, the Netherlands, England and France, came to Poland in 1775 and was initially employed by the wife of Marshal Lubomirski at Mokotów. In 1779, he laid out an English park at Dęblin for Michał Wandalin Mniszech and in 1781 he was appointed the steward of the King's gardens in Warsaw.

Moszyński's treatise had not been published, but its theses and recommendations became indirectly widespread in another form. This was the work of Szymon Bogumił Zug, who drew plans illustrating Moszyński's ideas, annexed to the text of the treatise. It does not seem that Moszyński introduced Zug to landscape gardening. Instead, it should be believed that the already formulated predilections of the architect encouraged Moszyński to ask him to work with him. Perhaps the new trends in garden layout came simultaneously from different directions. In 1771–1772 Zug was abroad; on that trip he might have had an opportunity to

Warsaw, draft design of the house of W. Arndt, S.B. Zug, 1787

33

Siedlec, draft design of the palace of the Krzycki family, J.Ch. Kamsetzer, c. 1790

come into contact with the fashion of picturesque gardens, as opposed to linear ones, which was then spreading all over Europe. Because he was very talented, receptive and with broad interests – this was soon reflected in his work. In an article on garden residences in Warsaw and its district, published in 1784 in *Theorie des Gartenkunst* by C.C.L. Hirschfeld, when describing Powązki, Zug pointed out still another source of new ideas, the role of Izabela Czartoryska in the shaping of the local landscape park. He wrote: "The trip to England helped this Lady to find ideas in great taste; she brought them along when she came back". Certainly, not only Czartoryska, but also other magnate patrons exerted significant influence not only on the general conception of the gardens designed, but also frequently on their motifs and particular park elements.

Doubtless, an enormous role in the spreading of the idea of decorative gardening was played by patterns contained in engraved publications, including the *Recueil des jardins anglo-chinois*, known in Poland and published in Paris in 1776–1788, and the richly illustrated publications of William Chambers.

The first landscape parks were laid out in the area of Warsaw in the early seventies. They included Solec, the property of the Prince Chamberlain Kazimierz Poniatowski, and Powązki, belonging to the Czartoryski family; there were also the gardens belonging to the Prince Chamberlain at Książęce and Góra nearby; the gardens of the Marshal's wife, Countess Lubomirska, at Mokotów; of Fryderyk Alojzy Brühl at Młociny; of Bishop, later Primate, Michał Poniatowski at Jabłonna; of the Commander-in-Chief's wife, Aleksandra Ogińska, at Aleksandria near Siedlce, and finally, of Helena Radziwiłł, at Arkadia near Nieborów. In his article of 1784, Zug distinctly emphasized that the design at Solec had been the first Polish garden in the English style (c. 1772). Arkadia was laid out in 1778, and was later transformed and expanded over many years. All of these parks and also others were connected with Zug. The parks which he designed were composed in keeping with the principles of the landscape park, with an irregular arrangement of paths, artificial streams with complicated meanders, freely grouped vegetation, meadows with clusters of trees and shrubs, clearings, waterfalls, pools with islets, ponds with irregular banks, bridges of varying shape, fountains, underground corridors, richly furnished and decorated, artificial grottoes from large boulders. Zug was unboundedly ingenious in his use of the features of the terrain, which was so greatly important in the design of landscape parks, and in the composition of surprising vistas and picturesque arrangements of architecture and vegetation.

There was an extreme richness and variety of architectural and decorative motifs in the parks

34

which Zug designed in his garden compositions in the seventies and eighties. They included a large number of ancient motifs – in temples and their ruins, Roman amphitheatres and circuses, ruins of triumphal arches and aqueducts; the architect also introduced the ruins of colonnades, single columns and groups of them; also broken columns, arcades, scenic monopter buildings, exedras, ancient altars, vases and urns, Roman sarcophagi and tombstones, motifs from catacombs, Egyptian motifs. Original ancient, Renaissance and also mediaeval sculptures and monuments were set within antiquating pavilions and garden decorations. These occured together with exotic Oriental-like pavilions – Chinese bowers, bridges, kiosks, and even a Chinese henhouse – and Turkish structures, such as minarets or the Imam's House which contained a kitchen; or even an "Indian" hut. Neo-gothic constructions included dwelling pavilions, small pseudo-mediaeval castles, a church with a tower, a grange with a small tower, separated towers, some of which housed pigeons. Finally, of timber and field stone there were peasant's or fisherman's cottages, byres, cow-houses and mills, gardener's lodges, inns and taverns. In his parks Zug also designed orangeries, pineries and bird-houses. He had a partiality for asymmetrical compositions, juxtaposing contrasting motifs and creating conglomerations of different forms. He was an outstanding artist in the field of decorative gardening in the Age of Enlightenment in Poland.

The further development of landscape parks was no longer related to Warsaw but to Puławy, which belonged to the Czartoryski family. New elements were introduced here into the old, neoclassical garden about 1775, when Powązki was constructed. It was then that "a wild promenade", with tangled arrangements of winding paths among trees, was made – but this was only an addition to a park of geometrical layout. It was not until 1786, when Puławy became a permanent residence, that Izabela Czartoryska undertook a complete reconstruction of the whole park, unifying its composition. Work was begun on its conversion to a sentimental landscape park and subsequently, with the work continuing till 1830, to a romantic one. When Powązki was destroyed during the Kościuszko Insurrection in 1794 and when Poland lost its independence the park at Puławy became the main centre of the artistic interests of Czartoryska and took a new expression – it was to reflect patriotic feeling and attachment to Polish traditions. Although it was enlivened by a Chinese bower, a fisherman's cottage, a hut by the stream, grottoes in the escarpment, an orangery, a Roman gate in the shape of a triumphal arch, English stairs, a sculpted group "Tancrede and Clorinda", as well as byres and "country" cottages built at Kępa beyond the Vistula

Warsaw, draft design of the palace of S. Poniatowski, called "Ustronie" (Secluded Spot), S. Zawadzki, before 1785

sandbank, its dominant elements were the neoclassical Sybil's Temple, constructed by Piotr Aigner in 1789–1801, which housed national relics, and the Gothic Cottage of 1809, with a collection of stone fragments, works of art and relics from various European countries. The inscription over the entrance to the Temple – "The Past for the Future" – carried a clear message.

Architects and gardeners collaborated with Czartoryska. Among them James Savage, who stayed at Puławy from 1791 to 1816, played the greatest role.

Czartoryska's book *Myśli różne o sposobie zakładania ogrodów (Various Reflections on the Manner of Making Gardens)*, published in 1805, greatly influenced the development of the landscape park in the first decades of the 19th century. Like Moszyński 30 years earlier, she too recommended an adaptation of the general principles of landscape gardening to the local landscape flora, which should set the course for the composition of Polish gardens. In her gardening practice she preserved paths lined with tall old linden trees and adjusted a large number of old elements of the park to the new compositions.

From the beginning of the 19th century numerous landscape parks were laid out in Volhynia and the Ukraine. Many of them were arranged by Dionizy MacClaire, also called Mikler, of Irish origin. They often covered large areas. MacClaire made 45 such parks, including those at Młynów, Poryck, Boremel and Mizocz. Zofiówka near Humań, on the estates of Szczęsny Potocki, became the most famous of all the parks in that region.

In the area of Warsaw, in 1806–1815 a large English park was laid out at Natolin, the work of Anna Potocka, née Tyszkiewicz, who also introduced considerable changes in the park at Jabłonna, which she inherited from Prince Józef Poniatowski. In those years, monuments and relics of the cult of heroes expressing patriotic feelings were a peculiar feature of Polish landscape romantic gardens. The parks at Puławy and Jabłonna commemorated Prince Józef Poniatowski; the Zofiówka park, Kościuszko; and Wilanów, the Raszyn Battle, to mention only the best-known examples.

The popularity of landscape gardening in Poland is evidenced by works of literature, among which one should note the earlier *Listy o ogrodach (Letters on Gardens)* by Krasiński,

Warsaw, draft design of the Ujazdów church – the Temple of Divine Providence, J. Kubicki, before 1791

Trembecki's works in verse devoted to Powązki, Zofiówka and Skrzetuski's Polanka, Wielądko's and Orański's description of the gardens at Mokotów, and finally the comprehensive publication by Franciszek Ksawery Giżycki *O przyozdobieniu siedlisk wiejskich (On the Adornment of Country Residences)* of 1827.

# The Painting of the Age of Enlightenment

As in architecture, in painting and sculpture neoclassical trends developed as a separate movement, from the Renaissance to the 19th century. Within the notion of neoclassical art, painting and sculpture were particularly characterized by a tendency towards static composition, by linearism and a predilection for sculptural modelling of figures in painting. It would not be correct to ascribe too much significance in the formation of new neoclassical versions in Polish painting and sculpture in the middle of the 18th century to an increasing interest in ancient culture. 18th-century theoreticians and admirers of the arts had in mind a new renaissance rather than imitation of works of ancient arts, which in addition was to a much lesser degree possible in painting than in sculpture and architecture. The Renaissance painting, Poussin's paintings and the works of the artists of Louis XVI were not part of those trends in the arts in which imitative features dominated, but were instead an expression of creative will. The neoclassical painting of the second half of the 18th century was by no means cold, impersonal, lifeless; nor was imitation of ancient art its purpose. It appeared in different versions and was not opposed to sentimental and preromanticist movements. It was only in the 19th century that a conflict developed between the classicists and the romanticists.

To the painters and sculptors of the Age of Enlightenment ancient art was not an end but rather a means; the study of classical culture was to help attain true simplicity, bring man closer to Nature, facilitate the creation of works full of truth, simplicity and purity. This inspired realistic trends that occurred in the painting and sculpture of that period; however, this art should not be interpreted only in terms of formal categories but rather as a phenomenon strictly connected with the contemporary ideology. Therefore, the content of the paintings is of significance, and it is only when a work of art is considered at the same time in terms of form and content that it is possible to understand it and to define correctly the character of its style. The old forms in art were not dropped immediately. In the early period of neoclassical painting and sculpture, in the 18th century, form evolved slowly and in a variety of ways.

Representations of virtuous, restrained life, uncorrupted simplicity, sacrifice, heroism and patriotism were typical subjects for neoclassical painting, faithfully reflecting the ideology of the Enlightenment. Scenes from classical mythology and history were most often allusions to topical events and important problems, to be given correct interpretation. Images from ancient and modern history satisfied purposes of political propaganda. The task of historical painting was to educate society, teach morality and advocate civic virtues, inspire contempt for danger with the good of the homeland at stake. History painting was set significant tasks and therefore it was given the highest rank in the academic hierarchy. The second place went to portrait painting, which was to show leaders and knights, scholars and philosophers, writers and good citizens. Genre scenes, landscapes, still life were relegated to a less important position. The arts were elevated very high and artists were called upon to serve not only individuals but also their nation and mankind. In addition to traditional portraits there were now also portraits where books, medical tools or manufactured goods appeared as accessories, and scenes from the life of simple people became a new theme. Towards the end of the 18th century patriotic and revolutionary themes became widespread in art.

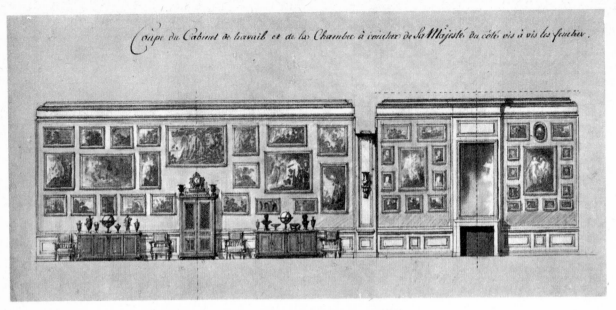

Warsaw, Royal Castle, draft design of the Bedchamber and Study, J.Ch. Kamsetzer, 1792

In Poland, it is particularly important to note the consciousness of the need for the creation of a national art which formed in the Age of Enlightenment. The credit for this is to a large extent due to the King who began to work towards it as soon as he came to the throne; this is one of the reasons why we consider his artistic patronage to have had features not only of court but also state patronage. Already the first project of the Academy of Fine Arts, which Bacciarelli drafted at the order of the King, included the significant view that it was not sufficient for foreign artists to be brought to Poland, so that fine arts could flourish here, but it was also necessary to produce a situation in which the natives of Poland would ply the arts. And in 1790 Antoni Albertrandi, when he published a handbook in Polish on painting skills, in verse, wrote in his preface: "...in order to satisfy the intentions of His Most Generous Royal Highness, feeling it my responsibility to take to the righteous ways the youth in my custody [...] that which I have long and dilligently pondered, that which I have found from my own experience, I am hereby presenting to it in my mother tongue."

From the middle of the 18th century Academies of Fine Arts arose in many a country of enlightened Europe, to mention only the Academy in Venice, founded in 1756, the Academy in St. Petersburg, 1757, and the Academy in Dresden, 1764. The Royal Academy in Warsaw was, according to the King's intention, to play a role which went beyond the limits of the arts; it was needed to ensure the undertaking of a broad programme not only in culture, but also in national education, which was an urgent necessity in the wake of the reigns of the Saxon kings. However, political circumstances and financial difficulties prevented the King from establishing the Academy of Fine Arts or the planned Academy of Sciences. Instead there arose an educational institution of a different nature, on a lower level of organization, called the Atélier or Royal Painting Studio, financed by the King and directed by Bacciarelli. The projected Academy was to have three departments: of painting, sculpture and architecture. In organizing the Atélier, the last of these was given up entirely. In the department of painting the project had envisaged the following professors: one expert in the composition of each of the following: history painting, portraiture, landscape and miniature painting. Since attempts to acquire a history painter had failed, of necessity Bacciarelli, whose specialty was portraiture, took over this department. Canaletto was considered a landscape painter, which was not exact, since he plied a peculiar version of it – *vedute*. The project envisaged the engagement of a professor of sculpture. André Le Brun took this post.

The Atélier was not basically a school to educate the young. Its essential purpose was to fulfill the King's artistic programme and to carry out his requests, whereas education was in a way an additional task. Thus, it is difficult to determine in some cases which of the artists and to what degree was engaged in didactic work. It is certain that as far as painters ago, Louis Marteau and Antoni Albertrandi also taught as well as Bacciarelli. Mateusz Tokarski was a copyist and curator of the Royal Gallery. Le Brun must have taught sculpture. We know the names of some thirty students who worked in the Atélier during the reign of Stanislas Augustus. None was particularly eminent, but some were quite good painters. The most important thing was the development of a community of Polish painters, which contributed to the formation at the beginning of the 19th century of a painters' centre in Warsaw and influenced the whole country, particularly aiding the development of painting in Vilna.

The Atélier at the Castle, which was founded soon after Stanislas Augustus had come to the throne and was directed by Bacciarelli, lasted longer than the King lived and was later run by Bacciarelli as his private studio. He failed to reopen it as an official atélier in the times of the Duchy of Warsaw, although he kept the studio and his apartment at the Castle, in the Kitchen Courtyard, until his death. The Royal Atélier preceded the first Polish artistic academy and was related symbolically to the latter by the person of Bacciarelli, who, in 1817, a few months before his death, was nominated honorary dean of the Department of Fine Arts at Warsaw University, which was founded at that time.

Marcello Bacciarelli played the most important role at the artistic court of King Stanislas Augustus and has become fixed in the memory of Poles, particularly because he had become so fully and truly polonized. It is to him and his workshop that most of the portraits of Stanislas Augustus – of which there were so many in Poland in palaces, churches and country mansions, and the numerous portraits of magnates and gentry – were attributed. In the 19th century and later his fame continued to be widespread in Poland, probably because his works filled the Royal Castle and Łazienki in Warsaw, possibly because in the contemporary and later view the portraits of this painter became so related to Polish mansions of the period of neoclassicism that they together constituted an important element of the Polish cultural landscape, and finally, too, because over the period when the role of Bacciarelli was predominant, Polish national art developed. The royal portraits and great paintings from the

Vilna, Cathedral, draft design for reconstruction, W. Gucewicz, 1783

history of Poland painted by Bacciarelli had preceded the history paintings of Franciszek Smuglewicz and his students, and also Matejko's series of royal portraits and his history paintings which have so deeply sunk into the national consciousness.

Born in Rome in 1731, as a young man he went in 1750 to Dresden, to the court of King Augustus III, and in 1756 he moved to Warsaw where he stayed (except for a short two-year break when he was in Vienna, in 1764–1766) until his death – 62 years in all. The King called him to the court as soon as he came to the throne in 1764, but Bacciarelli's obligations to the court in Vienna kept him there for some time. Only once, in 1787, did Bacciarelli leave Warsaw for a long time, when on behalf of the King he went to Italy. It can be said that for almost all his life he was connected with Warsaw; and his work was related, too, to Warsaw and the most important royal buildings.

Bacciarelli was the most prominent painter of the King but he also had much broader functions. It is said sometimes that he was as it were the royal minister on artistic matters. It is correct to say so, but only in reference to the royal court and royal patronage, and it does not apply to other artistic activities in Warsaw or other centres of cultural life in Poland. The patronage of the Czartoryski family, of the Warsaw burghers, of Massalski in Vilna, of the Branicki family in Białystok, of the wife of Marshal Lubomirski, of Stanisław Kostka Potocki, of primates and other dignitaries of the Church were not directed or inspired by the King; they developed independently, although still in some relation to the King. Still, as far as the activity of Stanislas Augustus in artistic culture goes, Bacciarelli was truly his favourite plenipotentiary. After August Moszyński, who had for the first few years of Stanislas Augustus's reign enjoyed the King's confidence in the field of the arts, had been dismissed, Bacciarelli played the major role at the royal court of artists – not only virtually but also, in time, formally, as in 1777 he was given the highest position in the Commission on Royal Buildings, assuming in 1784 the title of Director of Fine Arts; becoming in 1786 the Director General of workshops, constructions, brickyards, parks, gardens etc. He was closest to the King, and had similar tastes and understanding of the arts.

Bacciarelli exerted some influence on the formation of the Gallery and the Cabinet of Engravings, in whose collections he was all the more interested as from those engravings he often drew inspiration for his compositions, for the arrangement of details in his paintings, for the realia. Just how widely the artist drew on the engraved patterns as ancillary materials is evidenced by a 1783 catalogue that enumerates more than 1000 engravings from the royal collections which were then in his studio.

In characterizing Bacciarelli's work it is above all necessary to mention his great contribution to the composition of the beautiful interiors of Stanislas Augustus apartments at the Royal Castle. It would be wrong to say that these rooms were decorated with Bacciarelli's works or that they were hung there, for Bacciarelli's paintings constituted an integral part of the composition of the interiors and were conceived together with the architecture and sculpted decoration. This was most distinct in the Marble Chamber and the Knights' Hall, but it was also so in the Old Reception Chamber, the Bedchamber of the King and the great Ballroom.

When no greater work was undertaken at the Royal Castle after 1786, Bacciarelli was still able to create another interior where his paintings played a dominant role. As already mentioned, this room was at Łazienki and after the themes represented in Bacciarelli's paintings there it was called the Solomon Hall.

The set of paintings in the Solomon Hall formed a whole; they were in excellent relation to one another and in harmony with the interior. This was an outstanding achievement of Bacciarelli's, creative and original whole. Although evidence of his eclecticism could be seen there in borrowed motifs and ideas, the conception of the whole was his own, and the many portraits of dignitaries of the King who served as his models were among the best works of this artist. They were neoclassical paintings which derived from traditions of the Renaissance, the painters of the Bologna school and the French neoclassicists of the 17th century, and were still invested with the charm of rococo art.

When the Solomon Hall was finished in 1793, Bacciarelli began work on four tondoes which were to be set in the dome of the adjacent Rotunda. The tondoes, painted in 1793–1795, represented for the last time the motif of the personification of the virtues of an ideal ruler.

Much space has been devoted here to the work of Bacciarelli at the Castle and Łazienki, which carried out requests and ideas of the King, satisfying important political and social tasks. This was necessary to explain the character and role of those sets of paintings which, together with the architecture and sculpture, contributed to the formation of the two main centres of Polish cultural life in the Age of Enlightenment.

Bacciarelli's main sphere in painting were portraits painted from life, and it was in this field that he achieved his best artistic results.

His painting was formed in Dresden, which in the 18th century was not a centre of native Saxon art, but one of the cosmopolitan foci of European art, where, apart from Italians, the French dominated. As a portrait-painter Bacciarelli owed most to French art, of which he was fully conscious. His Polish contacts date from 1756–1764 and as early as those years he came in touch with the Poniatowski family; he then painted portraits of the male and female members of this family. How strong the effect of French painting was on Bacciarelli's portrait work was evidenced by his numerous images in which echoes of the portraiture of Nattier, Maurice Quentine de la Tour or François Boucher could be found.

What is very interesting and important is that in the portraits of men painted by Bacciarelli from his early years in Poland it was possible to discern a very strong effect of the portraits of the Sarmatian type. Also later this Sarmatian element penetrated into his art, by way of his studies on the old Polish portrait-painters, which were necessitated by the requirements of good work at the Castle.

Bacciarelli painted a large number of portraits of King Stanislas Augustus, even before he came to the throne, and particularly later, during his reign – in armour, in coronation dress, in the uniform of the mounted guards, in a hat with plumes. "The Portrait with an Hour-Glass" of 1793, which was tragic in expression and almost preromanticist in form, was different and of peculiar significance. Bacciarelli also painted self-portraits. The most popular of his self-portraits was that in a square-topped cap, which he painted after his return from Italy. As a portrait-painter he was inspired by a variety of influences and drew on various sources. However, his portraits had an individual character and his own style.

Was he an Italian in Poland, like Canaletto, or a Pole of Italian origin? There can be no doubt that he can be considered a Polish citizen (who later became a Polish nobleman) closely connected with Polish artistic culture, of which he was one of the creators in the Age of Enlightenment. He often declared that he considered Poland his homeland; following the partitions, he refused on principle to paint a portrait of the Prussian King, and in one of his letters in 1803, when Poland was in terrible decline, he said explicitly that it was his country.

In a review of the history of painting in the Age of Enlightenment, this preface has paid greater attention to only some phenomena – those related to the neoclassical movement and those which constituted parts of great artistic compositions, particularly at the Royal Castle and Łazienki in Warsaw. Therefore, the work of the eminent artist, Jean Pierre Norblin, whose descendant was Aleksander Orłowski, was not discussed and Canaletto only mentioned. Of Franciszek Smuglewicz it should still be added that he painted interesting portraits and scenes from peasants' life. It is also necessary to mention a large group of portraitists whose works often verged upon this version of painting which is called Sarmatian. The most eminent among them were Kazimierz Wojniakowski, Konstanty Aleksandrowicz, Józef Faworski, and then Józef Wall, Józef Peszka and Maciej Topolski. Much in the work of these painters, who were active in the Age of Enlightenment and at the turn of two epochs, augured the magnificent development of Polish painting in the 19th century.

# Directions in the Development of Polish Neoclassicism in the 19th Century

The partitions of Poland and the loss of its own statehood essentially affected the development of Polish art and artistic culture. There was no longer royal patronage, which had some features of state patronage and influenced to a greater or lesser extent the various centres in Poland. In the lands annexed by Prussia, and particularly by Austria, the infiltration of not only foreign officials but also of foreign artists brought by their governments could soon be felt. In view of such developments, it is possible to evaluate correctly the great significance of attempts to make the arts in Poland national, which were consciously undertaken and carried out systematically in the Age of Enlightenment. This was expressed in a great variety of phenomena and was perhaps most readily discernible in the Polish themes, historical and contemporary, in painting, sculpture and the graphic arts. But also particular significance should be ascribed to the emergence of a very large group of artists who were of Polish origin or were Polish from deep conviction. It would be superfluous to enumerate here the many names of Polish architects, painters, graphic artists, sculptors or authors of decorative art works. The question of the nationality of artists was all the more important as it was from the beginning of the 19th century that their social position changed essentially – they formed part of a new class of urban intelligentsia which would play such a great role in Polish history in the 19th and 20th centuries. Polish artists and Polish art were important under the partitions, in the struggle to keep the national identity. It was essential for our national survival that in a period of political catastrophes, for more than a hundred years, the development of national art was increasingly strong.

Although Poland was divided by borders, Warsaw remained its capital, with the highest concentration of cultural life influencing all the Polish lands. Despite the fact that Warsaw was no longer the capital of a state, it remained the capital of the nation. And apart from Warsaw, in the first thirty years of the 19th century, Vilna was another great centre of Polish culture.

In considering what was particularly important for the development of Polish art in the 19th century, it is above all necessary to mention the unbreakable ties with the cultural artistic ideas of the Age of Enlightenment, transmitted by artists, patrons and wide strata of society. If one attempted to determine which single artistic phenomenon in the first thirty years of the 19th century should be considered the most significant, one would have to mention the magnificent, monumental neoclassical architecture and neoclassical planning. The continuity of development was sustained by old artists and those who now entered the scene. Artists were now educated by as many as three schools: Warsaw University, Vilna University and Cracow University, and public exhibitions provided a new form of contacts between artists and society.

Thus, despite close relations to the Age of Enlightenment, changes occurring in art and artistic life were fundamental. It should be added that in the twenties of the 19th century, apart from the neoclassical movement, neo-gothic occupied an increasingly strong position. It was no longer related to neoclassicism, but to romanticism in literature.

The development of the arts from 1795 to 1831 can be divided into three periods connected

Falenty, draft design for the Ballroom at the palace of P. Fergusson Tepper, S.B. Zug, c. 1782–84

with political events, since obviously in 1795–1806 when Warsaw was under Prussian rule there were different conditions for culture from the times of the Duchy of Warsaw, and then different again, being most favorable, in the Kingdom of Poland.

When Poland lost independence and Warsaw ceased to be the capital – in the last years of the 18th century and the early years of the 19th century, until 1815 – there were fewer and fewer construction projects in Warsaw and other large towns. Instead there was a distinct development of rural building, including palaces, small and large mansions and farms. It was a continuation of those types which had been created in the Age of Enlightenment and which were often related to those conceptions, constituting a new stage in the development of the rural architecture of palaces and mansions. A great number of new neoclassical designs could be found in country palaces designed by Stanisław Zawadzki, to mention for instance the 1799 complex of buildings at Dobrzyca. New versions of the country park were created by Chrystian Piotr Aigner – Marynki at Puławy, 1791, and then about 1800, at Igołomia, and his reconstruction of Natolin in 1808–1812. His masterpiece was the rebuilding of the castle at Łańcut and the construction of park pavilions there in the early years of the 19th century. Jakub Kubicki also designed outstanding country residences: at Radziejowice and Bejsce in 1802, at Pawłowice in 1804 and at Młochów in about 1806; he also rebuilt the palace at Sterdyń. Only the most eminent architects and their well-known works have been mentioned here. The very numerous country residences, very large, large and small, could be divided into separate groups, but in any case, there emerged a general type of palace and mansion, very distinct, which can be called Polish. Soplicowo described by Mickiewicz in *Pan Tadeusz* was a good example of a modest Polish country manor.

Another example of the continuation of architectural ideas which were formulated in the Age of Enlightenment is the neoclassical type of a central church. This took shape for the first time in the Evangelical Church designed by Zug in Warsaw, in Szreger's church at Skierniewice and subsequently in the designs of the church at Ujazdów; it became monumental in the designs of the Temple of Divine Providence which was built to commemorate the passing of the Third of May Constitution. The edifice of the church, built to Kubicki's authorized design, was to be a domed central building. Its foundations have survived in a large excavation

in the Botanical Garden. Then Aigner took over in his two church buildings this idea which was so topical in the Age of Enlightenment (the large number of smaller churches which also drew on this conception will not be enumerated here). He built the first church, in the shape of a rotunda, covered with a flattened dome and with a Corinthian six-column portico, at Puławy in 1800. This church functioned as the sepulchral chapel of the Czartoryski family. And the last work of Aigner's in Warsaw, before he left Poland, was St. Alexander's Church, built in 1818–1820 – a rotunda with two equivalent elevations, the front one and that on the side of the chancel. The interior was made into a miniature of the Roman Pantheon. It is evident that after a lapse of 30 years, Aigner referred to Kubicki's designs of the church at Ujazdów and the Temple of Divine Providence. Only the political meaning of the founders' intentions was different. The Temple of Divine Providence was to commemorate patriotic reforms passed in order to preserve independence, whereas the church of 1818–1825 was built in memory of the entry of Tsar Alexander I, after the Kingdom of Poland had been established.

A turning point in planning and architecture came after the Kingdom of Poland was formed in 1815. Its government – it seems necessary to mention above all Duke Ksawery Drucki-Lubecki, who became in 1821 the President of the Government Commission on Revenue and Treasury – proposed an economic programme which was carried out with firm consistency and brought excellent results. The country, which had been only agricultural before, became agricultural and industrial, with great consequences also in planning and architecture. A new type of state patronage began to form and the activity of the central government could be seen most clearly in the expansion of Warsaw, but also affected provincial centres. The modernization of the state administration, the ordering of the economy and treasury, the development of cultural life, all exerted great influence on architecture, for which it was necessary to seek new forms. Certainly, there were still connections with the Age of

Enlightenment, but new problems required that new designs in planning and architecture should be sought. One of the characteristic phenomena of the new epoch was the destruction of mediaeval ramparts in Warsaw, Poznań, Cracow and Piotrków, in order to create large open areas and modern thoroughfares. Only in Cracow was the loss of the mediaeval walls partly compensated for by the formation of the Planty Park. New towns and estates which arose because of the industrial development required new designs in planning. An urgent need developed for the construction of town halls, courts of justice and other public buildings. The years 1815–1830 were with a great deal of justification called "a splendid chapter in the history of government in Poland".

The old architects whose work had taken shape in the Age of Enlightenment were still active in the early years of the Kingdom of Poland, particularly Kubicki and Aigner. Kubicki's last work was the Belweder Palace, a typical Polish neoclassical country manor, expanded to a palatial scale. In regulating the city boundaries of Warsaw and the roads out of the city in 1815 and later, Kubicki built toll-houses round Warsaw. When the question of ordering the premises of the Royal Castle arose, he designed a monumental project for its reconstruction. One of the elements of this design, an arcaded terrace at the foot of the Castle hill, was built. Aigner's activity also left distinct traces in the image of the city. In 1818–1819, he rebuilt the Governor's Palace; in 1816–1823, he exercised a great influence on the expansion of the University buildings; in 1817–1821, he built the mint in Bielańska Street; he rebuilt and expanded Marywil; he rebuilt St. Andrew's Church, and it is necessary to add that apart from Marywil, in 1823–1824, he constructed the "Market House", which so greatly affected the later conception of the façade of the Grand Theatre.

In the neoclassical architecture in the times of the Kingdom of Poland, however, the first place was taken by a young architect brought by Staszic from Florence to Warsaw in 1818, to build the edifice of the Society of the Friends of Science. He was Antonio Corazzi, then 26 years old, who remained in Warsaw for 27 years and whose architectural achievement was

Warsaw, draft design of the Main Store, W.H. Minter, c. 1800

related exclusively to Warsaw and Poland. It is sufficient to mention Bankowy Square, Teatralny Square and the last part of Krakowskie Przedmieście Street at the Nowy Świat Street end, all of which were shaped by Corazzi, to realize how many important elements the planning of Warsaw owes to him. In providing plans for the construction of large public edifices, he created monumental architecture, produced excellent basic shapes of buildings, ingeniously articulated but compact; with harmony he connected wall surfaces with great colonnades, complementing the whole with restrained decoration. His architecture showed both the taste of tradition and the breath of new times. The neoclassical architecture which he designed in Warsaw was then among the greatest achievements in Europe.

State patronage enabled him to create a large number of public edifices. It is sufficient to mention the edifices built in the twenties of the 19th century: the Government Commission on the Interior, rebuilt from the old palace of the Mostowski family, the Government Commission on Revenue and Treasury, the Directors' Palace (actually belonging to the minister Lubecki), and the imposing Polish Bank – the last three edifices constituting a truly exceptional neoclassical complex. If we add the house of the Supreme Board of Supervision at the corner of Nowy Świat Street and Jerozolimskie Avenue, the house of the Government Commission of the Warsaw District in Nowolipki, the edifice of the Government Commission in Radom and schools in Warsaw, Siedlce, Suwałki, Radzymin and Płock, we can declare that the work of Corazzi reflected perfectly the great trends in state policy, which worked towards the modernization of administration, providing foundations for the development of financial possibilities for industrialization in the country and also towards an acceleration in the great task of the spreading of education. In various districts of Warsaw, Corazzi built some twenty private houses, among which particular attention is due to the house of the archbishop Hołowczyc in Nowy Świat Street and two houses in Ujazdowskie Avenue. It can be said with complete certainty that Corazzi's contribution to neoclassical architecture in Warsaw was enormous. As his greatest achievement it is necessary to mention the Grand Theatre, one of the most beautiful theatre edifices in the world.

A few years after Corazzi, in 1822, Enrico (Henryk) Marconi, also 26 years old, came to Poland following a commission from General Ludwik Pac to build a neo-gothic palace at Dowspuda and to rebuild the palace in Miodowa Street, bought by Pac from Michał Radziwiłł; this reconstruction was carried out in 1824–1828. Only the latter palace, with its neoclassical front gate, can be included among the neoclassical buildings in Warsaw, since the whole rich work of Marconi belonged to a later period and was historicist.

At the threshold of the epoch in question, it is necessary to mention the little-known architect Fryderyk Albert Lessel, the author of the reconstruction of the Blue Palace in Warsaw in 1812–1819. If he is mentioned here after those architects who contributed most to the shaping of Warsaw neoclassicism, it is because he represented a very peculiar version of Polish architecture, which derived from the functional, purist French architecture of the early 19th century, most evident in the school of Jean-Nicolas-Louis Durand. This movement had less backing in Poland. Concluding this description of Warsaw neoclassicism in the 19th century, it seems necessary to mention the large colonnade of the Saxon Palace when it was rebuilt by Idźkowski in 1839–1842. There were still here echoes of the architecture of 1760–1831, as it is usually dated, but they had passed onto the sidelines.

A significant feature of 19th-century architecture, particularly its first thirty years, was the fact that even at the end of the 18th century sculpture and relief began to play an increasingly major role in architectural decoration. This sculpture was already neoclassically bereft of baroque reminiscences. The greatly increased need for sculpture could not be fulfilled by local artists, and therefore a large number of purchases or orders were made abroad and foreign artists brought to Poland. Paweł Maliński from Bohemia, who was brought to Warsaw

Warsaw, Royal Castle, draft design for expansion, J. Kubicki, 1816–18

by Stanisław Zamoyski in 1816, was an artist who exerted the greatest influence on neoclassical decorative sculpture in Poland. His first work in Poland was the frieze "Bacchus' Triumph" on the fronton of the Blue Palace. Subsequently he executed the Apollo group with the Muses of Art and Science in the old Kazimierzowski Palace, decorated with a frieze, the session room of the Society of the Friends of Science in the Staszic Palace, founded by Staszic, decorated with sculptures, the old palace of the Mostowski family, designed another frieze in the rotunda of the Polish Bank, and also – apart from a large number of his sculpted architectural decorations – he designed a large frieze over the entrance to the Grand Theatre, composed of more than 62 figures and representing Oedipus returning from the Olympic Games. It would be difficult to mention all the sculptures of architectural decoration with which he ornamented Warsaw buildings. These sculptures were not only related to state and reception buildings, but also to private houses and churches: the former Piarist church in Długa Street and Charles Boromeus' Church in Chłodna Street. Maliński also executed a number of sculpted tombstones for Warsaw cemeteries. One should give separate mention to the reliefs on the roadside obelisk, called the Monument of Labour, in Grochowska Street in Warsaw, and on a similar monument at Terespol. In the reliefs on these monuments Maliński managed to break with neoclassical traditions in favour of realistic trends in a representation of common people, workers and peasants, typical of the panorama of Warsaw, Siedlce and Brześć. Portrait sculpture of neoclassical character, but also with realistic expression, was a special field in his work. The sculptures with which Maliński decorated Warsaw complemented excellently the neoclassical architecture, particularly the work of Corazzi.

One should also mention Ludwik Kaufmann, the author of the frieze on the Pac Palace in Miodowa Street, representing Titus Quintus Flaminius in the act of declaring the independence of Greek cities; he was also the author of the female figure on the monument of Natalia Potocka at Natolin and of the sculptures representing the Vistula and Bug Rivers on the terrace of the Łazienki Palace. Among Polish artists the major place should go to Jakub Tatarkiewicz who after his studies in Warsaw completed his education in Rome with Bertel Thorvaldsen. Tatarkiewicz created outstanding neoclassical reliefs, numerous busts, a beautiful statue "Dying Psyche" and the tombstone sculptures of Stanisław Kostka Potocki and his wife on a monument at Wilanów.

As early as the second half of the 18th century, there were frequent and numerous imports of sculptures from Italy to Poland, and their significance increased greatly in the first decades of the 19th century. Antonio Canova sculpted a statue of the young Henryk Lubomirski as Amor (in the Łańcut collection) for a commission from Poland. For a great many decades Canova's Perseus remained in Poland, and in addition to a large number of other sculptures by this artist in this country one should also mention busts and tombstones produced by his students.

The work of Thorvaldsen was of particular significance for Polish art in the first half of the 19th century, not only in view of the large number of his sculptures made for Poland but also because of the close contacts, resulting both from public and private orders, which he had with Poles. In the minds of Polish society Thorvaldsen established himself as the author of public monuments. His relations with Poland began with an 1812 contract to make two caryatids for the Napoleon monument designed by Aigner for the Senatorial Hall at the Royal Castle in Warsaw. In 1817, the Public Committee asked Thorvaldsen to make an equestrian statue of Prince Józef Poniatowski, finished as late as 1829, which was returned to Warsaw and placed here after the First World War. In 1820 Thorvaldsen came to Warsaw and signed a contract with Staszic to produce the monument od Copernicus, which was unveiled in 1830. This set of public monuments was complemented by the numerous works Thorvaldsen made for private persons. One should above all mention the most outstanding of Thorvaldsen's sepulchral sculptures in Poland, the monument of Włodzimierz Potocki at the Wawel Cathedral, finished in 1830, one of the artist's best works. In addition the fact that to pay a visit to Thorvaldsen in Rome was part of the stay of almost all the eminent Poles who went there helps to explain the reasons why in the minds of Poles Thorvaldsen established himself not as a foreign sculptor, but as an artist most closely related to Polish cultural life.

Painting in the early 19th century took shape first within the traditions of the art of the Age of Enlightenment; over the first dozen-odd years Marcello Bacciarelli continued to be the major figure, in addition to whom one could mention particularly Maciej Topolski, Józef Peszka, Józef Oleszkiewicz, students of Franciszek Smuglewicz and outstanding portraitists. It would be difficult to relate to neoclassicism the work of Aleksander Orłowski, in which realistic and romanticist features dominated.

The main trend, representative of Polish painting in 1810–1830 and deriving from the spirit of the Age of Enlightenment, but already fully independent, was the mature Warsaw neoclassicism, with its leading artist Antoni Brodowski. Brodowski obtained his basic education in Paris, with the best contemporary artists, first Jacques-Louis David and subsequently François Gérard, the latter having had a dominant effect on his creative work. The gold medal at the 1819 exhibition and his subsequent professorship at the Department of Fine Arts at Warsaw University had established the status of this artist in the Warsaw artistic community. The important qualities of Brodowski's "Self-portrait" of 1813, his "Portrait of the Artist's Brother" of 1815 and the subsequent images in which realistic features of the artist's work were expressed, such as for instance the portrait of Ludwik Osiński of 1830 or that of Archbishop Hołowczyc of 1820, make it possible to deem Brodowski's work the crowning achievement of Polish portrait painting in 1820–1830. A strictly neoclassical trend was reflected in his large, antiquating compositions "Saul's Anger with David", "Leonidas", "Hector", "Paris and Helen". His contemporaries were particularly interested in "Oedipus and Antigone", painted for the 1823 competition, in which Brodowski competed with Aleksander Kokular and Antoni Blank.

Blank, who was also a neoclassical artist, was a very popular portrait painter. His best known works included the "Self-portrait with Wife and Two Daughters" and the "Portrait of Abraham Stern". Aleksander Kokular, whose work included above all portraiture, was a painter typical of his epoch.

In addition to Warsaw, individual painters' schools were formed in Cracow, Lvov and Vilna. The latter centre owed the beginning of its development to Franciszek Smuglewicz, who was working in Vilna as early as the 18th century and headed in 1798 the first department of painting at Vilna University. Under his influence the department developed an interest in portrait and history painting. In addition to Smuglewicz, his assistant Jan Rustem was active at Vilna University, taking over the department from the former and distinguishing himself in the field of portrait painting in Vilna.

The period of neoclassicism, which was contained approximately between 1760 and 1830, was of great significance for Polish culture. In Polish history this was a completely exceptional period when the fate of Poland was being decided; a period of patriotic reforms and political catastrophes, occupations and ephemeral attempts to call into being state organizations with smaller territory. It was in that period that the notion of national art was clearly defined and artistic education formed, and it was on the traditions of the Age of Enlightenment and neoclassicism, and later the romanticist art of the early decades of the 19th century, that the development of Polish art in the hardest years under the partitions was based.

*Stanisław Lorentz*

Illustrations

I WARSZAWA *J. Fontana*

II WARSZAWA *V. Louis*

IV WARSZAWA *V. Louis*

V WARSZAWA *V. Louis*

VII WARSZAWA *D. Merlini, J. Ch. Kamsetzer*

VIII NIEBORÓW *G. Quarenghi*

2. WARSZAWA *D. Merlini*

◀ 1. WARSZAWA *E. Szreger*

3. WARSZAWA
*J. B. Plersch*

5. WARSZAWA-Powązki

◀ 4. WARSZAWA D. Merlini, J. B. Plersch

6. WARSZAWA E. Szreger

7. ROGALIN

8. WARSZAWA *E. Szreger*

9. WARSZAWA *D. Merlini*

10. WARSZAWA *D. Merlini, J. Ch. Kamsetzer*

11. WARSZAWA ▶
*D. Merlini*
*J. Monaldi*
*A. Le Brun*

12. WARSZAWA *V. Louis, D. Merlini*

13. WARSZAWA *D. Merlini*

14. WARSZAWA *D. Merlini*
*J. B. Plersch*

18, 19. JABŁONNA *D. Merlini*  20. WARSZAWA *E. Szreger* ▶

*Vue de Jablonna*

21. WARSZAWA S. B. Zug

23. **SIEDLCE** *S. Zawadzki*

◀ 22. **SAMOTWÓR** *K. G. Langhans*

24, 25. KRAKÓW

26. WARSZAWA S. B. Zug, J. Ch. Kamsetzer

27, 28. WARSZAWA S. B. Zug

29. 30. 31. WARSZAWA *E. Szreger*

32. WARSZAWA *E. Szreger*　　　　　　　　33. PAWŁOWICE *J. Ch. Kamsetzer* ▶

34, 35, 36. PAWŁOWICE *J. Ch. Kamsetzer*

37. PAWŁOWICE *K. G. Langhans*

38, 39, 40. PAWŁOWICE *J. Ch. Kamsetzer*

41. WARSZAWA D. Merlini, J. Ch. Kamsetzer

42, 43. WARSZAWA *D. Merlini*

44, 46. SKIERNIEWICE *E. Szreger*

45, 47. KOCK *S. B. Zug*

48, 49. WARSZAWA-Natolin *S. B. Zug, S. K. Potocki*

50, 51. WARSZAWA-Natolin *S. B. Zug*

52. WARSZAWA *D. Merlini*

53. TULCZYN *Lacroix*

IX  WARSZAWA *Canaletto*

XIV *M. Bacciarelli*

XV *Dodin* ▶

XVI WARSZAWA *D. Merlini*

54, 55. WALEWICE *H. Szpilowski*

56, 57. MAŁA WIEŚ, *H. Szpilowski*

58, 59. MAŁA WIEŚ

60, 61. MAŁA WIEŚ

62, 63. MAŁA WIEŚ *H. Szpilowski,  J. B. Plersch (?)*

64. ŁAŃCUT V. Brenna

65, 66. ARKADIA S. B. Zug ▶

67, 68. ARKADIA *S. B. Zug*

69, 70, 71. WARSZAWA *S. B.* Zug

72. WARSZAWA *D. Merlini*

Vue du Palais à Lazienki
prise du Pont du Roi Jean III.

73. WARSZAWA *J. Ch. Kamsetzer*        74. WARSZAWA *D. Merlini, J. Ch. Kamsetzer*

75. WARSZAWA

77. WARSZAWA D. *Merlini* ▶

76. WARSZAWA *D. Merlini, J. Ch. Kamsetzer*

78. WARSZAWA *D. Merlini*

80. WARSZAWA
*J. Ch. Kamsetzer, A. d'Este*

◄ 79. WARSZAWA
*J. Ch. Kamsetzer*

81, 82. WARSZAWA *D. Merlini, J. B. Plersch*

83, 84, 85. WARSZAWA *J. Ch. Kamsetzer*

86. RACOT *D. Merlini*

87. SYCÓW
*K. G. Langhans*

88, 89. OLESIN *Ch. P. Aigner*

90. WARSZAWA *S. Zawadzki*　　　　　　　　　　　　91. DĘBLIN *D. Merlini* (?)

92, 93. WARSZAWA
*Ch. P. Aigner, S. K. Potocki*

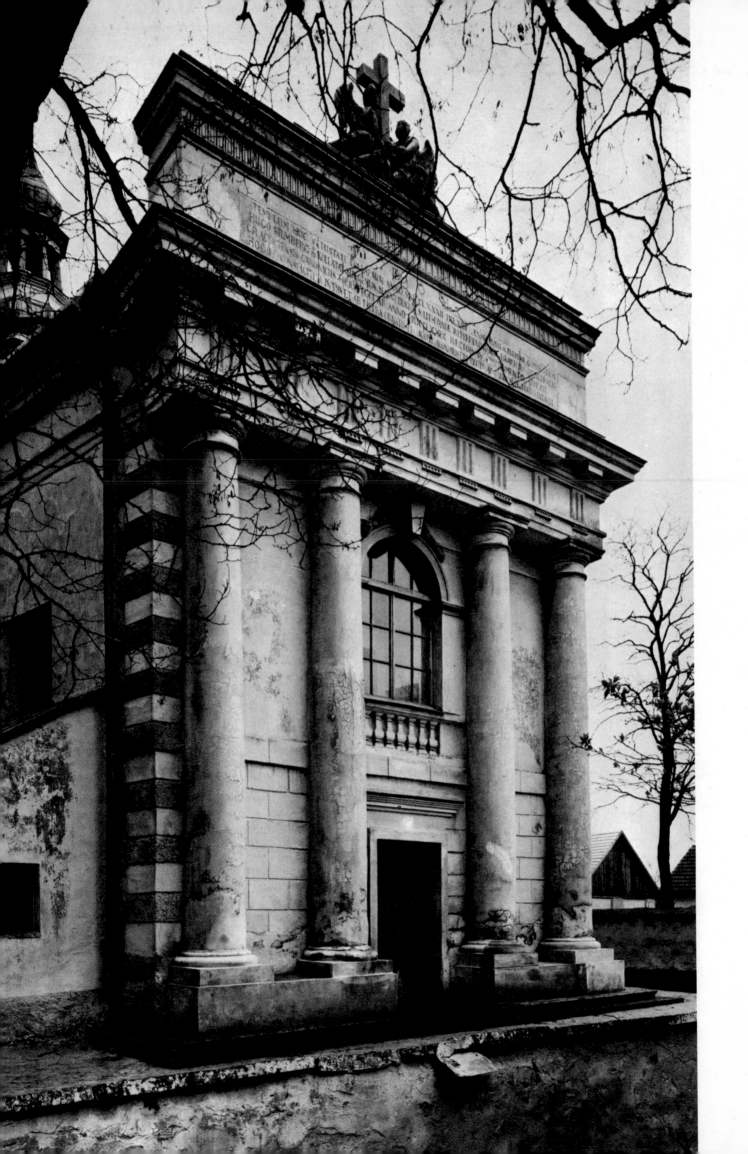

94. KRZYŻANOWICE *S. Zawadzki* 95, 96. POZNAŃ

97, 98. CZERNIEJEWO

99. POZNAŃ *J. Ch. Kamsetzer* ▶

102, 103. LEWKÓW

104, 105. WARSZAWA *J. Ch. Kamsetzer*

106, 107, 108. WARSZAWA *J. Ch. Kamsetzer*

109, 110. PUŁAWY *Ch. P. Aigner*

111, 112. CHOCZ

113. JAROGNIEWICE

114, 115. PAKOSŁAW

116. PETRYKOZY

117. SIEDLCE Z. *Vogel*

118. ŁAŃCUT S. B. *Zug*

119. WARSZAWA *J. Ch. Kamsetzer*

120. LUBOSTROŃ S. *Zawadzki*

121. LUBOSTROŃ

122, 123. DOBRZYCA *S. Zawadzki*

124. DOBRZYCA *S. Zawadzki*        125. DOBRZYCA *S. Zawadzki*, A. *Smuglewicz*

126. ŚMIEŁÓW S. Zawadzki

127. ŚMIEŁÓW *S. Zawadzki, A. Smuglewicz*

◀ 128. BIAŁACZÓW *J. Kubicki*

129. MOKOBODY *J. Kubicki*

130. MILICZ *G. Geissler*                        131. ŁAŃCUT *Ch. P. Aigner*

XVII ŁAŃCUT *V. Brenna*

XVIII WARSZAWA

XX WARSZAWA

XIX KORZEC

XXI  *J. Grassi*

XXII  *J. Peszka*

XXIII  *A. Kucharski*

XXIV  *P. Krafft*

XXV  *G. B. Lampi*

132, 133. IGOŁOMIA *Ch. P. Aigner*

134, 135. BEJSCE *J. Kubicki*

136. PUŁAWY *Ch. P. Aigner*

137. ŁAŃCUT
*Ch. P. Aigner,*
*F. Baumann*

138, 139. ŁAŃCUT
*Ch. P. Aigner, F. Baumann*

140, 141. ŁAŃCUT *Ch. P. Aigner, F. Baumann*

142. WARSZAWA-NATOLIN *W. Baumann*

143, 144. WARSZAWA-NATOLIN
*Ch. P. Aigner, W. Baumann*

145. WARSZAWA *F. A. Lessel*

146. WARSZAWA *J. Kubicki*

147. WARSZAWA *Ch. P. Aigner*

148. WARSZAWA
*Ch. P. Aigner*

149, 150. WARSZAWA *J. Kubicki*

151. WARSZAWA *J. Kubicki* ▶

152. WARSZAWA *A. Corazzi*

153. WARSZAWA *H. Szpilowski*

154. **WARSZAWA** *A. Corazzi*

155. **WARSZAWA** *Ch. P. Aigner*

156. KALISZ *S. Szpilowski*

157. RADOM *A. Corazzi*

158. WROCŁAW *K. F. Langhans*          159. WARSZAWA *J. Lessel*

160, 161, 162. WARSZAWA A. *Corazzi*

163, 164, 165. WARSZAWA A. Corazzi

166. WARSZAWA *H. Marconi*

167. ŁOWICZ

168, 169. ŁOWICZ B. Witkowski

170. WARSZAWA A. *Kropiwnicki*                                              171. KALEŃ

172. RADZIEJOWICE

173. PŁOCK

174. KRAKÓW *P. von Nobile*                    176. WARSZAWA-NATOLIN *H. Marconi* ▶

175. WARSZAWA *A. Idźkowski, W. Ritschel*

177. F. Smuglewicz

178. *F. Smuglewicz*

179. *F. Smuglewicz*

180. *J. P. Norblin*

181. *J. P. Norblin*

182. *J. P. Norblin*

183. *K. Wojniakowski*

184. *K. Wojniakowski*

185. *M. Topolski*

186. *J. Faworski*

187, 188. *M. Bacciarelli*

189. *J. B. Plersch*

190. *J. Wall*

191. *A. Orłowski*

192. *A. Orłowski*

193. *J. Gładysz*

194. *A. Blank*

XXVI  SIEDLCE *S. B. Zug (Z. Vogel pinxit)*

XXVII  *F. Smuglewicz*

XXVIII  *K. Aleksandrowicz*

XXIX  *A. Brodowski*

XXX *K. Wojniakowski*

XXXI *J. Rustem*

XXXII  *A. Kokular*

XXXIII  *A. Brodowski*

196, 197. A. Le Brun

198. *A. Le Brun*

200. J. Regulski

199. J. Monaldi

201. A. Canova

202.
B. Thorvaldsen

203.
B. Thorvaldsen ▶

204. B. Thorvaldsen

205. J. Tatarkiewicz

205. J. Tatarkiewicz

206. J. Tatarkiewicz

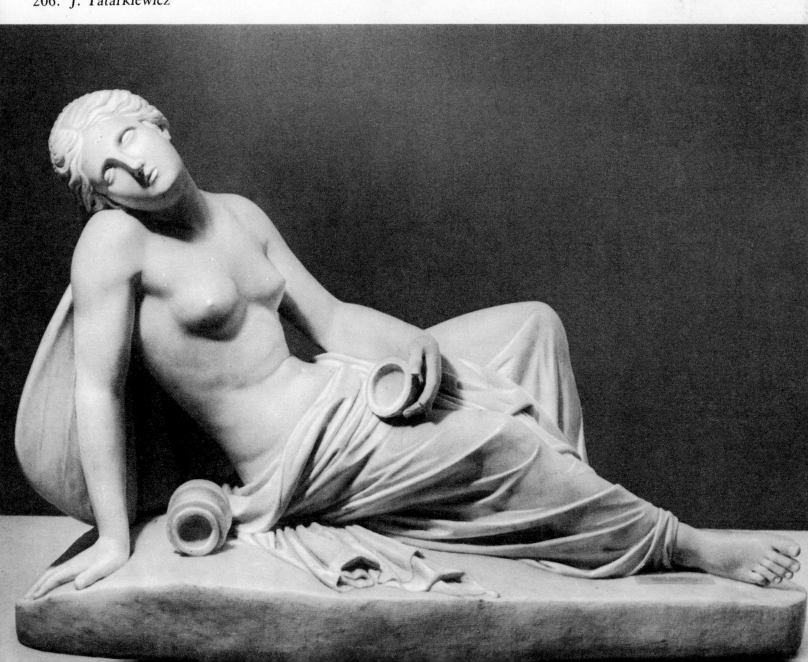

◀ 207. *L. Kaufmann*

208, 209. *L. Kaufmann*

213. *J. Ch. Kamsetzer*

214. *J. L. Prieur*

◄ 212. *Ph. Caffieri*

215. *J. J. Bandau*

216. *J. Skalski*

217. *T. Pawłowicz*

218. BARANÓWKA

219, 220. URZECZE

221. WARSZAWA

# Catalogue

*by Andrzej Rottermund*

## Bibliographic Abbreviations and Glossary

**1.** A. Bartczakowa, *Jakub Fontana, architekt warszawski XVIII wieku* (*Jakub Fontana, a Warsaw Architect of the 18th Century* – in Polish), Warsaw 1970 – Bartczakowa, *J. Fontana*

**2.** Z. Bobrowski, *Budynki użyteczności publicznej w Polsce wieku Oświecenia* (*Public Buildings in Poland in the Age of Enlightenment*), (in:) *Studia i materiały do teorii i historii architektury i urbanistyki* (*Studies and Materials for the Theory and History of Architecture and Townplanning* – in Polish), III, 1961 – Bobrowski, *Public Buildings*

**3.** A. Chyczewska, *Marcello Bacciarelli. 1731–1818* (in Polish), Wrocław–Warsaw–Cracow–Gdańsk 1973 – Chyczewska, *M. Bacciarelli*

**4.** T. Dobrowolski, *Nowoczesne malarstwo polskie* (*Modern Polish Painting* – in Polish), vol. 1, Wrocław–Cracow 1957 – Dobrowolski, *Modern Polish Painting*

**5.** S. Iskierski, *Bronzy Zamku Królewskiego i pałacu Łazienkowskiego w Warszawie* (*Bronzes in the Royal Castle and Łazienki Palace in Warsaw* – in Polish), Warsaw 1929 – Iskierski, *Bronzes*

**6.** T.S. Jaroszewski, *Architektura doby Oświecenia w Polsce, nurty i odmiany* (*Polish Architecture in the Age of Enlightenment, Trends and Versions* – in Polish), Wrocław–Warsaw–Cracow–Gdańsk 1971 – Jaroszewski, *Architecture in the Age of Enlightenment*

**7.** T.S. Jaroszewski, *Chrystian Piotr Aigner* (in Polish), Warsaw 1970 – Jaroszewski, *Ch.P. Aigner*

**8.** D. Kaczmarzyk, *Rzeźba polska od XVI do początku XX wieku. Katalog zbiorów Muzeum Narodowego w Warszawie* (*Polish Sculpture from the 16th to the Beginning of the 20th Centuries. Catalogue of the Collections of the National Museum in Warsaw* – in Polish), Warsaw 1973 – Kaczmarzyk, *Polish Sculpture*

**9.** *Katalog rysunków architektonicznych ze zbiorów Muzeum Narodowego w Warszawie* (*A Catalogue of Architectural Drawings in the Collection of the National Museum in Warsaw* – in Polish), ed. A. Rottermund, Warsaw 1970 – *Catalogue of Drawings*, ed. A. Rottermund

**10.** *Katalog rysunków z Gabinetu Rycin Biblioteki Uniwersyteckiej w Warszawie*, cz. 1, *Varsaviana* (*A Catalogue of Drawings in the Cabinet of Drawings of the Warsaw University Library* – in Polish), part 1, *Varsaviana*, eds. T. Sulerzyska and S. Sawicka, with cooperation of J. Trenklerówna, Warsaw 1967 – *Catalogue of Drawings*, part 1, *Varsaviana*

**11.** *Katalog rysunków z Gabinetu Rycin Biblioteki Uniwersyteckiej w Warszawie*, cz. 2, *Miejscowości różne* (*A Catalogue of Drawings in the Cabinet of Drawings of the Warsaw University Library*, part 2, *Various Localities* – in Polish), ed. T. Sulerzyska, Warsaw 1969 – *Catalogue of Drawings*, part 2, *Various Localities*

**12.** *Katalog wystawy "Polonia: arte e cultura dal medioevo all' illuminismo* (*Catalogue of the Exhibition "Polonia: arte e cultura dal medioevo all' illuminismo"*), Rome 1975 – *Catalogue of the Exhibition "Polonia: Arte e Cultura"*

**13.** Z. Kossakowska-Szanajca, B. Majewska-Maszkowska, *Zamek w Łańcucie* (*Łańcut Castle* – in Polish), Warsaw 1964 – Kossakowska-Szanajca, Majewska-Maszkowska, *Łańcut Castle*

**14.** A. Król, *Zamek Królewski w Warszawie, od końca XIII wieku do roku 1944* (*The Royal Castle in Warsaw, from the End of the 13th Century to 1944* – in Polish), Warsaw 1969 – Król, *Royal Castle in Warsaw*

**15.** M. Kwiatkowski, *Mazowiecka grupa pałaców klasycystycznych* (*The Mazovian Group of Neoclassical Palaces* – in Polish), "Biuletyn Historii Sztuki", XXV, 1963, no 2, pp. 158–169 – Kwiatkowski, *Mazovian Group of Palaces*

**16.** M. Kwiatkowski, *Szymon Bogumił Zug, architekt polskiego Oświecenia* (*Szymon Bogumił Zug, Polish Enlightenment Architect* – in Polish), Warsaw 1971 – Kwiatkowski, *S.B. Zug*

**17.** M. Kwiatkowski, *W sprawie autorstwa niektórych pałaców grupy wielkopolskiej. Ze studiów nad klasycyzmem polskim* (*On the Authorship of Some Palaces of the Great Poland Group. Studies in Polish Neoclassicism* – in Polish), "Biuletyn Historii Sztuki", XXIV, 1962, no 2, pp. 156–170 – Kwiatkowski, *On the Authorship*

**18.** M. Kwiatkowski, *Zapowiedzi romantyzmu w architekturze polskiej drugiej połowy XVIII wieku* (*Pre-Romanticist Elements in the Polish Architecture of the Second Half of the 18th Century*), (in:) *Romantyzm, studia nad sztuką drugiej połowy wieku XVIII i wieku XIX* (*Romanticism, Studies in the Arts of the Second Half of the 18th and the 19th Centuries* – in Polish), Warsaw 1967, pp. 219–235 – Kwiatkowski, *Pre-Romanticist Elements*

19. S. Lorentz, *Architektura wieku Oświecenia w świetle przemian w życiu gospodarczym i umysłowym* (*The Architecture of the Age of Enlightenment in the Light of Changes in Economic and Intellectual Life* – in Polish), "Biuletyn Historii Sztuki", XIII, 1951, no 4, pp. 5–38 – Lorentz, *Architecture of the Age of Enlightenment*

20. S. Lorentz, *Domus Aurea Nerona i Villa Laurentina* (*Nero's Domus Aurea and Villa Laurentina* – in Polish), "Meander", I, 1946, no 6, pp. 314–324 – Lorentz, *Domus Aurea and Villa Laurentina*

21. S. Lorentz, *Natolin* (in Polish), Warsaw 1948 – Lorentz, *Natolin*

22. S. Lorentz, *O importach rzeźb z Włoch do Polski w pierwszej połowie XIX w. i o Thorvaldsenie* (*On the Sculpture Acquisitions from Italy to Poland in the First Half of the 19th Century and on Thorvaldsen* – in Polish), "Biuletyn Historii Sztuki", XII, 1950, nos 1–4, pp. 289–309 – Lorentz, *On the Sculpture Acquisitions*

23. S. Lorentz, *Prace architekta Louisa dla Zamku Warszawskiego* (*The Work of the Architect Louis for the Warsaw Castle* – in Polish), "Biuletyn Historii Sztuki", XIII, 1951, no 4, pp. 39–74 – Lorentz, *Work of Louis*

24. S. Lorentz, *Wawrzyniec Gucewicz. Na marginesie monografii: E. Budreika, Architektas Laurynas Stuoka Gucevicius, Vilnius 1954* (*Wawrzyniec Gucewicz. Side-notes on the Monograph: E. Budreika, Architektas Laurynas Stuoka Gucevicius, Vilna 1954* – in Polish), "Biuletyn Historii Sztuki", XX, 1958, nos 3/4 – Lorentz, *W. Gucewicz*

25. I. Malinowska, *Stanisław Zawadzki* (in Polish), Warsaw 1953 – Malinowska, *S. Zawadzki*

26. B. Maszkowska, *Z dziejów polskiego meblarstwa okresu Oświecenia* (*The History of Polish Furniture-making in the Age of Enlightenment* – in Polish), Wrocław 1956 – Maszkowska, *History of Polish Furniture-making*

27. A. Miłobędzki, *Zarys dziejów architektury w Polsce* (*A Concise History of Polish Architecture* – in Polish), Warsaw 1968 – Miłobędzki, *Concise History*

28. Z. Ostrowska-Kębłowska, *Architektura pałacowa drugiej połowy XVIII wieku w Wielkopolsce* (*The Palace Architecture in Great Poland in the Second Half of the 18th Century* – in Polish), Poznań 1969 – Ostrowska-Kębłowska, *Palace Architecture*

29. K. J. Pilchowie, *Zabytki Dolnego Śląska* (*Monuments in Lower Silesia* – in Polish), Wrocław–Warsaw–Cracow 1962 – Pilchowie, *Monuments in Lower Silesia*

30. *Portrety osobistości polskich znajdujące się w pokojach i w Galerii pałacu w Wilanowie. Katalog* (*Portraits of Polish Personages in the Rooms and Gallery of the Wilanów Palace. Catalogue* – in Polish), Warsaw 1967 – *Portraits of Polish Personages*

31. A. Ryszkiewicz, *Polski portret zbiorowy* (*Polish Group Portrait* – in Polish), Warsaw–Wrocław–Cracow 1962 – Ryszkiewicz, *Polish Group Portrait*

32. K. Sroczyńska, *Zygmunt Vogel, rysownik gabinetowy Stanisława Augusta* (*Zygmunt Vogel, Court Drawing Artist of King Stanislas Augustus* – in Polish), Wrocław–Warsaw–Cracow 1969 – Sroczyńska, *Z. Vogel*

33. W. Tatarkiewicz, *Dominik Merlini* (*Domenico Merlini* – in Polish), Warsaw 1955 – Tatarkiewicz, *Merlini*

34. "Biuletyn Historii Sztuki" (Bulletin of Art History) – BAH

35. The Cabinet of Drawings at the Library of Warsaw University – Cabinet of Drawings, Warsaw Univ. Lib.

The dimensions of objects described in the catalogue are given in cm, height times width.

Every entry in the catalogue includes a number in square brackets which corresponds to the sequence of illustrations in the book.

# Architectural Draft Design

## Jakub Fontana (1710–1773)

**1** [I] Warsaw, Royal Castle, Marble Chamber, view of the northern wall, 1770–1771

Inventory of the northern wall, drawing by J. Ch. Kamsetzer, 1784, India ink and water colour, 24×50; the inscription on the jacket refers to a set of 5 drawings: "Projet pour la Chambre de Marbre en 1768. V Feuilles" and "par Fontana en 1768"; Cabinet of Drawings, Warsaw Univ. Lib., Royal Collection, T. 189 no 16

The Marble Chamber was situated in the eastern wing on the side of the courtyard. In the reign of Ladislas IV it was used for reception purposes and was damaged later on. It was rebuilt in 1770–1771 to a design by J. Fontana of 1768. The royal portraits were painted by M. Bacciarelli, the ceiling painting by M. Bacciarelli and J.B. Plersch, sculptures by A. Le Brun, stucco work by A. Bianchi and Merck, stone work by Dollinger. At the order of Paskewich the Chamber was stripped of marble and furnishings and the royal portraits taken away to Russia. In 1922, part of the furnishings of the Chamber were returned to the Castle where they remained until September 1939.

If it is accepted, following Batowska, that J. Ch. Kamsetzer drew them, then they were made in 1784 when Kamsetzer was carrying out measurements at the Castle. The Chamber was conceived of as a reception hall which commemorated Polish monarchs. As in the Knights' Hall, also here the King intended to have the many centuries of the history of the Polish state recalled to the contemporaries. A return to history was one of the major tendencies in the Age of Enlightenment, which was particularly strongly reflected in the closest entourage of King Stanislas Augustus.

*Bibliography:* N. and Z. Batowski, M. Kwiatkowski, *Jan Chrystian Kamsetzer, architekt Stanisława Augusta* (*Jan Chrystian Kamsetzer, Architect of Stanislas Augustus* – in Polish), Warsaw 1978, p. 100

## Victor Louis (1731–1800)

**2** [p. 7] Warsaw, Royal Castle, draft design of the Ballroom, 1765

Cross-section with a view of the window wall; India ink and water colour, 20×34.5; with the inscription: "Coupe de la Salle de Bal No 11; par Louis à Varsovie en 1765"; Cabinet of Drawings, Warsaw Univ. Lib., Royal Collection, T. 192 no 18

The interior which was to become the Ballroom was formed as a result of the extensive reconstruction and expansion under Augustus III, but it was left unfinished at that time. This was a two-storey reception hall on a rectangular plan with rounded corners. Louis intended to decorate it with 48 Ionic wall columns which would have stood all round it, supporting the gallery. The shafts of these columns were to be fluted and garlanded. The Hall, despite the noticeable reserve in decoration, makes the impression of a rococo room rather than a neoclassical one. The idea of the rhythmical articulation of the interior with wall columns all round it was undertaken in 1777 by the architects who took part in a competition for the decoration of the Ballroom.

*Bibliography: Catalogue of Drawings,* part 1, *Varsaviana,* item 262, p. 83; Lorentz, *Work of Louis,* pp. 39–74

## Victor Louis

**3** [IV] Warsaw, Royal Castle, draft design of the Throne Room, 1766

The wall with the royal throne; India ink and water colour, 30×77.5; with the inscription: "Development de la chambre du Dais No 12. du côté du Trône. env. de Paris en 1766"; Cabinet of Drawings, Warsaw Univ. Lib., Royal Collection, T. 192 no 36

The designs which Louis made for the interiors of the Castle were never carried out. However, some elements of the decoration and furnishings of the interiors designed by Louis, such as bronzes, furniture, textiles, vases, sculpted woodwork etc., continued to be brought in from Paris until 1778. D. Merlini used these elements in the interiors which he designed. In the Throne Room, which was to be situated next to the Ball Room (in the place where the Knights' Hall was later sited), there were early neoclassical motifs of laurel wreaths, wreathed eagles, fasces and doors with a motif of crossed standards. Some dissonance was introduced into the early neoclassical wall composition by two niche sculptures in traditional baroque pose.

*Bibliography:* Lorentz, *Work of Louis,* pp. 39–74; *Catalogue of Drawings,* part 1, *Varsaviana,* item 285, p. 87; F. G. Pariset, *Jeszcze o pracach Wiktora Louisa dla Zamku warszawskiego* (*More About the Work of Victor Louis for the Warsaw Castle* – in Polish), BAH, XXIV, 1962, no 2, pp. 137–148.

## Victor Louis

**4** [V] Warsaw, Royal Castle, draft design of the Bedchamber, 1766

The wall with the King's bed; India ink and water colour, 25×66; with the inscription: "Development de la chambre a coucher No. 14. du côté du Lit.", "Paris 1766"; Cabinet of Drawings, Warsaw Univ. Lib., Royal Collection T. 192 no 28

In this design the Bedchamber was situated in the place of the later Throne Room. The composition of the interior was typical of the early stage of neoclassicism with its frequent reference to the architecture of the times of Louis XVI. New decorative elements drawn from classical buildings were introduced and at the same time the typically rococo, extremely intensive colour was preserved in the interiors. Paintings and sculpture of rococo form and theme were also quite frequent. The interior of the Bedchamber designed by Louis is a good example of the transition from baroque to neoclassicism.

*Bibliography:* Lorentz, *Work of Louis*, pp. 39–74; *Catalogue of Drawings,* part 1, *Varsaviana,* item 293, p. 88

## Victor Louis

**5** [II] Warsaw, Royal Castle, draft design of the King's Dressing Room, 176
The wall with the window; India ink and water colour, 59×70; with the inscription: "Developement de la moitié du Boudoir, No 15, Paris 1766"; Cabinet of Drawings, Warsaw Univ. Lib., Royal Collection, T. 192 no 56

The Dressing Room was designed for the place where the Conference Closet would later be. The artistic expression of this room was constituted by the interior decoration where neoclassical motifs (eagles, garlands, rosettes, palmettes in side-view) combined with paintings of rococo mood and very intensive colour.

*Bibliography:* Lorentz, *Work of Louis*, pp. 39–74; *Catalogue of Drawings,* part 1, *Varsaviana,* item 295, p. 88

## Jakub Fontana

**6** [p. 8] Warsaw, Royal Castle, draft design for reconstruction (the so-called 5th design by Fontana), 1772
Perspective view, drawn by J. Ch. Kamsetzer, 1773; India ink, 51.5×72.5; with the inscription: "Elevation du Chateau Royal de Varsovie suivant le dernier dessein du défunt Mr. de Fontana executé par J. C. Kamsetzer. Varsovie le 25 Juillet 1773"; Cabinet of Drawings, Warsaw Univ. Lib., Royal Collection, T. 191 no 30

In the last of his designs Fontana achieved a solution which was simple in arrangement, but at the same time monumental in terms of architecture and layout. By straightening out the bend between the southwestern and northeastern wings he brought the courtyard to rectangular form, and by demolishing the western wing and replacing it by an openwork colonnade he linked the internal courtyard to the square in front of the Castle. Fontana drew the idea of using an extended colonnade from neoclassical French and Italian architecture. However, he modified their designs by placing a helmeted tower over the main entrance. Fontana's designs were never used and further attempts to find a solution were put forward by E. Szreger and D. Merlini.

*Bibliography: Catalogue of Drawings,* part 1, *Varsaviana,* item 244, pp. 79–80; Bartczakowa, *J. Fontana,* p. 242

## Szymon Bogumił Zug (1733–1807)

**7** [p. 10] Warsaw, Solec Garden, draft design of an artificial ruin and wooden mill, c. 1772
View of the buildings from the side of the garden with a pond in the foreground; India ink and water colour, 22.1×66.2; with the inscription: "voilla le Dessain de Cug", signed "SGZ"; Cabinet of Drawings, Warsaw Univ. Lib., Inw. G.R. 146, Jeżewski Collection, 415

In 1772 Zug began work on the embellishment of the residence of Duke Kazimierz Poniatowski, the Crown Chamberlain. He expanded the palace, designing in the vicinity, among other things, a colonnade in the form of an artificial ruin and a wooden mill, and composed a landscape garden. The Solec design was the first spatial solution in Poland in which a fundamental role was played by asymmetrical buildings, made up to look apparently worn by the passage of time. The garden was also composed quite freely, with an irregular arrangement of paths, streams and clusters of trees and shrubs. This type of garden design was repeatedly used later by Zug and the contemporary Polish architects.

*Bibliography: Catalogue of Drawings,* part 1, *Varsaviana,* item 1105; p. 210, Kwiatkowski, *S.B. Zug,* pp. 45–49, 325–326, 345–347

## Domenico Merlini (1730–1797)

**8** [p. 13] Warsaw, Royal Castle, draft design for reconstruction and expansion (the so-called first design by Merlini), 1773
Perspective view; India ink and pencil, 60.2×101.5; with the inscription: "Idees de Merlini pour le Chateau depuis la mort de Fontana"; Cabinet of Drawings, Warsaw Univ. Lib., Royal Collection, T. 191 no 44

After Jakub Fontana's death, Merlini began to design the Castle. In 1773–1788 he executed six general designs for its reconstruction and expansion. In his first design he retained the previous five-sided shape, adding colonnades in the outer parts of the west elevation He intended to have the Church of Bernardine Nuns demolished and replaced by a long wing, parallel to the south elevation, which would have housed a theatre hall. The new wing was to be linked with the Castle by a colonnade, with the entrance to the Senate Hall at its centre. This would have given a spacious courtyard, divided by an openwork balustrade from the square. The strict axiality of the composition, with Great order wall divisions and the profusion of sculpted elements would have created the impression of a stately and monumental design. However, the tall baroque (Sigismund) tower was in distinct dissonance with the spatial composition based on ancient patterns. For the next dozen or so years Merlini looked for a better solution. Unfortunately, none of his designs have ever been built.

*Bibliography: Catalogue of Drawings,* part 1, *Varsaviana,* item 405, pp. 103–104

## Efraim Szreger (1727–1783)

**9** [p. 11] Warsaw, Royal Castle, draft design for a reconstruction and novel shaping of the Castle square, 1777
Perspective view; India ink and water colour, 45.5×58; with the inscriptions: "de Schröger Architecte", "Projet de Schröger pour la place des Bernadins et l'entrée du Chateau en 1767 et 1777"; Cabinet of Drawings, Warsaw Univ. Lib., Royal Collection, T. 189 no 74

Szreger's design introduced sweeping changes into the

western part of the surroundings of the Castle. They required the demolition of the Cracow Gate, the building up of the courtyard in front of the western elevation of the Castle and the elimination of some of the buildings in Świętojańska Street, including St. John's Church. At the entrance to the Castle square Szreger intended to set, symmetrically to the column of Sigismund III, a column with a statue of John III Sobieski, with a triumphal arch between them. In the centre of the square an equestrian statue of Stanislas Augustus was to stand and the imposing edifice of the cathedral was to close the area from the north. The architectural forms of Szreger's royal forum exhibited some influence of early neoclassical French architecture; the idea itself has strong echoes of Renaissance and baroque layouts.

*Bibliography: Catalogue of Drawings*, part 1, *Varsaviana*, item 386, pp. 100–101

## Domenico Merlini

**10** [p. 14] Warsaw, draft design of the edifice of the Academy of Sciences, c. 1774–1776
Perspective view; pencil and India ink, 16.6×70; with the inscription: "Projet de Façade du Palais de l'Academie"; Cabinet of Drawings, Warsaw Univ. Lib., Royal Collection, P. 186 no 196

This draft design of the edifice of the Academy of Sciences was closely related to the projected formation of a centre which would gather scholars and make their research possible.
The moderate neoclassical architecture of the building was broken by a neo-mediaeval tower, housing an astronomical observatory, in its central part. This kind of "style" contrast between architectural structures was rather characteristic of garden buildings. In the case of the Academy of Sciences the intention of this design may have been to emphasize the many centuries of the tradition of Polish scholarship (reaching back to mediaeval times).

*Bibliography: Tatarkiewicz, Merlini*, pp. 10, 19, 29; *Catalogue of Drawings*, part 1, *Varsaviana*, item 820, p. 163; Bobrowski, *Public Buildings*, pp. 90, 99, 101; Lorentz, *Architecture of the Age of Enlightenment*, pp. 33–34

## Szymon Bogumił Zug

**11** [p. 15] Warsaw, draft design of the edifice of the National Theatre, c. 1776
Front elevation; India ink, water colour and sepia, 39.3×53; with the inscription: "Façade de l'Entrée principal du Theatre", signed "SGZ"; Cabinet of Drawings, Warsaw Univ. Lib., Royal Collection, P. 186 no 169

This draft design of the theatre can be recognized as one of the most outstanding examples of public building in the Age of Enlightenment. It combined formal and functional values. In the austere outline shape of the building, three functional systems, entrance, auditorium and stage, were distinguished. The purpose of the building was emphasized by the introduction of suitably chosen inscriptions,

reliefs, medallions and statues. The public buildings which arose in the Age of Enlightenment were characterized by building shapes with a comprehensible function and appropriate iconographic programmes for the elevation. This principle was resumed by 19th-century public architecture.

*Bibliography:* Lorentz, *Architecture of the Age of Enlightenment*, p. 36; B. Król, *Budynek Teatru Narodowego (The Edifice of the National Theatre –* in Polish) (1779–1833), "Pamiętnik Teatralny", VII, 1958, no 1, pp. 68–69; Bobrowski, *Public Buildings*, pp. 121–125; *Catalogue of Drawings*, part 1, *Varsaviana*, item 941, p. 84; Kwiatkowski, *S.B. Zug*, pp. 167–168

## Szymon Bogumił Zug

**12** [p. 16] Głosków (Warsaw District), draft design of a villa for Piotr Tepper Sr., c. 1775–1780
Front elevation; India ink and water colour, 37×54.4; with the inscriptions: "Façade du Côte de l'Entrée", "Project pour Głosków faite pour le vieux Tepper", signed "SGZ"; Cabinet of Drawings, Warsaw Univ. Lib., Inw. G.R. 292, Jeżewski Collection, 90

The villa which Zug designed at Głosków was an example of the dependence of Polish architecture on the architectural ideas of Andrea Palladio, which were current here in the second half of the 18th century. Of Palladio's works, which were then the recognized patterns, his central villa, the so-called Villa Rotonda, near Vicenza, was the most significant. Zug was one of the first Polish architects related to the principle of its composition and, compared with other designs imitative of the Villa Rotonda (Królikarnia, Lubostroń), he proposed, both in the interior arrangement and in the roof form, a solution closest to the ideal. In turn the elevation of the building, with its austere Doric portico, horizontal rustication of the walls and small-scale decorative motifs was his own work.

*Bibliography:* Lorentz, *Architecture of the Age of Enlightenment*, pp. 19–21, T.S. Jaroszewski, *Ze studiów nad problematyką recepcji Palladia w Polsce w drugiej połowie XVIII wieku (Studies on the Problems of the Reception of Palladio in Poland in the Second Half of the 18th Century)*, in: *Klasycyzm (Neoclassicism –* in Polish), Wrocław–Warsaw–Cracow 1968, p. 143; *Catalogue of Drawings*, part 2, *Various Localities*, item 203, p. 62; Kwiatkowski, *S.B. Zug*, pp. 138–141, 355–356

## Marcin Knakfus (1742 – after 1821)

**13** [p. 18] Vilna, draft design of a parish teachers' training college, 1776
From elevation of the main building; India ink, 20.2×36.3; with the inscription: "Faciata Szkoły Nauczycielów Parafialnych", signed "M. Knackfus Prof: Ar: Prak: ułożył" (designed by M. Knackfus, Professor of Practical Architecture); Cabinet of Drawings, Warsaw Univ. Lib., Royal Collection, P. 186 no 202

The parish teachers' training college was designed at the request of the Committee for National Education and was strictly related to its programme, one of the most important aims of which was the creation of secular teachers. In the history of Polish architecture, this was one of the first examples of a building design with a deliberate functional programme adapted to a modern education system. The architecture of the building was in its general arrangement related to the tradition of palatial form. The designer only emphasized the modern character of the edifice by introducing monumental form and austere Tuscan order in the decoration. Unlike the palace architecture, he placed service courtyards on either side of the main building.

*Bibliography*: Lorentz, *Architecture of the Age of Enlightenment*, p. 31; Lorentz, *W. Gucewicz*, p. 372; *Catalogue of Drawings*, part 2, *Various Localities*, item 916, pp. 208–209; Bobrowski, *Public Buildings*, pp. 86–89

## Szymon Bogumił Zug

**14 [p. 20]** Warsaw, draft design of the Aleksandria palace of Janusz and Karolina Sanguszko, c. 1778
Front elevation; India ink and water colour, 41.1×59.2; with the inscription: "Façade nach den Hoffe"; Cabinet of Drawings, Warsaw Univ. Lib., Inw. G.R. 2262, Patek Collection, 594

17 drawings with designs of the palace, among which 5 versions can be found, have been preserved. The palace was built after 1780, according to the last version. It burned down after 1788 and then fell into ruin. Analysis of the various versions of the design indicates that Zug tried to free himself from the baroque conception of palace architecture. For the first time he introduced a four-column portico with a triangular fronton, simple semi-circular arcades in the French windows on the ground floor, and he covered the large wall surfaces with austere rustication. The modest decorative motifs consisted of stone vases and two medallions on a tall plinth rising out of the attic over the portico. The façade sheltered functional interiors, among which it is interesting to note a round salon on the axis on the side of the garden, and the precedent square vestibule with a circular colonnade.

*Bibliography*: Kwiatkowski, *S.B. Zug*, pp. 112–121; *Catalogue of Drawings*, part 1, *Varsaviana*, item 1009, p. 195

## Vincenzo Brenna (1747–1820)

**15 [III]** Warsaw-Natolin, draft design of the wall polychromy for the Oval Chamber, after 1780
View of the wall; India ink and water colour, 51.1×99.5; with the inscription: "Pittura Prospettica, della Pariete da dipingersi nella Camera Ovale, distesa sopra la sua superficie, da una Colonna all altra, nella sua estremita", signed "Vincentius Brenna Romanus: Architectus et Pictor: inventor et delineavit"; National Museum in Warsaw, WAF, 80, Fig. 5248

The conception of the polychromy for the Oval Chamber owed very much to the baroque decoration composition. Brenna painted illusionistic architecture of a distinctly theatrical character. The whole was complemented by the richness of ornate motifs used and decorative elements of baroque outline. However, among baroque and rococo forms there were conspicuous neoclassical motifs based on ancient patterns. These included above all the decoration of the plinth frieze (the motif of griffin and candelabrum) and that of the entablature frieze (eagles).

*Bibliography*: Lorentz, *Natolin*, pp. 42–54

## Vincenzo Brenna

**16 [VI]** Rome, draft design for the reconstruction of one of the rooms of the ancient villa of Pliny the Younger (Laurentinum), c. 1777–1778
View of the wall; India ink and water colour, 56.7×93.2; National Library in Warsaw, WAF, 68. Fig. 5028

The draft designs for the reconstruction of the villa of Pliny the Younger, called Laurentinum (after Laurentum, a town about 25 km from Rome, on the Latin coast) were made at the initiative and under close supervision of Stanisław Kostka Potocki. A description of the villa had been known from Pliny's letter to Gallus; Scamozzi (17th century) and Felibien des Avaux (early 18th century) had also written about it; the villa had further been studied by Krubsacius, an architect of the Saxon court in Warsaw. For the purposes of his work Potocki employed Polish artists who were then working in Rome and also Italian architects. Vincenzo Brenna was Potocki's main collaborator and it is to him that we owe the most beautiful inventory drawings. The set of illustrations related to the villa of Pliny the Younger originally included 49 pieces, of which only 28 have survived. We may assume that the illustrations were being prepared for publication; for unknown reasons, however, the inventory was never published. Because of this, the time-consuming reconstruction could not have affected to any large extent the crystallization of the new style and was only reflected in the designs of Brenna himself, e. g. in the draft design of the decoration for the palace at Natolin.

*Bibliography*: Lorentz, *Nero's Domus Aurea and Villa Laurentina*, pp. 314–324

## Jakub Kubicki (1758–1833)

**17 [p. 22]** Warsaw, Castle Square, draft design of a triumphal arch, 1781
Elevation; pencil and water colour, 43.2×55.9; with the inscription: "Projet d'illumination pour le retour du Roi de Wiśniowiec", "à Varsovie en 1781", signed "J Kubicki Fecit"; Cabinet of Drawings, Warsaw Univ. Lib., Royal Collection, P. 186 no 89

The triumphal arch was one of the several elements of "occasional" architecture designed for the return of King Stanislas Augustus from Wiśniowiec in September 1781. The architecture was inspired by ancient triumphal arches. The design of "occasional" buildings, executed for a variety of state and private ceremonies, was part of the duties of all the artists connected with the royal and magnate courts. These were most frequently triumphal arches and gates, castra doloris, banquet and fireworks pavilions, pillars, obelisks and thanksgiving altars.

Bibliography: *Catalogue of Drawings*, part 1, *Varsaviana*, item 1370, p. 255

## Szymon Bogumił Zug

**18** [p. 24] Warsaw (Rymarska Street, No 739 in the record of land-ownership), draft design of the "White Eagle" Hotel, 80's of the 18th century
Longitudinal cross-section and part of the elevation from Na Tłomackiem Square; India ink and water colour, 37.3×53.4; with the inscription: "Durchschnit, Ansicht vom Hoffe", signed "SGZ"; Cabinet of Drawings, Warsaw Univ. Lib., Inw. G.R.44, Jeżewski Collection, 280

Schultz's house, where the "White Eagle" Hotel was, was part of a larger spatial composition, designed by Zug in the eighties of the 18th century. Within the complex of buildings round Na Tłomackiem Square, the hotel building was conspicuous with its large mass and architecturally diversified elevation. The "White Eagle" Hotel differed from other hotel and restaurant buildings in Warsaw. In this buildig there was a distinct division of the restaurant from the accommodation and the entertainment and recreation part. The functional design of which the "White Eagle" Hotel was representative, was an intermediate type in the development of hotel architecture between the old inn and a hotel in the modern meaning of the term.

Bibliography: *Catalogue of Drawings*, part 1, *Varsaviana*, item 844, pp. 167–168; Kwiatkowski, *S.B. Zug*, pp. 201–203; A. Rottermund, *Pierwszy nowoczesny hotel w Warszawie* (*The First Modern Hotel in Warsaw*), (in:) *Sztuka 2. połowy XIX wieku* (*The Art of the Second Half of the 19th Century* – in Polish), Warsaw 1973, pp. 118–119

## Szymon Bogumił Zug

**19** [p. 25] Warsaw (38/40 Długa Street, No 556 in the record of land-ownership), draft design of the Ballroom at the so-called "Four Winds" Palace of Piotr Fergusson Tepper, c. 1784
Longitundinal cross-section and half the ceiling; India ink and water colour, 37.3×53.5; with the inscription: "Troisieme Project, Coupe de la Salle a danser, Plafon", signed "SGZ"; Cabinet of Drawings, Warsaw Univ. Lib., Inw. G.R. 2301, Patek Collection, 564

Zug designed the Ballroom on the first floor, in the new part, on the side of the garden. Three design versions of the room have been preserved; none was ever built. The common feature in all the versions was a colonnade all round the room. In the first version, the room was on a circular plan; in the second, on a rectangular plan with a semicircular end; and in the third, rectangular with semicircles on either side. In addition to the design of the salon at the Sanguszko palace and that of the Ballroom at the Royal Castle, the draft design of the Ballroom at the Tepper palace was the most carefully detailed interior design in the whole of Zug's career.

Bibliography: Kwiatkowski, *S.B. Zug*, pp. 234–237; *Catalogue of Drawings*, part 1, *Varsaviana*, item 1214, p. 228

## Jan Samuel Becker

**20** [p. 27] Różana (now in the USSR), draft design of the Theatre Room at the palace of the Sapieha family, c. 1784
Longitudinal cross-section of the auditorium; India ink, sepia and water colour, 41.2×61.7; signed "inv: dess: et execut: par J.S. Becker Lieutenant Architecte"; Cabinet of Drawings, Warsaw Univ. Lib., Sapieha Collection T. 7 no 25

A dozen or so designs of theatre halls, both court and public, from the second half of the 18th century have survived in Poland. Theatre buildings and halls were designed, for instance, by D. Merlini, J. Ch. Kamsetzer, A. Moszyński, S.K. Potocki, J. Kubicki and S.B. Zug. The architectural theme of a theatre building was one of the most popular in the Age of Enlightenment. Among the preserved designs there is the outstanding theatre hall for the palace of the Grand Chancellor of Lithuania, Aleksander Sapieha, at Różana. It is above all interesting to note the monumental character of the two-storey auditorium, mainly achieved as a result of massive columns round it and the extremely economical, austere architectural detail.

Bibliography: *Catalogue of Drawings*, part 2, *Various Localities*, item 751, p. 169

## Szymon Bogumił Zug

**21** [p. 28] Raszyn (Warsaw District), draft design of an inn, c. 1784–1790
Front elevation; India ink and water colour, 29.7×49; with the inscription "Ansicht von der Strasse", signed "SGZ"; Cabinet of Drawings, Warsaw Univ. Lib., Inw. G.R. 310, Jeżewski Collection, 82

Here, the building of the inn was one of several elements in the architectural programme for this small town belonging to Piotr Fergusson Tepper, known as Tepper the Younger. In addition to the inn, a church, a presbytery and a post office were built here. The architecture of the Raszyn inn had an interesting functional programme. In the main building, the hotel, restaurant and ball parts were separated and the service buildings (stables etc.) were in the wings flanking the courtyard. This programme was later developed in hotel buildings in the course of the 19th century.

Bibliography: Lorentz, *Architecture of the Age of Enlightenment*, p. 21; Bobrowski, *Public Buildings*, pp. 22–23; *Catalogue of Drawings*, part 2, *Various Localities*, item 725, p. 116; Kwiatkowski, *S.B. Zug*, p. 228

## Wawrzyniec Gucewicz (1753–1798)

**22** [p. 30] Vilna, draft design of the town hall, 1785–1786
Side elevation; India ink and water colour, 60.4×90; with the inscription: "Facyata Boczna od Niemieckiey Ulicy Ratusza Wileńskiego. w proiekcie Starych Murów z dodatkiem wieży na fundamentach już wymurowanych" (Side façade of the Vilna Town Hall from German Street, in the design of the old walls with the addition of a tower on foundation made earlier); Cabinet of Drawings, Warsaw Univ. Lib., Royal Collection, P. 188 no 66

Gucewicz rebuilt the old building of the town hall. He made three design versions, of which King Stanislas Augustus accepted the third. The construction of the town hall was begun in 1786 and continued until 1789. Those studying the architecture of the Age of Enlightenment have drawn particular attention to the first version of the reconstruction, which the King rejected. They have stressed the extremely economical forms of the building, above all the conscious contrast between the massive structure of the edifice and the slender tower in the back elevation. His tendency to a bold contrast between austere building outlines indicates the kinship of Gucewicz with the most avant-garde achievements of European architecture among architects at the time of the French Revolution.

Bibliography: Lorentz, W. Gucewicz, p. 373; Kwiatkowski, Pre-Romanticist Elements, p. 226; Jaroszewski, Architecture in the Age of Enlightenment, pp. 140–141; Catalogue of Drawings, part 2, Various Localities, item 909, p. 207

## Stanisław Zawadzki (1743–1806) and Stanisław Kostka Potocki (1755–1821)

**23 [p. 31]** Warsaw (20/22 Miodowa Street, No 487/488 in the record of land-ownership), draft design for the reconstruction of the Piarist college, 1786
Front elevation; India ink, 46×96.3; Cabinet of Drawings, Warsaw Univ. Lib., Royal Collection, P. 186 no 198

The edifice of the Collegium Nobilium was built as a result the endeavours of Stanisław Konarski, to a design by Jakub Fontana, in 1743–1754. The new façade was built in 1783–1786 to a design by Stanisław Zawadzki, with whom Stanisław Kostka Potocki worked closely together. The new version showed moderation in decorative motifs and a simple, lucid composition of each particular part of the building.

Bibliography: Lorentz, Architecture of the Age of Enlightenment, pp. 31–32; Malinowska, S. Zawadzki, pp. 28–29; Catalogue of Drawings, part 1, Varsaviana, item 851, p. 169

## Jan Chrystian Kamsetzer (1753–1795)

**24 [p. 32]** Sierniki (Piła District), draft design of the palace of Katarzyna Radolińska, née Raczyńska, 1786–1788
Front elevation; India ink, 27.7×44.2; with the inscription: "Façade de la maison de Campagne à Siernik"; National Museum in Warsaw, Nieb. 215/1

The external composition of the palace and the interior arrangement by Kamsetzer had become a prototype design for a number of palaces built later all over the Commonwealth. The essential features of this palace type were a rectangular plan, a projection on the axis on the side of the garden and a four-pillar portico in the front. The interior arrangement, where only the vestibule and salon on the central axis emphasized symmetry, did not correspond to the strict symmetry of the external architecture. The other rooms were in freer arrangement. Kębłowska attempted to identify the origin of this design type by proposing as the patterns of the external architecture the works of the

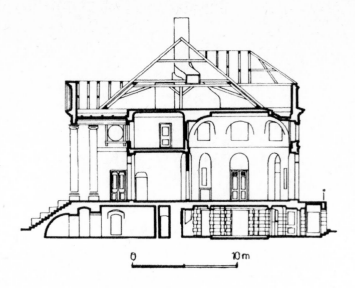

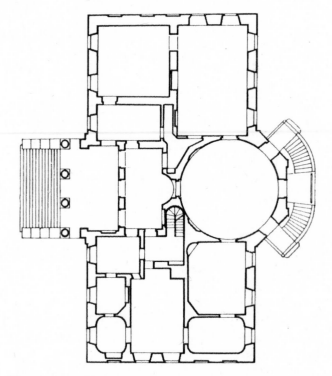

The palace at Sierniki, cross-section and ground plan

English imitators of Palladio (e.g. Campbell, Ware, Chambers, Adam), and with regard to the interior arrangement, the works of French architects (Blondel, Briseux).

Bibliography: Kwiatkowski, On the Authorship, pp. 156–170; Ostrowska-Kębłowska, Palace Architecture, pp. 131–148; Catalogue of Drawings, ed. A. Rottermund, items 615–616, p. 112

## Szymon Bogumił Zug

**25 [p. 33]** Warsaw (Mazowiecka Street, No 1348 in the record of land-ownership), draft design of the house of Wilhelm Arndt, c. 1787
Elevation from Królewska Street (detail of the illustration); India ink, 34.2×48.4; Cabinet of Drawings, Warsaw Univ. Lib., Inw. G.R. 2351, Patek Collection, 566

Zug has been suggested as its designer by the authors of the

"Catalogue of Drawings...", who have dated the design at about 1780. The monographer of Zug, M. Kwiatkowski, has accepted this attribution, changing the date of the design to about 1787 and finally establishing the customer as August Wilhelm Arndt. The house was pulled down in 1868 because of the construction of Kronenberg's palace. Among the rather schematic elevation designs in Warsaw burghers' houses, those of the Arndt house were distinguished by individual detail.

*Bibliography: Catalogue of Drawings*, part 1, *Varsaviana*, item 1322, p. 245; Kwiatkowski, *S.B. Zug*, pp. 217–219

## Jan Chrystian Kamsetzer

**26** [p. 34] Siedlec (Poznań District), draft design of the palace of the Krzycki family, c. 1790
Front elevation; India ink and pencil, 38.5×50; National Museum in Warsaw, Nieb. 216/1

This design of Kamsetzer's completed a building which had been begun in 1770–1775. Thus, when he began work, the form of the palace had to a large extent been determined (overall outline of building, interior layout). The architect moderated the centripetal composition of the edifice by stressing its lateral parts (adding one storey). This composition with taller lateral parts was chosen under the influence of English architecture, mainly the works of Campbell and Kent. Unlike Kamsetzer's palace at Sierniki, the type represented by the Siedlec palace hardly found any reflection in Polish architecture.

*Bibliography*: Kwiatkowski, *On the Authorship*, p. 161; Ostrowska-Kębłowska, *Palace Architecture*, pp. 183–186; *Catalogue of Drawings*, ed. A. Rottermund, items 613–614, p. 112

## Stanisław Zawadzki

**27** [p. 35] Warsaw (Piękna Street, No 1755 in the record of land-ownership), draft design of the palace of Stanisław Poniatowski, called "Ustronie" (Secluded Spot), before 1785
North elevation; copperplate, 50.5×72.5 (plate); with the inscriptions: "Facciata verso il Cortile, segnata in pianta sulla Linea C.D", "IV", signed "Zawadzki Architectus Inv. et del., Christophorus ab Aqua Vincentinus Sculp. 1786"

Stanisław Zawadzki designed for Stanisław Poniatowski a large complex of architecture and garden, consisting of the palace, the adjacent service rooms (stables etc.) and the garden. Despite the symmetry of particular elevations, this architectural design was asymmetrical as a whole. In the Polish architecture of the Age of Enlightenment, Ustronie was one of the first examples of a conscious break with symmetry in residential buildings. The use of this type of design can be explained by the situation of the complex on the edge of an escarpment descending in terraces, and by the wish to stress the picturesque character of the whole. In the architecture of the palace, it is interesting to note the mansard roof shapes, characteristic of the buildings de-

signed by Stanisław Zawadzki (see Dobrzyca, Śmiełów).

*Bibliography*: Malinowska, *S. Zawadzki*, pp. 8, 29–38

## Jakub Kubicki

**28** [p. 36] Warsaw, draft design of the Ujazdów church – the Temple of Divine Providence, before 1791
Front elevation (with variants stuck on: dome with a drum, dome, dome top); pencil and sepia, 60.6×48; Cabinet of Drawings, Warsaw Univ. Lib., Royal Collection, T. 193 no 17

The first designs of the Ujazdów church, which was to stand not far from the Ujazdów Castle, on the edge of a ravine (the later Agrykola Street), were made in 1775. The design work was continued in 1781–1782 and 1784–1785. It was finally finished in 1791 when it was decided to build a "Temple of Divine Providence", to commemorate the Third of May Constitution. Among some dozens of designs, one of those proposed by Jakub Kubicki was chosen. The cornerstone was laid on the first anniversary of the passing of the Constitution. Unfortunately, the construction was stopped and never resumed again.
Most preserved designs proposed a building on a circular plan, covered by a dome, with a Ionic or Corinthian colonnade surrounding the body of the church. This pattern, based on ancient works (Vesta temples in Rome, the temple at Tivoli, the Pantheon in Rome), was popular in the architecture of the Age of Enlightenment. Kubicki's design was characteristic of this type.

*Bibliography*: Z. Batowski, *Świątynia Opatrzności z r. 1791 (The Temple of Divine Providence of 1791)*, (in:) *Sprawozdania z posiedzeń Towarzystwa Naukowego Warszawskiego (Proceedings of Sessions of Warsaw Scientific Society – in Polish)*, XXIII, Dept II, pp. 1–3; *Catalogue of Drawings*, part 1, *Varsaviana*, item 95, pp. 59–60

## Jan Chrystian Kamsetzer

**29** [p. 38] Warsaw, Royal Castle, draft design of the Bedchamber and Study, 1792
Cross-section with a view of the walls facing the windows; India ink, 29.5x48.2; with the inscription: "Coupe du Cabinet de travail et de la Chambre à coucher de Sa Majesté du côté vis à vis les fenêtres. Tab. II"; Cabinet of Drawings, Warsaw Univ. Lib., Inw. G.R. 2042, Patek Collection, 429

Kamsetzer intended to furnish the King's Bedchamber and Study on the first floor, in the wing on the side of the Vistula. The implementation of this design was begun in 1793–1795, but it seems that it was left unfinished. Its characteristic principle of interior decoration deviated from those then current in Poland. In the rooms designed by Kamsetzer an essential role was played by carefully chosen art objects and a very deliberate arrangement of them: paintings, furniture, sculptures, vases etc. The architectural decoration was reduced, only to provide a discrete frame for the works of art. Kamsetzer's manner of interior decoration was widely used in English palaces.

He had become acquainted with interiors of this type during his visit to England.

Bibliography: Catalogue of Drawings, part 1, Varsaviana, item 470, p. 113; ASAD, Archiwum Kameralne (Small Archives), III/483

## Domenico Merlini with collaboration of Jan Chrystian Kamsetzer

**30** [VII] Warsaw, Royal Castle, draft design of the Knights' Hall, 1784–1786
Inventory of the western wall; drawn by Hilary Szpilowski(?), c. 1809; India ink and water colour, 42.6×58.6; Cabinet of Drawings, Warsaw Univ. Lib., P. 186 no 217

The Hall was situated in the eastern wing, on the side of the Vistula, between the Throne Room and the Ball Room. It was furnished to Merlini's design, with the cooperation of Kamsetzer including frontons and applied ornaments. Work in the Hall was begun in 1784 and finished in 1786. Historical paintings and the portraits of famous Poles were by M. Bacciarelli; the busts of distinguished Poles, by Le Brun and J. Monaldi; the statue of Chronos was the work of Monaldi; that of Fame was sculpted by Le Brun. The stucco work was by J. Amadio and P. Casasopra. Part of the decoration – for example, the painted group of famous Poles and historical paintings – was taken away to Russia in 1832. They were returned to Poland in 1922. In addition to the Marble Chamber, the Knights' Hall had the highest thematic content among interiors of the Castle. Stanislas Augustus devoted it to the memory of the most eminent persons of the Polish nation and the most glorious events in the history of Poland.

Bibliography: Król, Royal Castle in Warsaw, pp. 121–127, 172, 183; Catalogue of Drawings, part 1, Varsaviana, item 440, p. 109

## Wawrzyniec Gucewicz

**31** [p. 39] Vilna, draft design for the reconstruction of the Cathedral Church of St. Stanislas, 1783
Perspective view; India ink, 19.1×31.4; signed: "Arch. G. del:", with the inscriptions: "Kathedra Wileńska" (Vilna Cathedral), "Widok optyczny, iak ma bydź Cathedra Wileńska, w Roku 1786. wykonany." (Optical view of how Vilna Cathedral is to be, in 1786 made); Cabinet of Drawings, Warsaw Univ. Lib., Royal Collection, P. 186 no 164

In 1783, Gucewicz took over the reconstruction of the ruined Vilna Cathedral from Józef Sacco and, according to Lorentz, as early as this Gucewicz must have elaborated his own, new draft design. Although the general layout of the building depended on the old design, still the architectural decoration was completely new and based on neoclassical forms. The prototype for the design of the front elevation of the Cathedral might have been a composition shown in the popular album by the French architect M.-J. Peyre, "Oeuvres d'Architecture" (Paris 1765).

Bibliography: Lorentz, W. Gucewicz, pp. 367–380; Jaroszewski, Architecture in the Age of Enlightenment, pp. 119–121; Catalogue of Drawings, part 2, Various Localities, item 904, p. 206

## Szymon Bogumił Zug

**32** [p. 43] Falenty (Warsaw District), draft design of the Ballroom at the palace of Piotr Fergusson Tepper, c. 1782–1784
Cross-section; India ink and water colour, 32.9×47.8; with the inscription: "Project zum Saale in Falęty"; Cabinet of Drawings, Warsaw Univ. Lib., Inw. G.R. 229, Jeżewski Collection, 29

In the present state of research it is difficult to determine whether the design was put into effect since the palace at Falenty underwent fundamental reconstruction in the 19th century. In the draft design the Ballroom was on a rectangular plan, with a Ionic colonnade inscribed along an elliptic circumference. Compared with the design of the ballrooms at the Royal Castle and Tepper's palace in Warsaw the Falenty design was much more simple and economical in decorative elements. The painted decoration represented landscapes, in order to create the impression of direct contact with the park surrounding the country residence. The motif of garden's "invasion" into the interior occurred a few times in Zug's works, which can be explained by the predilection of this architect for theatrical effects.

Bibliography: Kwiatkowski, S.B. Zug, pp. 257–261; Catalogue of Drawings, part 2, Various Localities, item 161, p. 54

## Giacomo Quarenghi (1744–1817)

**33** [VIII] Nieborów (Skierniewice District), palace of the Radziwiłł family, draft design for reconstruction and expansion, c. 1800
Front elevation; India ink and water colour, 36.8×64; National Museum in Warsaw, Nieb. 236/1

Giacomo Quarenghi was one of the most eminent European architects active in the second half of the 18th century. Although his work was related to his long stay in Russia, some of his designs were also connected with Poland. The Radziwiłł family managed to gather a large collection of Quarenghi's drawings on 44 plates, including the design for the reconstruction of the palace at Nieborów. These drawings influenced the work of two Polish architects: S.B. Zug and H. Ittar. Quarenghi drew his inspiration from the classical period and the works of the great Italian architects of the 16th century, particularly Palladio. There was repeated evidence of this in his works. Such was his project for the reconstruction of the Nieborów palace. On the basis of the Palladian principles he subordinated two lower lateral wings to a strongly emphasized central part and gave very austere shape to two towers, in a way which was very typical of the neoclassicism of about 1800.

Bibliography: M. Kwiatkowski, Polski zbiór projektów architektonicznych Giacomo Quarenghiego (The Polish Collection of Architectural Designs of Giacomo Quarenghi – in Polish), BAH, XII, 1960, no 2, pp. 166–169; Catalogue of Drawings, ed. A. Rottermund, item 448, p. 88

## Henryk Ittar (1773–c. 1850)

**34** [p. 44] Arkadia (Skierniewice District), draft design of the Tomb of Illusions, c. 1800

Front elevation and plan; India ink and water colour, 43×28; National Museum in Warsaw, Nieb. 236/59

An important architectural and ideological motif of sentimental parks was an imposing tomb (frequently with the inscription "Et in Arcadia ego"). This introduced the motif of "death in Arcadia", mainly known from Vergil's and Boccaccio's poetry and Poussin's painting, a death which comes even in a country of love and happiness. Helena Radziwiłł, née Przeździecka, ordered a design of the tomb, which she called the "Tomb of Illusions", from S.B. Zug and subsequently from H. Ittar. Ittar's draft designs were more mature. The architect tried as much as possible to unify the overall shape of the tomb, giving up excessive decoration. As a result, he achieved a very economical structure: on a square plan, with a vestibule opening to the outside through an ogival arcade.

*Bibliography:* T.S. Jaroszewski, A. Rottermund, *Hempel, Lessel, Ittar, Minter* (in Polish), Warsaw 1974, pp. 140–144

## Wilhelm Henryk Minter (1777–1831)

**35** [p. 45] Warsaw (Smocza Street, No 2492a in the record of land-ownership), draft design of the Main Warsaw Store, c. 1800

Front elevation; pencil and water colour, 38×46.3; signed: "WM"; Cabinet of Drawings, Warsaw Univ. Lib., Inw. G.R. 2211, Patek Collection, 841

The Main Warsaw Store was built about 1807 and pulled down in the course of the 19th century. This building can be considered one of the most economical, almost purist, architectural designs in Poland at the turn of the 18th and 19th centuries. Minter's design was characterized by simplicity in means of expression, reduced decoration and rejection of the traditional architectural orders. These were the essential features of the "cubic" style of the turn of the 18th and 19th centuries. Apart from Minter, F. A. Lessel and H. Ittar were the main representatives of this trend in Poland.

*Bibliography:* T.S. Jaroszewski, A. Rottermund, *Hampel, Lessel, Ittar, Minter* (in Polish), Warsaw 1974, pp. 189–191; *Catalogue of Drawings,* part 1, *Varsaviana,* item 863, p. 171

## Jakub Kubicki

**36** [p. 47] Warsaw, 1 Zamkowy Square, Royal Castle, draft design for expansion, 1816–1818

East elevation; India ink and water colour, 24×46; with the inscription: "E. Elévation projettée du Chateau Royal de Varsovie du Cote de la Vistula", signed "par j Kubicki"; State Art Collections in the Hermitage, Leningrad (USSR)

The drawing comes from a set of six plates showing a draft design for the reconstruction of the Castle and its surroundings, which Kubicki carried out as Director General of Royal Buildings at the Royal Commission for Supervision of Construction. The architect proposed a monumental neoclassical façade on the side of the Vistula, with a 7-arcade terrace and an embankment park. This design, although never fully carried out as only the terrace was built in 1818–1820, was nevertheless evidence of the great energy with which Warsaw was reconstructed and expanded in the time of the Kingdom of Poland. The façade, which was to be as much as almost 200 m wide, acquired more expression with four lateral projections and a central domed one. They moderated the monotony of the horizontal block. Altogether, this architecture was uninteresting, repeating the long obsolete composition arrangement of a wall with a rusticated ground floor and two upper storeys linked by pilasters.

*Bibliography:* E. Szwankowski, *Kubickiego plany przebudowy Zamku warszawskiego (Kubicki's Draft Designs for the Reconstruction of the Warsaw Castle* – in Polish), BAH, 1957, no 4, pp. 386–389

# Architecture

## Efraim Szreger

**37** [1] Warsaw, 52/54 Krakowskie Przedmieście Street, Carmelites' Church of the Assumption and St. Joseph the Bridegroom, front elevation, after 1762

The present church was constructed in several stages: the first in 1661–1672, the second in 1677, and continued in 1680–1682. The façade was finished in 1782 to Efraim Szreger's design of 1761–1762, sponsored by Michał and Karol Radziwiłł.

The front elevation of the Carmelites' Church was one of the earliest examples of how the neoclassical style was taking shape in Poland. The composition of the whole was based on the principle of a two-storey church façade articulated by pairs of columns or pilasters. This principle, which derived from Jesuit churches, was transformed by 17th-century French architects (e.g. the church of Val-de-Grace), towards making the composition more classical and quiet. Scholars have also pointed out the dependence of the façade of the Warsaw church in terms of composition on the triumphal arch in the Place de Trone in Paris. However, Szreger updated his design by wider spacing of the outer pairs of pilasters, introduction of rectangular panels with garlands and small corner belfries in simplified form.

*Bibliography:* S. Lorentz, *Materiały do historii kościoła Karmelitów Bosych na Krakowskim Przedmieściu (Materials on the History of the Church of the Discalced Carmelites in Krakowskie Przedmieście Street* – in Polish), "Rocznik Warszawski", III, 1962, pp. 26–41; Z. Bieniecki (commentary), *op. cit.*, pp. 41–44; Jaroszewski, *Architecture in the Age of Enlightenment,* pp. 79–82

## Domenico Merlini

**38** [2] Warsaw, Łazienki, White Pavilion, south elevation, c. 1765–1774

The White Pavilion was the first pavilion built by Stanislas Augustus in the Łazienki park. The year 1774, which has been assumed as its date by the experts on Łazienki, has raised an objection from the most recent monographer on the Łazienki complex, M. Kwiatkowski, who thinks that some architectural forms in the White Pavilion were obsolete as early as 1774 and that it is impossible that the King accepted them at that time. Kwiatkowski believes that the idea of the pavilion arose about 1765, the construction work may have begun in the late sixties and the external finish may have been carried out in 1774–1775. The interiors were thus decorated in 1775–1776, and the paintings produced in 1777. The interior decoration was the work of J.B.. Plersch and J. Ścisło.

This two-storey building on a square plan had identical rusticated elevations. The architecture of the White Pavilion is related to early neoclassical villas, and similar designs in terms of architecture and decoration could be found in French architectural pattern-books in the sixties of the 18th century.

**39** [3, 4] White Pavilion, Dining Chamber, view of the interior, 1775–1777

The Dining Chamber is a richly decorated interior on the ground floor of the pavilion, in the southeast corner. The grotesque painted decoration was carried out by J.B. Plersch. It is related to classical and Renaissance grotesque paintings, imitated in the second half of the 18th century, and was one of the earliest decorations of this type in Poland, which became widespread here only at the turn of the 18th and 19th centuries. In 1777 an antique statue of Venus Anadiomene, a Roman copy from the early 2nd century, was set in a niche opposite the window.

*Bibliography*: W. Tatarkiewicz, *Łazienki warszawskie* (*Łazienki in Warsaw* – in Polish), Warsaw 1957, pp. 58–62; M. Kwiatkowski, *Łazienki* (in Polish), Warsaw 1972, pp. 38–58

## Unknown architect

**40** [7] Rogalin (Poznań District), palace of the Raczyński family, garden elevation, 1768–1773

The palace was built in 1768–1773 for Kazimierz Raczyński. The imposing edifice of the palace and the outbuildings were connected in 1782–1783 with quarter-circular galleries, forming a spatial system of the Palladian type (see Pawłowice, the Primate's Palace in Warsaw, Śmiełów, Białaczów). In 1788–1789 a new staircase nad a salon on the first floor were built to J. Ch. Kamsetzer's design. In the middle of the elevation on the side of the garden work was begun on stairs, also to Kamsetzer's design. This work was stopped and the stairs pulled down in 1865. In 1862–1963 the stairs were reconstructed from the original design. They are the only fully neoclassical motif against the background of the late baroque outline of the palace at Rogalin.

*Bibliography*: Ostrowska-Kębłowska, *Palace Architecture*, pp. 63–75, 116–117, 220–221

**41** [5] Warsaw, garden of Izabela Czartoryska, née Fleming, a× Powązki, from 1771
Unknown author, view of the cottage of the Duchess from the southeast, last quarter of the 18th century; ink, 22.3× 61.8; Cabinet of Drawings, Inw. zb. d. (Old Collections) 476

The garden was laid out in the area bounded by the present Powązkowska, Elbląska, Pieńkowska and Libawska Streets. When the Czartoryski family took it over in 1770 this was a wooded area, with natural elevations and water reservoirs. Work on the layout of the garden was begun in 1771. Its design has been usually connected with the architects E. Szreger and S.B. Zug, the painter J.P. Norblin and the owner herself, Izabela Czartoryska, née Fleming. The natural advantages of the area made it possible to create a diversified spatial composition with the essential elements of the spacious pond and two large islands. On one of the islands the cottage of the Duchess, a complex of small houses, an artificial ruin, a triumphal arch, an amphitheatre in ruin and a fisherman's hut were built. On the other island, linked by a small bridge with the former, there was a picturesque cottage. On the land, near the shore of the pond, a gothic grange, a gardener's lodge and a mill were built. In constructing the pavilions and other elements of architecture, two sources were drawn upon: the classical period and primitive rural architecture. These were, however, no exotic forms. Among the gardens executed in Poland in the seventies and eighties of the 18th century, Powązki was closest to the English manner of shaping the garden space.

*Bibliography*: M. Kwiatkowski, *Powązki* (in Polish), "Rocznik Warszawski", vol. IX, Warsaw 1969, pp. 123–161; M. Kwiatkowski, *S B. Zug*, pp. 76–83, 375; *Catalogue of Drawings*, part 1, *Varsaviana*, item 1391, p. 261

## Efraim Szreger

**42** [6] Warsaw, 55/59 Puławska Street, villa of Izabela Lubomirska, née Czartoryska, at Mokotów, 1772–1774
Z. Vogel, Palace at Mokotów, 1806, etching; 24.9 × 29.8; signed "S. Vogel delin: J. Frey sculp"; with the inscription: "Pałac w Monkotowie. Le palais de Monkotow"

The small palace, built in 1772–1774, was completely reconstructed in 1822–1825 to H. Marconi's design in neo-gothic forms, and the latter was applied when it was rebuilt in 1960–1964. It is, however, Lubomirska's small neoclassical palace that was significant in the history of Polish architecture, since it was one of the earliest buildings in Poland with the function of a suburban villa. This type gained popularity in the architecture of the last quarter of the 18th century. Such suburban villas included, for example, the small palace of the banker Łyszkiewicz at Fawory (designed by E. Szreger), the small palace at

Natolin (designed by S.B. Zug) or the small palace at Głosków (designed by S.B. Zug).

*Bibliography:* Lorentz, *Natolin,* p. 13; B. Majewska-Maszkowska, *Mecenat Izabeli z Czartoryskich Lubomirskiej. 1736–1816 (The Patronage of Izabela Lubomirska, née Czartoryska, 1736–1816 – in Polish),* Wrocław 1976, pp. 157–187

## Efraim Szreger

**43** [8] Warsaw, Miodowa Street, Tepper's house, front elevation, 1774, L. Schmidtner, Tepper's house, lithograph, (in:) *Zbiór celniejszych gmachów miasta stołecznego Warszawy (A Collection of the Handsomer Edifices in the Warsaw Capital Town – in Polish),* Warsaw 1823

The house was built for the banker Piotr Tepper, reconstructed in the course of the 19th century, burnt down in 1944 and pulled down in 1947 in connection with the construction of the W-Z thoroughfare.

Tepper's house was the key building in early neoclassical architecture in Poland. In addition to the noteworthy values of the composition of the façade, with lucid horizontal and vertical divisions, it is particularly interesting to note the functional programme of the building. The ground floor housed banking counters, offices and store-rooms, there were reception apartments to rent on the first floor and the luxurious apartments of the owner on the second floor. This functional programme, with commercial or banking rooms on the ground floor and rooms to rent on one of the upper storeys, contained the essential features of the future urban tenement house. E. Szreger's banking house was distinct from the previous houses in Miodow Street, becoming the most important motif in one of the major streets of the capital. It was with the scale of the architecture of the building itself that Tepper wanted to manifest the important position of his banking firm in the life of the town and the country.

*Bibliography:* Lorentz, *Architecture of the Age of Enlightenment,* pp. 5–14

## Domenico Merlini

**44** [X] Warsaw, Royal Castle, Chapel, 1774–1777

The Chapel, which is on the first floor of the Grodzka Gate, consists of the square room of the nave and a small chancel on a circular plan. The Chapel was decorated at the same time that work was carried out in the Canaletto Hall and the Old Reception Chamber, i.e. in 1774–1777. The execution of the Castle Chapel was evidence of the great skill of the designer, who managed to monumentalize the very small interior and at the same time, by means of delicate colour (the willow green of the column shafts, the red of the walls and the gilded ornamentation), to give it the expression of artistic subtlety, so typical of the Stanislas Augustus style. The Chapel was destroyed in 1939–1944 and rebuilt within the reconstruction of the Castle in 1971–1983.

*Bibliography:* Król, *Royal Castle in Warsaw,* p. 112; *Zamek Królewski w Warszawie (The Royal Castle in Warsaw* – in Polish), collective work, edited by A. Gieysztor, Warsaw 1972, p. 130

## Domenico Merlini

**45** [9] Warsaw, Royal Castle, Old Reception Chamber, 1774–1777

In terms of its composition and style this interior was among those most typical of the Stanislas Augustus style. Here, Merlini combined monumental painting by M. Bacciarelli and J.B. Plersch and easel painting with the delicate outline of architectural divisions and the patterned floor. The theme of the ceiling painting was the flourishing of the arts, sciences, agriculture and commerce in the reign of Stanislas Augustus. Four ovate frontons represented the allegories of the monarch's virtues: "Faith", "Justice", "Power" and "Order Arresting the Impetuosity of Youth". The programme was complemented with the portraits of the parents of King Stanislas Augustus and with four busts of Henry IV, Elisabeth I, John III Sobieski and Catherine II. Within this framework the designer composed the decoration of the interior. In terms of style, as M. Kwiatkowski has pointed out, "neoclassicism with the hallmark of the baroque" co-existed here with an "augury of the Empire style" (eagles over the mirrors).

*Bibliography: Zamek Królewski w Warszawie (The Royal Castle in Warsaw* – in Polish), collective work, edited by A. Gieysztor, Warsaw 1972, pp. 130–131; M. Kwiatkowski, *Problemy wystroju architektonicznego wnętrz stanisławowskich – Louis, Fontana, Merlini i Kamsetzer (Problems of the Architectural Decoration in Stanislas Augustus Interiors – Louis, Fontana, Merlini and Kamsetzer),* (in:) *Siedem wieków Zamku Królewskiego w Warszawie (Seven Centuries of the Royal Castle in Warsaw* – in Polish), Warsaw 1972, pp. 180–182; Chyczewska, *M. Bacciarelli,* pp. 71–76

## Domenico Merlini

**46** [XI] Warsaw, Royal Castle, Bedchamber, 1772–1774

The Bedchamber was situated in the east wing on the side of the Vistula River, between the Old Reception Chamber and the King's Dressing Room. It was the first interior by Merlini, showing a large number of traditional features, such as the rounded corners of the alcove, the outline of the panels etc. The painted compositions in the Bedchamber were the work of M. Bacciarelli. They were four paintings whose content drew on the Old Testament: "Rebecca and Eleazar", "Esther Faints before Ahasuerus", "Hagar with Her Son on Her Lap" and "The Angel Shows the Spring to Hagar".

*Bibliography: Zamek Królewski w Warszawie (The Royal Castle in Warsaw* – in Polish), collective work, edited by A. Gieysztor, Warsaw 1972, p. 132; M. Kwiatkowski, *Problemy wystroju architektonicznego wnętrz stanisławowskich – Louis, Fontana, Merlini i Kamsetzer (Problems of the Architectural Decoration in Stanislas Augustus Interiors – Louis, Fontana, Merlini and Kamsetzer),* (in:) *Siedem wieków Zamku Królewskiego w Warszawie (Seven Centuries of the Royal Castle in Warsaw* – in Polish), Warsaw 1972, pp. 178–179; Chyczewska, *M. Bacciarelli,* pp. 71–76

## Domenico Merlini with collaboration of Jan Chrystian Kamsetzer

**47** [10] Warsaw, Royal Castle, Ballroom, 1777–1781

The spatial layout of the room dates from about the middle of the 18th century when the wing of the Castle on the side of the Vistula River was built. The earliest designs of the room were the work of V. Louis (1765) and J.B. Plersch (1765); in 1777 King Stanislas Augustus proposed an architectural competition for its design. The competitors included J.B. Plersch, S. Zawadzki, S.B. Zug, E. Szreger and D. Merlini. None of their designs was accepted and finally the room was decorated to a new design by Merlini; work was begun in 1777 and as it proceeded new details of the interior decoration and new objects of art were introduced. Kamsetzer contributed to their design. The stucco work was by J.M. Graff, the ceiling painting "Jove Brings the World Out of Chaos" by M. Bacciarelli and the sculptures by A. Le Brun and J. Monaldi.

The architecture of the Ballroom was an outstanding wo k in the "Stanislas Augustus style"; its combination of architectural, painted and sculpted decoration achieved a full harmony of composition. It is interesting to note the harmonious colour in the interior, where the yellowish shafts of the columns and a frieze the same colour stand out against the background of white walls; there was the delicate outline of golden ornamentation and the whole was dominated by a ceiling painting in warm colours.

Bibliography: Zamek Królewski w Warszawie (The Royal Castle in Warsaw – in Polish), collective work, edited by A. Gieysztor, Warsaw 1972, pp. 139–140; Catalogue of Drawings, part 1, Varsaviana, pp. 82–83, 99–102, 106–108; M. Kwiatkowski, Problemy wystroju architektoniczne-go wnętrz stanisławowskich – Louis, Fontana, Merlini i Kamsetzer (Problems of the Architectural Decoration in Stanislas Augustus Interiors – Louis, Fontana, Merlini and Kamsetzer), (in:) Siedem wieków Zamku Królewskiego w Warszawie (Seven Centuries of the Royal Castle in Warsaw – in Polish), Warsaw 1972, pp. 186–187

## Victor Louis, Domenico Merlini

**48** [12] Warsaw, Royal Castle, Ballroom, the so-called "doors with banners", 1766, adapted for the Ballroom in 1777–1781

A great number of objects of the decoration of the interiors of the Castle which Louis designed were executed and sent from Paris to Warsaw. Louis designed the doors with the banners for the Throne Room in 1766. Merlini used those ready elements for the Room in his design.

Bibliography: F.G. Pariset, Jeszcze o pracach Wiktora Louisa dla Zamku warszawskiego (More about the Works of Victor Louis for the Royal Castle – in Polish), BAH, 1962, no 2, pp. 136–137

## Domenico Merlini

**49** [11] Warsaw, Royal Castle, Ballroom, recessed doorway

The recessed doorway was the most important element of the composition of the Ballroom. Merlini used here an architectural solution which resembled the one that he used in the composition of the elevation of the Myślewice palace. Over the door there was a sculpted group representing the allegorical figures of Peace and Justice (by J. Monaldi) which supported a medallion with the profile of Stanislas

Augustus (by A. Le Brun). On either side of the door, between columns, there were A. Le Brun's statues, Apollo on the left and Minerva on the right. As a result of a very harmonious combination of the sculpture with the elements of architectural decoration, the recessed doorway of the Ballroom can be considered one of the most outstanding architectural and sculpted designs of Polish neoclassicism.

Bibliography: Zamek Królewski w Warszawie (The Royal Castle in Warsaw – in Polish), collective work, edited by A. Gieysztor, Warsaw 1972, pp. 139–140

## Domenico Merlini

**50** [13] Warsaw, Łazienki, Myślewice palace, front elevation, 1775–1776

The palace was built in stages. The main body was completed in 1775; the lateral pavilions were added in 1776 and linked to the main body with quarter-circular wings, and in 1783 another storey was added to the wings. Before the Palace on the Island was expanded, the Myślewice palace had been the most imposing building at Łazienki. It is one of the outstanding examples of early neoclassical architecture in Poland. It is interesting to note the good proportions of the cubic outline of the main body and the unusual design of the façade with a recess over the whole height.

**51** [14] Myślewice palace, Dining Chamber, 1778

The Dining Chamber is situated on the ground floor, in the back suite of the main body. In 1778 J. B. Plersch painted on the walls three large compositions representing "The View of St. Michael's Bridge in Rome", "The Casino of Pius VI at the Vatican", and "The View of Venice from St. Mark's Square". The type of decoration which included large compositions with picturesque views of towns, mainly Italian, was, apart from arabesque-grotesque decoration, the most popular interior decoration in neoclassicism. In their work painters drew on popular engraved publications.

Bibliography: W. Tatarkiewicz, Łazienki warszawskie (Łazienki in Warsaw – in Polish), Warsaw 1968, p. 18; M. Kwiatkowski, Łazienki (in Polish), Warsaw 1972, pp. 60–69

## Szymon Bogumił Zug

**52** [15] Warsaw-Wilanów, Guardhouse, 1775–1776

At the request of Izabela Lubomirska, née Czartoryska, Zug built three buildings at Wilanów: Guardhouse, Kitchen and Bath-house. These buildings are situated on the right of the courtyard. Chronologically, the Guardhouse came first; it was a two-storeyed building on a rectangular plan with a small inner courtyard. It is interesting to note the very individual form of the elevation. The whole surfaces of the walls of the projections and corners were rusticated and the motifs of Doric entablature, panels, discs and knobs introduced as decorative elements. These motifs became part of the formal repertory of Zug's design. Both the conception of the inner courtyard and the individual form of the elevation indicate that in the seventies Zug was experimenting in overall forms and the surfaces of the walls of buildings.

*Bibliography:* Kwiatkowski, *S.B. Zug*, pp. 145–147, 348

## Szymon Bogumił Zug

**53** [16] Warsaw-Wilanów, Bath-house of Izabela Lubomirska, née Czartoryska, interior of the Bedchamber, 1775–1776

The building of the Bath-house is asymmetrically adjacent to the south wing of the palace. It was designed on a plan close to a square and was originally a single-storey building, to which Leandro Marconi, who also reconstructed the interiors, added another storey in 1893. As a result of the building and conservation work in 1965–1967, the main interiors of the bath apartment: Bathroom, Cabinet and Bedchamber, regained their original appearance. Most elements of the original decoration were preserved in the Bedchamber, a small square interior in the suite on the side of the courtyard. Its white varnished walls were covered with gilded decorative motifs. The set of these motifs, e.g. the wreath around the mirror, garlands, a full-blown bell flower with ears of corn, pairs of wreaths hung on a ribbon, ornamental listels and the composition of the panels were characteristic of Zug's individual style.

*Bibliography:* W. Fijałkowski, *Łazienka wilanowska marszałkowej Izabeli Lubomirskiej* (*The Wilanów Bath-house of Izabela Lubomirska, Wife of the Marshal*), (in:) *Muzeum i Twórca* (*Museum and Creator* – in Polish), Warsaw 1969, pp. 251–275; Kwiatkowski, *S.B. Zug*, pp. 147–149

## Demenico Merlini

**54** [19] Jabłonna (Warsaw District), palace, front elevation, 1775–1779
F. Smuglewicz, The Palace at Jabłonna from the front c. 1784–1794; India ink, pen and brush, 24.1×37; with the inscription: "Vue de Jabłonna"; Cabinet of Drawings, Warsaw Univ. Lib., Royal Collection, T. 175, no 31

Smuglewicz's drawing shows the palace from the perspective of the drive. The outbuildings are seen on either side of the courtyard of honour and on the right, on a hill, there is a Chinese bower. The palace at Jabłonna, built for Primate M. Poniatowski, was reconstructed in 1837 by Henryk Marconi (who adjusted the two wings of the palace in the front and rebuilt the interiors).
The most characteristic features of the architecture of the palace are its small scale and the strong emphasis on the central axis given by a tower with an ornate helmet.

*Bibliography:* *Catalogue of Drawings*, part 2, *Various Localities*, item 233, p. 70

**55** [17, 18] Jabłonna, palace, garden and front elevations – the present-day state

The garden elevation is dominated by the central part, housing the projecting Ballroom, which is one storey taller than the rest. This design of the central part of a palace building was employed in 18th-century French and English architecture. In Polish palace architecture it developed in a number of versions. The composition of the garden elevation at Jabłonna was one of the earliest neoclassical designs of this type in Poland.
This elevation is in contrast with the front elevation, which is less uniform in terms of composition. The latter elevation resembles rather the rococo designs of park pavilions, although the rococo features were moderated by introducing austere architectural divisions.

*Bibliography:* S. Lorentz, *Jabłonna* (in Polish), Warsaw 1957

## Efraim Szreger

**56** [20] Warsaw, 45 Krakowskie Przedmieście Street, Skalski's house, 1775–1780

The house was built for Józef Skalski, the court apothecary and the doctor of King Stanislas Augustus. It was destroyed in 1944 and rebuilt in 1948–1949, under the supervision of Mieczysław Kuźma.
Skalski's house shows the most fully developed set of forms, which makes it distinct among the late baroque and early neoclassical houses in Warsaw. In the façade Szreger used simple frames around openings, restrained neoclassical ornamentation and an austere attic coping. In the (not preserved) interiors, the architect introduced stucco decoration and ornamental motifs drawn from the classical repertory, and in the bathroom, coloured marbled walls, a type of decoration which was later adopted by others, notably J. Ch. Kamsetzer.

## Stanisław Zawadzki

**57** [23] Siedlce, palace, front elevation, 1776–1782

The palace was reconstructed and expanded from an earlier mansion, for Aleksandra Ogińska, in 1776–1782 (or, as M. Kwiatkowski dates it, in 1783–1784). It was burnt down in 1944 and rebuilt in 1950.
The building consists of a two-storey main body, perpendicular wings and single-storey annexes on either side of the wings. The main body, divided by pilasters of the Great order, has a four-pillar Ionic portico. The palace at Siedlce was the only known building designed by Zawadzki in Mazovia. It represents a modest design, which includes, however, the essential elements of this type of neoclassical palace: a simple, cubic solid, pillared portico and a projecting salon on the axis.

*Bibliography:* Kwiatkowski, *Mazovian Group of Palaces*, p. 163; *Katalog zabytków sztuki w Polsce* (*A Catalogue of Art Monuments in Poland*), vol. X, *woj. warszawskie* (*Warsaw District*), no 22, *pow. siedlecki* (*Siedlce County* – in Polish), edited by I. Galicka, M. Sygietyńska, D. Kaczmarzyk, Warsaw 1965, pp. 30–32

## Szymon Bogumił Zug (?)

**58** [XXVI] Siedlce, garden of Aleksandra Ogińska, 1776–1781

Z. Vogel, View of a Part of the Garden at Siedlce; water colour, 39×58.3; signed "S.P. 1791"; with the inscription in the margin: "Vue d'une partie du Jardin à Siedlce"; Cabinet of Drawings, Warsaw Univ. Lib., Royal Collection, T. 175 no 225

The landscape garden, called "Aleksandria" after the name of the owner, was laid out at the back of the residence of the Ogiński family at Siedlce. Its design has been attributed to Zug. The composition of the garden with its developed water system and a variety of pavilions was characteristic of the work of this architect. It included Fisherman's House, Dairy, Turkish Presbytery, Mosque and Oak with a small room. A small house with a broken column on top was built on an artificial rock in which a grotto was made. The interesting conception of a building combining naturalist motifs and a neoclassical structure with the symbolic expression of the broken column indicated the undoubted freedom in associating contradictory formal elements. In the 19th century the garden was reshaped to Walerian Kronenberg's design.

*Bibliography:* Kwiatkowski, *S.B. Zug*, pp. 101–102; Sroczyńska, *Z. Vogel*, p. 158; *Katalog zabytków sztuki w Polsce* (*A Catalogue of Art Monuments in Poland*), vol. X, *woj. warszawskie* (*Warsaw District*), no 22, *pow. siedlecki* (*Siedlce County* – in Polish), edited by I. Garlicka, H. Sygietyńska, D. Kaczmarzyk, Warsaw 1965, p. 33

## Szymon Bogumił Zug

**59** [21] Warsaw, garden of Kazimierz Poniatowski at Książęce, 1776–1779

Z. Vogel, The View of the Gardens of Prince Kazimierz Poniatowski at Książęce; 1785–1786, water colour, lost in World War II, before the war the property of the National Museum in Warsaw, inv. no 18 1797; the archives contain a water coloured photograph, inv. no 77 008

The garden was laid out on an escarpment, on the north side of the present-day Książęca Street. The architect took advantage of the relief of the terrain, separating the service part, situated closer to the present-day Nowy Świat Street, from pavilions concentrated on the very edge of the escarpment. Among Zug's dozen-odd designs, the garden at Książęce was distinguished by the considerable concentration of the buildings and at the same time by their unusual stylistical diversification. Side by side, there was a grotto with a cascade, linked by an underground passage with the room of the so-called Eliseum, a kitchen the shape of a small mosque with two minarets (called the Imam's House), a minaret which dominated the whole, a Chinese bower, a dairy with a pigeon-house, a thatched country inn and a small, round pillared temple. Only the latter was related to an ancient prototype; buildings the other all were an expression of an interest in forms which were neoclassical: Chinese and Middle-Eastern exoticism,

forms of rural architecture and naturalist motifs.

*Bibliography:* Sroczyńska, *Z. Vogel*, p. 146; Kwiatkowski, *S.B. Zug*, pp. 49–55

## Karl Gothard Langhans (1732–1808)

**60** [22] Samotwór (Wrocław District), palace, front elevation, 1776–1781

The palace at Samotwór was built for Major Gottlob Albrecht Sauern and his wife Maria Franciszka Ernestyna Countess Clairon d'Haussonville.

In the general layout of the main body of the building and the interior of the palace, the architect made reference to Palladian and English patterns. The composition of both porticoes (in the front and the garden elevations) was based on the principle of the so-called Palladian motif. The English influence was most distinct in the interior decoration of the oval salon. The palace underwent slight reconstruction in 1919.

*Bibliography:* M. Staszewska, *Pałac w Samotworze* (*The Palace at Samotwór*), (in:) *Muzeum i Twórca* (*Museum and Creator* – in Polish), Warsaw 1969, pp. 475–484

## Unknown architect

**61** [24, 25] Cracow, Main Market Place, palace of the Potocki family (also of the Wodzicki, Jabłonowski and Zbaraski families), elevation facing the Market Place, 1777–1783

This three-wing palace was integrated in the 16th and 17th centuries from older houses, and the porch was added in 1620–1631. In 1777–1783 the palace was given new decoration of the front façade and in some interiors on the first floor. The principle of its baroque composition consisted in the division of the façade by Great order pilasters, its crowning with a tympanum and a balustraded attic. However, decorative motifs from the classical formal repertory gave a new expression to this elevation, one characteristic of early neoclassical compositions. Apart from the palace of the Wodzicki family in Św. Jana Street, the elevation of that of the Potocki family is the most outstanding example of this stage of neoclassicism in Cracow.

*Bibliography:* T. Dobrowolski, *Sztuka Krakowa* (*The Arts in Cracow* – in Polish), Cracow 1959, pp. 454–456; J. Łoziński, A. Miłobędzki, *Atlas zabytków architektury w Polsce* (*An Atlas of Architectural Monuments in Poland* – in Polish), Warsaw 1967, p. 106

## Szymon Bogumił Zug

**62** [27, 28] Warsaw, 2 Małachowskiego Square, Evangelical-Augsburg Church, general view and portico, 1777–1781

This was bombed and burnt down in September 1939 and reconstructed in 1948–1958 to Teodor Bursze's design. In its plan and mass the Church is related to the Roman Pantheon. The classical theme was for the architect the starting point for a very individual scheme of architecture. Quite freely, Zug gathered here a variety of shapes: the

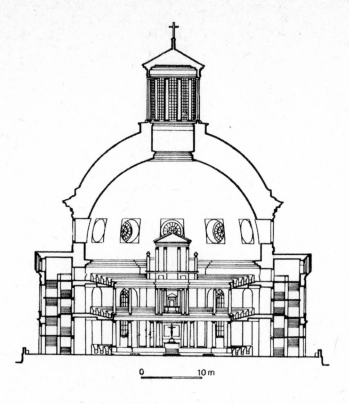

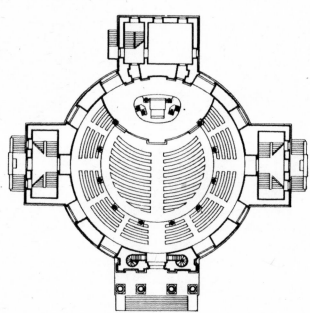

The Evangelical-Augsburg Church in Warsaw, cross-section and ground plan

central cylinder, the lateral annexes and the lantern in the form of a small pillared temple. The surface of the building with its diversified texture and the Doric order portico emphasized the austere nature of the Church. The Evangelical Church in Warsaw was the leading work of Polish neoclassicism in its most austere expression.

*Bibliography:* Kwiatkowski, *S.B. Zug,* pp. 159–162; T.S. Jaroszewski, *Nurt awangardowy architektury polskiej doby Oświecenia (The Avant--garde Movement in Polish Architecture in the Age of Enlightenment* – in Polish), "Rocznik Historii Sztuki", VIII, 1970, pp. 264–267

## Szymon Bogumił Zug, Jan Chrystian Kamsetzer
**63** [26] Warsaw, 14 Senatorska Street, palace of Piotr Blank, staircase, 1777

Blank's palace was reconstructed by Zug in 1762–1764 from an earlier building, for Filip Nereusz Szaniawski. In 1777 it was built by Piotr Blank. The neoclassical decoration of the interiors of the palace dates from this period. The decoration has been attributed to Kamsetzer or Zug. It is particularly interesting to note the vestibule and the staircase, separated by two Doric columns. The interior decoration already included motifs characteristic of the mature stage of neoclassicism.

*Bibliography:* Z. Niesiołowska-Rothertowa, *Pałac Blanka. Dawna Warszawa w odnowionej formie (Vlank's Palace. Old Warsaw in Reconstructed Form* – in Polish), Warsaw 1949, p. 9; Kwiatkowski, *S.B. Zug,* pp. 32–35, 150

## Efraim Szreger
**64** [30] Warsaw, Senatorska Street, Primate's Palace, view from Senatorska Street, after 1777 until 1783, work finished by S.B. Zug until 1786
Z. Vogel, View of the Primate's Palace, 1789; water colour, 30.9×54.5; with the inscription: "Widok II-gi Pałacu prymasowskiego" (2nd view of the Primate's Palace); National Museum in Warsaw, inv. no 181 765

An old mansion – built at the end of the 16th century for Bishop Wojciech Baranowski and rebuilt after 1691, possibly to a design by Tylman of Gameren, for Primate Michał Radziejowski – was expanded, by adding a pillared portico and wings ending in pavilions, to E. Szreger's design, for Primate Antoni Kazimierz Ostrowski. The construction was finished by S.B. Zug. It was burnt down in 1939 and rebuilt in 1949–1952 under the supervision of Kazimierz Saski, when its appearance at the end of the 18th century was restored. Such a design in which the main body of a palace is contained between quarter-circular galleries ending in pavilions has been called the Palladian layout. The Primate's Palace was the first neoclassical version of this design in Poland.

**65** [29, 31] Primate's Palace, elevation in its present-day state and detail

As a result of the reconstruction in 1777–1786, the palace acquired restrained neoclassical decoration, limited to Fames in low relief, panels in low relief in the attics and the motifs of oak garlands and fasces, which decorated the projections of the wings.

**66** [32] Primate's Palace, Ballroom

The Ballroom in the Primate's Palace, designed by E. Szreger, was one of the most magnificent works of Polish neoclassicism. Like most of E. Szreger's works, it is

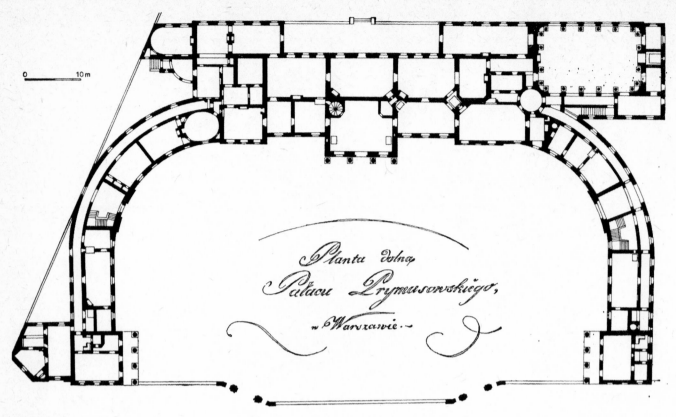

The Primate's Palace in Warsaw, ground plan

marked by lucid composition and economy in decoration. J.Ch. Kamsetzer collaborated with E. Szreger on the decoration of this interior.

*Bibliography*: K. Saski, *Odbudowa dawnego pałacu Prymasowskiego w Warszawie* (*The Reconstruction of the Old Primate's Palace in Warsaw* – in Polish), "Ochrona Zabytków", XX, no 3, pp. 20–38; T.S. Jaroszewski, *Ze studiów nad problematyką recepcji Palladia w Polsce* (*Studies on the Problems of the Reception of Palladio in Poland*), (in:) *Klasycyzm* (*Neoclassicism* – in Polish), Wrocław–Warsaw–Cracow 1968, p. 150; Sroczyńska, *Z. Vogel*, p. 152; S. Lorentz, *Pałac Prymasowski* (*The Primate's Palace* – in Polish), Warsaw 1982

## Karl Gothard Langhans

**67** [37] Pawłowice (Leszno district), palace of the Mielżyński family, view of the palace and outbuildings from the front, 1779–1787

This palace complex was built to Langhans's design for Maksymilian Mielżyński. The spatial layout of the design, which consisted in linking the main body with the outbuildings by means of quartercircullar galleries, was derived from Palladio's architecture. The design executed at Pawłowice was one of the first of this type in Poland; it became very popular later on (see Śmiełów, Białaczów, Żelazków). The architectural expression of the palace was determined by the flat mansard roof, the short lateral projections and above all a four-pillar Ionic wall portico crowned by a full attic with statues. This composition of the façade was most probably inspired by contemporary English designs with which Langhans had become acquainted during his stay in England.

## Jan Chrystian Kamsetzer

**68** [33] Pawłowice, palace of the Mielżyński family, Columnar Chamber, 1789–1792
The Chamber is on the first floor, in the suite facing the garden, on the main axis of the palace; built in 1779–1783.

It was finished and decorated to Kamsetzer's design in 1789–1792. The stucco work was carried out by Giuseppe Amadio and Giuseppe Borghi with their team. The extent to which the Chamber was already complete when Kamsetzer began his work on it has not been determined. It may be presumed that the situation of the columns was based on Langhans's design. The origin of the conception of the interior of the Columnar Chamber, which was a combination of Langhans's design and Kamsetzer's decoration, should be sought in English architecture in the school of Robert Adam. Following the destruction of the interiors of the Royal Castle in Warsaw and in other Warsaw palaces, the Columnar Chamber is the only example in Poland of an original interior from the end of the 18th century which was built as a result of the activity of architects from the royal court.

**69** [36] Columnar Chamber, detail of wall decoration

As in the Warsaw interiors designed by Kamsetzer (see the palaces of the Tyszkiewicz or Raczyński families), so at Pawłowice the characteristic feature is the combination of stucco decoration with architecture, with simultaneous complete lack of painted decoration. The decorative motifs

254

and limited colour were characteristic of Kamsetzer and his workshop. The motifs included puttoes in low relief leading animals, trophies, eagles with garlands and bands, and hanging fruit.

**70** [34, 35, 38, 39, 40] Palace of the Mielżyński family, ceiling decoration

In the complex of the interiors of the palace at Pawłowice it is interesting to note the decoration of ceilings, with geometrical divisions (rectangles, circles, diamonds triangles), into which arabesque-grotesque decorative motifs have been composed. This type of design was inspired by the interiors designed by Robert Adam, one of the most outstanding European architects, from whom Kamsetzer took only the general principle of composition; the interpretation of motifs, boldness in composing new arrangements and the richness of elements introduced were the individual achievement of the Polish architect.

*Bibliography:* Kwiatkowski, *On the Authorship*, pp. 164–168; Ostrowska-Kębłowska, *Palace Architecture*, pp. 99–112, 200–224

## Domenico Merlini

**71** [42, 43] Warsaw, Royal Castle, Throne Room, 1781–1786

The Throne Room was set in the south projection of the east wing on the side of the Vistula River. It was executed to a design probably from 1781, using a number of ready elements of decoration and furnishing which V. Louis had designed in 1765–1766 and which continued coming from Paris to Warsaw until as late as 1778 (rose-patterned wainscoting, clock table, chandeliers with eagles etc). Among the Stanislas Augustus interiors, the Throne Room had the richest interior decoration and was at the same time composed with classical discipline, which determined the lucid composition of the walls, ceiling and the beautifully patterned floor. After its complete destruction in World War II it was rebuilt in 1971–1983.

*Bibliography: Zamek Królewski w Warszawie* (*The Royal Castle in Warsaw* – in Polish), collective work, edited by A. Gieysztor, Warsaw 1972, pp. 132–133; *Catalogue of Drawings*, part 1, *Varsaviana*, p. 109; M. Kwiatkowski, *Problemy wystroju architektonicznego wnętrz stanisławowskich – Louis, Fontana, Merlini i Kamsetzer* (*Problems of the Architectural Decoration in Stanislas Augustus Interiors – Louis, Fontana, Merlini and Kamsetzer*), (in:) *Siedem wieków Zamku Królewskiego w Warszawie* (*Seven Centuries of the Royal Castle in Warsaw* – in Polish), Warsaw 1972, pp. 188–190

## Domenico Merlini with collaboration of Jan Chrystian Kamsetzer

**72** [41] Warsaw, Royal Castle, Library, interior, 1779–1782 and after 1784

This room, in a separate building situated along a wing of the Tin Roof Palace, was built to Merlini's design, with some work by Kamsetzer (interior decoration, including fire places). Medallions, designed by J.B. Plersch (one

dated 1782), were made by J. Monaldi, F. Pinck, G. Staggi and J.M. Graff. The Library was built for the royal collection of books – 16 thousand volumes – and a set of more than 70 thousand drawings. It was the only Stanislas Augustus interior in the Castle to survive the destruction of World War II. Its architectural forms were influenced by neoclassical English architecture from the last quarter of the 18th century. It was devastated by Cherkess troops in the 19th century, partly destroyed in 1944 and renovated in 1961–1965.

*Bibliography:* W. Olszewicz, *Biblioteka króla Stanisława Augusta* (*The Library of King Stanislas Augustus* – in Polish), "Przegląd Biblioteczny", V, 1931, pp. 14–57; B. Kaczorowska, *"Specyfikacja malowania" Jana Bogumiła Plerscha dla Stanisława Augusta* ("*The Specification of Painting" by Jan Bogumił Plersch for Stanislas Augustus* – in Polish), BAH, XXIX, 1967, no 4, pp. 556–558; Król, *Royal Castle in Warsaw*, pp. 141–150

## Szymon Bogumił Zug

**73** [45] Kock, palace of Anna Jabłonowska, née Sapieha, c. 1780

Z. Vogel, The Palace at Kock Seen from the Front, 1796, pen, brush, India ink, 33.9×49.2; with the inscription in the margin: "Vue de Kotsko" and, on the back, "Vogel Zygmunt Widok Kocka (View of Kock)"; National Museum in Warsaw, inv. no 46938

Zug's transformation of the old building consisted in making its architecture more classical, by adding a Ionic portico in the front elevation, a terrace supported by Tuscan columns in the garden elevation and full attics over the central part of the garden elevation and over the projections of the front elevation. Zug also reconstructed the lateral outbuildings, linking them with the main body of the palace by quarter-circular columnar galleries. This type of palace design with quarter-circular galleries, defined as Palladian, was typical of Polish residential architecture in the last quarter of the 18th century (see the Primate's Palace in Warsaw, Pawłowice, Rogalin, Tulczyn, Białaczów). Kock was one of the earliest examples of this type of design. It was reconstructed by H. Marconi in the 19th century.

## Szymon Bogumił Zug

**74** [47] Kock, parish church, 1779–1782, and town hall, c. 1780

Z. Vogel, The Market Place with Church and Town Hall at Kock, 1796, water colour, 36×53; National Museum in Warsaw, inv. no 159107

Vogel's water colour shows the view of the market place at Kock with the church and town hall a dozen-odd years after the construction work had been finished. At present, only the façade of the church has preserved the original elements; the town hall was pulled down as early as the 19th century.

The church was designed on an elongated rectangular plan, with a six-pillar portico along the entire façade. In his design Zug referred directly to a pattern contained in J.F. Neufforge's publication, which was popular in the period of neoclassicism. This type of church architecture, the first example of which in Poland was the church at Kock, was later repeated several times by Zug himself, and also by H. Szpilowski and Ch.P. Aigner. The composition of the building of the town hall, consisting of a two-storey central part, emphasized by a tower with an obelisk, and lower side parts, suggests the division of the functions of the building. The central part housed offices; the other, commercial rooms. Zug repeated this principle in other town halls.

Bibliography: Kwiatkowski, *S.B. Zug*, pp. 180–183, 318; Sroczyńska, *Z. Vogel*, pp. 177–178; Jaroszewski, *Architecture in the Age of Enlightenment*, pp. 105, 109

## Efraim Szreger

**75 [44] Skierniewice, Parish Church of St. James, south elevation, 1780–1781**

The Church, founded by Primate Antoni Ostrowski, was built in 1781 (according to the date on a slab in the façade). To the new solid Szreger adapted the gothic tower and designed full interior decoration of the Church, including the altar, pulpit, wall polychromy and baptistry. The Church was conceived of as the mausoleum of Primate A. Ostrowski. The outline shape of the Church was composed of contrasting simple and economical geometrical structures. The lucid composition of shapes was emphasized further by a rhythmical system of windows and restrained architectural detail.

**76 [46] Parish Church of St. James, interior towards the chancel**

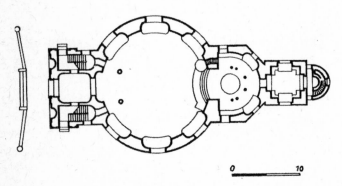

The church at Skierniewice, ground plan

The external composition of the architecture of the church is in harmony with the interior with unified expression. Simplicity, economy, composition values and harmony between the external shape and the interior, all put the church at Skierniewice among the most outstanding examples of neoclassical architecture in Poland.

Bibliography: S. Lorentz, *Skierniewice w okresie klasycyzmu* (*Skierniewice in the Period of Neoclassicism* – in Polish), "Kwartalnik Architektury i Urbanistyki", VI, 1961, no 1, pp. 3–22; T.S. Jaroszewski, *Nurt awangardowy architektury polskiej doby Oświecenia* (*The Avant-garde Movement in Polish Architecture in the Age of Enlightenment* – in Polish), "Rocznik Historii Sztuki", VIII, 1970, pp. 280–283

## Szymon Bogumił Zug

**77 [50, 51] Warsaw-Natolin, palace, park elevation, 1780–1782**

The palace was built in 1780–1782 for the then owners of nearby Wilanów, Duke August Czartoryski and his daughter Izabela Lubomirska. The painted decoration of some interiors was the work of the well-known Italian architect and decorator V. Brenna. The palace was rebuilt in 1806 (the front elevation, the vestibule and the first-floor apartments) to Stanisław Kostka Potocki's design, and to Ch.P. Aigner's in 1808 with collaboration of S.K. Potocki (the decoration of the Open Salon, the Parlour, the Mosaic Cabinet and the Dining Room). At that time Natolin was a residence of Aleksander and Anna Potocki. The palace at Natolin is an example of the early neoclassical magnate summer residences which appeared in the area of Warsaw in the last quarter of the 18th century. The most characteristic element of its architecture, which was patterned on English and French buildings of this type, is the semi-open oval salon on the side of the park. It is interesting to note the picturesque situation of the palace on the edge of a steep escarpment.

**78 [48, 49] Warsaw-Natolin, palace, general view and elevation from the courtyard, 1780–1782 and 1806**

In the elevation on the side of the courtyard, an open terrace is contained between two long projections. The exit from the terrace was through a triple-arcaded doorway. In 1806 the elevation was given new architectural decoration, designed by Stanisław Kostka Potocki. With this decoration the elevation acquired a completely different character from that of the other external walls of the palace This difference was the result of Doric order elements. The change to the more simple and austere decoration agreed with the general contemporary tendencies towards architecture which was economic in decoration and austere in expression.

Bibliography: Lorentz, *Natolin*; B. Majewska-Maszkowska, *Jeszcze o Natolinie – Bażantarnia Augusta Czartoryskiego i jego córki Izabeli Lubomirskiej* (*More about Natolin. The Pheasant-House of August Czartoryski and His Daughter Izabela Czartoryska – in Polish*), BAH, XXVIII, 1966, no 2, pp. 193–201

## Domenico Merlini

**79 [52] Warsaw, 113 Puławska Street, palace at Królikarnia, 1782–1786**

The palace was built for Karol de Valery Thomatis, Director of Royal Theatres. After the fire of 1879 it was partly reconstructed (interiors) to Józef Huss's design. It was burnt down and destroyed in 1939 and 1944; it was rebuilt in 1959–1964 to Jan Bieńkowski's design.
This two-storey, domed building on a square plan, with a four-pillar Ionic portico, was related to the famous work of Palladio, the Villa Rotonda near Vicenza. Among the

Palladian patterns which were popular in Poland in the second half of the 18th century, the Villa Rotonda type was built relatively less frequently, occurring, apart from Merlini's designs, also in the work of S. Zawadzki, S.B. Zug and Ch.P. Aigner. It is believed that the lesser popularity of buildings of this type was for purely utilitarian reasons, i.e. the rather inconvenient arrangement of interiors.

*Bibliography:* Jaroszewski, *Architecture in the Age of Enlightenment,* pp. 95–101

## Lacroix (second half of the 18th century)

**80** [53] Tulczyn (now in the USSR), palace, 1775–1782
J. Richter, View of the Palace at Tulczyn from the Front, 1835, sepia and water colour, 27.3×40.2; signed "J. Richter", in Warsaw, inv. no Polish Drawings, 1716

Among the large number of Palladian-type designs which were built for Polish customers, the palace at Tulczyn, built by an architect whom we know only by the name of Lacroix for Szczęsny Potocki, was particularly important, since this design can be included among the most monumental neoclassical palace designs in Poland.
The horizontal block of the main body, with its ten-pillar recessed portico, was linked here by short galleries with the outbuildings, which were as large as the central part. The relatively early date of the building (earlier, for example, than that of the reconstruction of Łazienki) makes the palace at Tulczyn one of the most important works of Polish neoclassicism.

*Bibliography: Widoki architektoniczne w malarstwie polskim 1780–1880. Katalog wystawy w MNW (Architectural Views in Polish Painting. 1780–1880. The Catalogue of the Exhibition in the National Museum in Warsaw – in Polish),* Warsaw 1964, item 354, p. 103; Jaroszewski, *Architecture in the Age of Enlightenment,* p. 108

## Hilary Szpilowski (1753–1827)

**81** [54, 55] Walewice (Skierniewice District), palace of the Walewski family, view of the palace from the front, 1783

The palace was built for Anastazy and Magdalena Walewski, née Tyzenhauz (there is a slab under the fronton of the portico which gives names of the founders, the architect and the date). The residence at Walewice was one of the earliest buildings in Poland to follow the design of a two--storey palace on a rectangular plan, with a pillared portico and the ground floor serving reception purposes. This type became widely used all over Poland until the forties of the 19th century. Very rare, original wall paper from the early 19th century has been preserved in the lateral pavilions. Walewice was related to Maria Walewska, née Łączyńska, the second wife of Anastazy Walewski. Maria Walewska, the "Polish wife of Napoleon", lived (from time to time) in this palace in 1805–1812.

*Bibliography:* S. Hiż, *Zarys życia i twórczości Hilarego Szpilowskiego (A Concise Outline of the Life and Work of Hilary Szpilowski – in Polish),* BAH, XVI, 1954, no 3, pp. 335–339; Kwiatkowski, *Mazovian Group of Palaces,* p. 161

## Hilary Szpilowski

**82** [56, 57] Mała Wieś (Radom District), palace of the Walicki family, view from the front, 1783–1786

The palace was built for Bazyli Walicki and his wife, née Nieborska, in the place of an earlier wooden mansion. It was an early example of a typical neoclassical country two-storey design on a rectangular plan, with a pillared portico in the front. It was built simultaneously with another palace designed by Szpilowski at Walewice. These two works constituted the beginning of a large group of Szpilowski's palaces with essentially similar elements. The painted decoration in two rooms on the ground floor, the walls on a landing on the staircase and five rooms on the first floor (also stucco work in the Golden Salon) were carried out in the late 18th century and about 1808.

**83** [62, 63] Palace of the Walicki family, Pompeian Chamber

The Pompeian Chamber is a rectangular interior on the first floor, in the suite from the west, with a reduced corner. There is grotesque decoration on the walls, on the panels of the doors, on the facet and on the ceiling, with scenes from Ovid's *Metamorphoses* and the allegories of painting, sculpture, music and architecture composed into ovals, tondoes and rectangles. This type of decoration was related, for example, to the Pompeian styles (hence the name of the Chamber) and was one of the most popular kinds of wall decoration after the eighties of the 18th century. The author of the decoration at Mała Wieś is unknown, but, in view of the good workmanship and the composition of motifs, J.B. Plersch may have been a contributor.

**84** [58, 59] Palace of the Walicki family, Golden Salon

The Golden Salon is an interior on the first floor, in the suite facing the garden. The interior was richly ornamented with stucco work which constituted the frames of openings, mirrors and panneaux; over which there was a painted frieze with motifs of eagles, garlands with wreaths and a facet with the motif of an acanthus leaf and laurel wreaths. The stucco work at Mała Wieś was one of the earliest examples of the fully mature neoclassical decoration of the palace interior. The motifs which were used here would be employed until the 19th century (see Natolin, the Mosaic Cabinet).

**85** [60, 61] Palace of the Walicki family, Warsaw Chamber

The Warsaw Chamber is an interior on the first floor; in the suite facing the garden. The walls and the ceiling were ornamented with polychromy representing in illusionistic frames a view of Warsaw and a view of Naples with Mt Vesuvius. Fantastic landscapes with ancient ruins or views of picturesque Italian towns were, apart from grotesque decoration, often used in the decoration of the walls of neoclassical interiors. A unique thing in the decoration was the panorama of Warsaw. The painter used as his pattern the well-known panorama of Warsaw from the Praga side of the Vistula River, as painted by Bernardo Bellotto, called Canaletto.

*Bibliography:* Lorentz, *Natolin*, pp. 156–157; Kwiatkowski, *Mazovian Group of Palaces*, pp. 159–163; *Katalog zabytków sztuki w Polsce* (*A Catalogue of Art Monuments in Poland*), vol. X, *woj. warszawskie* (*Warsaw District*), no 5, *powiat grójecki* (*Grójec County* – in Polish), edited by I. Galicka and H. Sygietyńska, Warsaw 1971, pp. 42–45

## Vincenzo Brenna

**86** [64] Łańcut (Rzeszów District), Castle, Brenna Room I, mural, eighties of the 18th century

This interior in the north wing of the Castle, on the ground floor, was rebuilt in the eighties of the 18th century and was at that time given painted decoration designed by Brenna. In Room I the decoration covered the four surfaces of the walls and the spaces over the doorways. The themes of the composition were ruins, ancient buildings and monuments against the background of a landscape. On one of the paintings there is the signature "V. BRENNA ROMAN [us] PIN [xit]". The composition of the decoration and the themes of the paintings were characteristic of neoclassical decorative painting based on knowledge of classical murals.

**87** [XVII] Brenna Room II, walls with paintings

In the room adjacent to the former the walls and the ceiling were covered with grotesque decoration; this type, which was related to the so-called Pompeian Styles, was popular in wall decoration as early as the eighties of the 18th century. In decoration of this type, compositions were symmetrical, with fields bounded by frames and border bands beside larger surfaces. The most frequent motifs were vases, sphinxes, dolphines, wound kerchiefs and the figures of dancers in rhomboid or mandorla frames. In addition, there was vegetal ornamentation in strictly symmetrical, often candelabral, arrangements. The type of decoration which Brenna introduced in the Łańcut interiors was popular in the decoration of Polish neoclassical palaces until the middle of the 19th century.

*Bibliography:* Lorentz, *Natolin*, pp. 34–64; Kossakowska-Szanajca, Majewska-Maszkowska, *Łańcut Castle*, pp. 144–145

## Szymon Bogumił Zug

**88** [67] Arkadia (Skierniewice District), Diana's Temple, north elevation, 1783

Arkadia, a park with pavilions, 4 km from Nieborów, is one of the most interesting Polish parks which was laid out in the last quarter of the 18th century, on the orders and under the personal supervision of Helena Radziwiłł, née Przeździecka, and was to be a dreamland of love and happiness, which was, however, interrupted by the death which was inevitable for all men. The Diana's Temple, situated on the pond, is the central point of the spatial disposition of the park, and the free, asymmetrical composition of the shape and plan of the building emphasized the romanticist ideas of the Arkadian park design.

**89** [68] Arkadia, Diana's Temple, portico on the side of the pond and south elevation, 1783

The Diana's Temple was built as the main pavilion in the Arkadia park. Its particular role in the composition of the design affected the careful selection of the final form of the Temple. It was to close the axis of vision from within the park, and on the other side of the building there was to be a spacious view of the pond and the island. The architect's purpose was to combine two types of Roman temples, monopteral building and porticoed temple, enriched further by an irregular triangular projection in the south elevation. This way of shaping the outline form of the Temple at Arkadia was an example of the tendency in Polish neoclassicism towards the breaking up of the unified composition of a shape.

*Bibliography:* J. Wegner, *Arkadia* (in Polish), Warsaw 1948, pp. 18, 21; Jaroszewski, *Architecture in the Age of Enlightenment*, pp. 144–145; Kwiatkowski, *S.B. Zug*, pp. 244–251, 331–332, 389

## Szymon Bogumił Zug

**90** [65] Arkadia, Aqueduct, 1781–1784, reconstructed in 1950–1952

Antiquity was for the neoclassicism of the second half of the 18th century not only a pattern of forms, proportion and ornamentation, but also a source of architectural structures, quite often in the shape of a ruin. The aqueduct was one of the building types. In the Arkadia park it was an essential element of composition, providing an optical counterpart to the main pond viewed from the steps of the Diana's Temple.

*Bibliography:* Catalogue of Drawings, part 2, *Various Localities*, item 35, p. 27; Kwiatkowski, *S.B. Zug*, pp. 251, 331; *Katalog zabytków sztuki w Polsce* (*A Catalogue of Art Monuments in Poland*), vol. IX, *woj. łódzkie* (*Łódź District*), no 5, *pow. łowicki* (*Łowicz County* – in Polish), Warsaw 1953, p. 6

## Szymon Bogumił Zug

**91** [66] Arkadia, Greek Arch, 1783–1785

One of the most picturesque spots in the park of Arkadia was the point from which there was the view towards the Diana's Temple. On a path, near the Temple, an arch in the shape of an arcade was set from irregular stones. The use of this material was meant to emphasize the impression of an old building. Apart from the irregular shapes of pavilions, artificial ruins and structures drawn from the architecture of previous ages were the most frequent elements in the parks in the second half of the 18th and the beginnings of the 19th century.

Bibliography: Catalogue of Drawings, part 2, Various Localities, item 38, p. 27; Kwiatkowski, S.B. Zug, p. 245

## Szymon Bogumił Zug

**92** [69] Warsaw, house of Jan Michał and Franciszek Roesler and Gaspar Hurtig, 79 Krakowskie Przedmieście Street, 1784–1785, façade from Miodowa Street, 1886–1887

The house of the Roeslers and Hurtig was one of the most outstanding achievements of the architecture of Polish neoclassicism. With its design and function, this building augured a big city tenement-house, which was to become typical of 19th-century Warsaw, and its high composition values put Zug's work among the best architectural designs in the period of neoclassicism. In the house of the Roeslers and Hurtig, there were the most characteristic features of a big city tenement-house: a deep courtyard, commercial interiors on the ground floor, the owner's apartments on the first floor and apartments to rent on the upper floors. In his layout of the façade Zug gave up the baroque tradition of axial composition and, deliberately avoiding dominating accents, broke its unity of composition.

**93** [70] Warsaw, house of the Roeslers and Hurtig, ground-floor windows

The motif of a tripartite opening, called *serliana*, was mostly used in architectural designs as the central element. In its use by Zug as a continuous motif, it was to emphasize the very individually worked out ground floor, and thus contribute to the disintegration of the unity of composition of the whole façade. In purposefully working towards such a solution, the architect was directly opposed to the baroque principles of composition. It is also interesting to note the restrained interpretation of the motifs used, above all the austere baseless Tuscan columns.

Bibliography: Kwiatkowski, S.B. Zug, pp. 209–211, 388, 401; Lorentz, Architecture of the Age of Enlightenment; Catalogue of Drawings, part 1, Varsaviana, pp. 232–233; Bobrowski, Public Buildings, p. 15; T. Grygiel, Pałac Małachowskich i Dom Roeslera (The Palace of the Małachowski Family and Roesler's House – in Polish), Warsaw 1982

## Szymon Bogumił Zug

**94** [71] Warsaw, water-tower at the former Tłomackie, so-called "Fat Kate", now in Świerczewskiego Street, 1783–1787

In the eighties Zug designed, and partly built for Karol Schultz, a complex of commercial and hotel buildings. He located the complex round a square called "Na Tłomackiem" (At Tłomackie). In the centre of the square a small, cylindrical structure was built, to house a spring. With its geometrized solid and austere elaboration of the wall surface, the architect achieved here the effect of some monumentalism. As a result of this, the building became the most important decorative element of the square. Zug's water-tower is now the only preserved relic from the former "Na Tłomackiem" square and one of the few examples of buildings of this type from the second half of the 18th century to have been preserved until the present day.

Bibliography: Kwiatkowski, S.B. Zug, pp. 192–205; Bobrowski, Public Buildings, pp. 69–73

## Domenico Merlini

**95** [72, 74] Warsaw, Łazienki, Palace on the Island, bird's eye view and south elevation, 1784

Originally the Bath-house (Łazienka) of Stanisław Herakliusz Lubomirski, it was built in 1683–1689 to a design by Tylman of Gameren (the interiors with baroque decoration: vestibule, Bacchus Room, bathroom have been preserved until today). Its neoclassical reconstruction and expansion, to serve as King Stanislas Augustus' residence, to Merlini's design, was carried out in several stages: the first, 1775–1776, consisted in the addition of the first floor from the south; the second, 1784, in the working out of the south elevation; the third, in the construction of lateral wings, north elevation and belvedere; and the fourth, in the addition of two pavilions linked with the palace by colonnades over the canals. The interiors from 1788–1795 were the work of D. Merlini (including the Rotunda and the Solomon Hall) and J.Ch. Kamsetzer (including the Ballroom); the painted decoration was carried out by M. Bacciarelli and J.B. Plersch, and the sculpted decoration by A. Le Brun and J. Monaldi. The palace was fully renovated in 1921–1922. It was burnt down in 1944. After World War II, it was reconstructed under the supervision of J. Dąbrowski, with the work finished in 1965. It is now a branch of the National Museum in Warsaw.

In the second half of the 18th century, Łazienki – the park with the palace, pavilions and park buildings – was a summer residence of Stanislas Augustus. Under his personal supervision it took a shape which, with only slight changes, it has preserved until the present day. The palace and park complex at Łazienki was one of the most interesting Polish residences constructed in the Age of Enlightenment. The architecture of the Palace on the Island was imitated in the course of the 19th century, and the building was valued for its historic as well as artistic importance. Here, in the Dining Chamber on the ground floor, meetings of scholars and artists, called "Thursday Dinners", chaired by the King himself, were held. In World War II the Germans closed the park to Poles and devastated the palace and pavilions, taking the precious collections away to Germany. In December 1944, before leaving Warsaw, they bored 800 holes for explosives in the walls of the palace, meaning to blow up the building. In view of the rapid advance of the front, they did not manage to do so, burning the palace down instead before they fled. Immediately after the liberation the walls of the palace were secured and subsequently reconstruction work was begun on the building and interior decoration, the latter including objects which have been preserved, complemented by those from the collections of the National Museum and paintings salvaged from the Gallery of Stanislas Augustus.

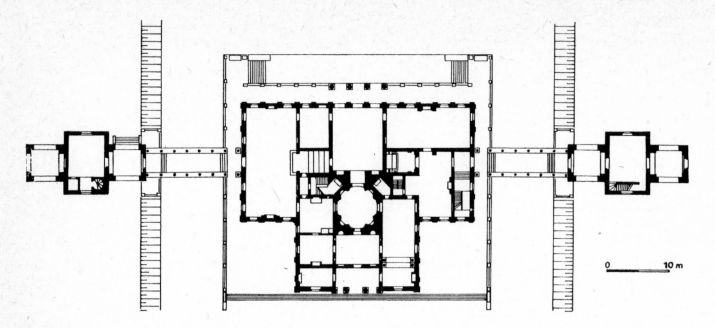

Łazienki, Palace on the Island, ground plan

## Jan Chrystian Kamsetzer, Domenico Merlini

**96** [73] Warsaw, Łazienki, Palace on the Island, north elevation, 1788
Z. Vogel, View of the Palace at Łazienki from the Bridge of King John III, water colour, 41.7×57.6; signed on the back: "Dessine d'après Nature par S. Vogel dit Ptaszek au mois d'Aout 1794"; State Art Collection Hermitage, Leningrad, USSR, inv. no 27.001

In 1787 King Stanislas Augustus set Merlini and Kamsetzer the task of further expansion of the Palace on the Island. This involved, among other things, the design of a new elevation of the palace from the north. M. Kwiatkowski has established that the conception of the north elevation was the work of Kamsetzer. The new elevation was characterized by greater simplicity, linearism and discipline of composition. The walls were articulated by flat pilasters over both of the storeys and the central part was accentuated by a four-pillar portico. The sculpture, limited to the figures of Mars and Athene in the portico and the relief filling the tympanum, stressed the architecture with economy; statues, the personifications of the four continents, were set on the attic wall crowning the palace, and the belvedere included statues symbolizing the four elements. The new north terrace was decorated by two sculptures representing fighting gladiators.

## Domenico Merlini

**97** [77] Warsaw, Łazienki, Palace on the Island, Dining Chamber, 1784–1788

This interior in the south suite, in the east part, was enlarged and decorated with stucco in the course of the expansion of the palace in 1784–1788. The parts with which the Chamber was enlarged were separated by pairs of columns facing one another; this effected an optical foreshortening of the excessively elongated interior. The very economical architecture of the Chamber was enriched with a subtly matched composition of white and red stucco. The lucid composition of the interior of the Dining Chamber makes it distinct among Merlini's works, characterized by more diversified arrangements of architecture and decoration.

## Domenico Merlini, Jan Chrystian Kamsetzer

**98** [76] Warsaw, Łazienki, Palace on the Island, Gallery, 1788–1793

This room in the north suite, in the east part, arose in the course of the extension of the palace carried out by Merlini in 1788. Until 1793 it was decorated by Kamsetzer, being meant to house a gallery of paintings densely spaced in rows, on the three walls of the room. The gallery has restrained architectural decoration. The most intense motif is a black marble fireplace and, over it, above the mirror, a medallion with the image of Antinoos (a copy of the relief at the Villa Albani near Rome). The copies of classical sculptures (Venus and a Faun) at either side of the fireplace emphasize the austere character of the room, inspired by classical patterns. Like other works of Kamsetzer's, this interior is an example of more mature neoclassicism compared to that in Merlini's designs.

## Domenico Merlini

**99** [78] Warsaw, Łazienki, Palace on the Island, Solomon Hall, 1788–1793 (photograph taken before 1939)

This interior on the axis of the palace, in the north suite, was created in the course of the expansion of the palace in 1788. It was named after a cycle of paintings devoted to King Solomon's life, executed by Marcello Bacciarelli.

"Solomon's Dream" on the ceiling was painted in 1788–1789, the two paintings on the walls: "Solomon Makes an Offering to Idols at the Request of His Concubines" and "The Consecration of the Temple in Jerusalem by Solomon" were executed in 1790–1791; the three representations on the facets: "The Judgement of Solomon", "The Queen of Sheba Visits Solomon" and "Solomon in Council with King Hiram over the Construction of the Temple", in 1792–1793.

The paintings in the Solomon Hall, which were among the best achievements of Marcello Bacciarelli, were burnt down in 1944. They glorified Stanislas Augustus, whom Bacciarelli represented in the figure of King Solomon. The other figures in the cycle were given the features of persons in the immediate entourage of the King. Bacciarelli's cycle was complemented by painted decoration carried out by J.B. Plersch and richly gilded stucco work. The composition of the Solomon Hall, which linked the surfaces of the paintings with ornamental decoration, gilded stucco work and the richness of uniformly designed furnishings, was characteristic of the reception interiors of Stanislas Augustus (see the Knights' Hall and the Ballroom at the Royal Castle in Warsaw). These interiors were related both in form and ideas, to the arts of the court of Louis XVI.

## Domenico Merlini

**100** [XVI] Warsaw, Łazienki, Palace on the Island, Rotunda, 1788–1795

This two-storey interior is in the central part of the palace, and housed a grotto with a fountain at the time of Lubomirski's ownership. The new architectural composition consisted in the articulation of the walls by eight Corinthian half-columns, among which there were four doorways and four niches with royal statues. The Rotunda was covered with a dome. The appearance of the interior was determined above all by a rich combination of the colours of stucco work and marble. The white column shafts stood against the background of golden walls with grey panels. The marble floor and the compositions painted inside the dome were also intense colour effects.

In the niches were set the statues of Polish kings: Casimir the Great (by J. Monaldi), Sigismund the Old and Stephen Báthory (by A. Le Brun) and John III (by F. Pinck to Le Brun's design). Over the doorways there were set three busts of Roman emperors: Trajan, Titus and Marcus Aurelius. The frieze round the Rotunda contains the inscription "UTILE MUNDO EDITI IN EXEMPLUM" (a quotation from Book X of Lucan's *Pharsalia*). Inside the dome Bacciarelli painted four tondoes, the allegories of Wisdom, Courage, Justice and Kindness. The meaning of the room was clear: the author of the subject matter, doubtless the King himself, wanted to express a conception of government based on the glorious Polish traditions and the political patterns of ancient Rome.

## Jan Chrystian Kamsetzer

**101** [79] Warsaw, Łazienki, Palace on the Island, Ballroom, interior, 1788–1793

This two-storey rectangular room was built in the west part of the palace in the course of its expansion in 1788. Its architecture was designed by Kamsetzer (the date of the end of the work, 1793, can be seen over the doorway), its sculpted decoration by A. Le Brun and painted decoration by J.B. Plersch.

The interior is characterized by simplicity in composition, harmonious combinations of decorative elements and reduction of stronger colour effects in favour of delicate and light hues. The architectural, sculpted and painted decoration of the room are related to familiar classical and Renaissance patterns, e.g. Plersch's frescoes derived from the Logge painted by Raphael at the Vatican. Along with the Columnar Chamber at Pawłowice and the interiors of the palace of the Tyszkiewicz family in Warsaw, the Ballroom is the most outstanding example of the interior architecture of mature neoclassicism in Poland.

**102** [80] Ballroom, fireplace with Apollo Belvedere

Over the fireplace in the north wall the designer set a statue of Apollo Belvedere, a copy of the calssical sculpture by Antonio d'Este. A. Le Brun sculpted the figures of King Midas and the satyr Marsias for the mantelpiece. Over the fireplace in the opposite wall, the statue of Farnese Hercules (a copy of the classical sculpture by Giuseppe Angelini) was placed between two caryatids, Centaur and Cerberus. Both of the compositions have symbolic meaning: the first symbolizes the superiority of spirit over stupidity and pride; the other, the power of man over the forces of Hell and the elements.

Bibliography: Łazienki warszawskie (Łazienki in Warsaw – in Polish), Warsaw 1968; W. Tatarkiewicz, Wiadomości o życiu i pracach Dominika Merliniego (On the Life and Work of Domenico Merlini – in Polish), "Rocznik Historii Sztuki", vol. 1, 1956, pp. 369–423; L. Niemojewski, Wnętrza architektoniczne pałaców stanisławowskich (The Architectural Interior Decoration of Stanislas Augustus Palaces – in Polish), Warsaw 1927; J. Szablowski, Łazienki Królewskie, widoki, plany, projekty (The Royal Łazienki, Views, Plans, Draft Designs – in Polish), Warsaw 1937; M. Mrozińska, Pierwowzory graficzne łazienkowskich stiuków figuralnych (The Graphic Prototypes of the Figurative Stucco Work at Łazienki – in Polish), BAH, XV, 1953, no 2, p. 33 and others; T.S. Jaroszewski, O naśladowaniu pałacu na Wyspie w Łazienkach (On the Imitations of the Palace on the Island at Łazienki), (in:) Muzeum i Twórca, Studia z Historii Sztuki i Kultury ku czci prof. dra Stanisława Lorentza (Museum and Creator. Studies on the History of Art and Culture Dedicated to Prof. Dr Stanisław Lorentz – in Polish), Warsaw 1969, pp. 311–325; S. Mossakowski, Rezydencja Ujazdowska Stanisława Herakliusza Lubomirskiego (The Ujazdów Residence of Stanisław Herakliusz Lubomirski – in Polish), BAH, XXXI, 1969, no 4, pp. 363 and others; M. Karpowicz, Łazienka St. Herakliusza Lubomirskiego (The Bath-house of Stanisław Herakliusz Lubomirski – in Polish), BAH, XXXI, 1969, no 4, pp. 393 and others; M. Kwiatkowski, Łazienki (in Polish), Warsaw 1972; A. Chyczewska, Marceli Bacciarelli. Katalog wystawy (Marcello Bacciarelli. The Catalogue of the Exhibition – in Polish), Poznań 1970

## Domenico Merlini

**103** [81, 82] Warsaw, Łazienki, Theatre in the Orangery, auditorium, 1784–1788

The Orangery was situated in the west part of the park, on a semicircular plan. Two wings were added to the Orangery itself: one housed the theatre, the other was to serve as apartments. The auditorium of the theatre consisted of the ground floor amphitheatre and nine boxes on the first floor. The walls of the auditorium were divided by pilasters, and over the cornice, on the axis of the first-floor boxes, nine illusionistic boxes were painted. These paintings, also the large ceiling painting representing Apollo in a quadriga, and the other elements of painted decoration were carried out by J.B. Plersch. All the architectural elements were covered with polychromy imitative of marble. The rich gamut of the colours in the interior was dominated by gold, cream, blue and beige. The painted decoration was complemented with plaster-of-Paris statues of eight female figures holding gilded candelabra. The latter were carried out by A. Le Brun, with collaboration of J. Monaldi and P. Staggi. The decoration was finished in early September, 1788, and on October 19, 1788 the theatre was opened to the public. The Theatre in the Orangery is one of the few examples of a preserved 18th-century court theatre in the world.

*Bibliography:* B. Król-Kaczorowska, *Łazienkowski Teatr w Pomarańczarni* (*The Łazienki Theatre in the Orangery* – in Polish), Warsaw 1961; M. Kwiatkowski, *Łazienki* (in Polish), Warsaw 1972, pp. 172–180

## Jan Chrystian Kamsetzer

**104** [84, 85] Warsaw, Łazienki, Amphitheatre, auditorium, 1790–1791

The Amphitheatre was ceremoniously inaugurated on September 7, 1791, with the historical ballet *Cleopatra*. The auditorium of the theatre was patterned after that at Herculaneum. The statues on the ballustrade round the auditorium were made in 1793 by T. Righi to A. Le Brun's design. There were 18 of them, with eight representing ancient playwrights, eight statues of modern ones and two which personified Comedy and Tragedy (now there are eight statues).

It is interesting to note the functional design of this auditorium and the semicircular surrounding structure which is austere in elaboration and fully expressive.

**105** [83] Amphitheatre, view of the stage

The stage of the amphitheatre was inspired by the ruins of Jove's Temple at Baalbek in Lebanon. As a result of the original separation of the stage from the auditorium by water and the inclusion of the surrounding natural water landscape into the stage dècor, Kamsetzer's work was of high artistic rank. The Amphitheatre at Łazienki is one of the few buildings of this type in the world.

*Bibliography:* W. Tatarkiewicz, *Łazienki Warszawskie* (*Łazienki in Warsaw* – in Polish), Warsaw 1968; M. Kwiatkowski, *Łazienki* (in Polish), Warsaw 1972

## Stanisław Zawadzki

**106** [90] Warsaw, Dzika Street, Barracks of the Artillery of the Crown, 1784–1788, view from the north
Z. Vogel, View of the Barracks of the Artillery of the Crown, water colour, 28.8×49.8, with the inscription: "Widok II-gi Koszar Artylerii Koron" (Second View of the Barracks of the Artillery of the Crown); National Museum in Warsaw, inv. no 181787

Between 1781 and 1795 S. Zawadzki was active in designing military buildings, constructing or reconstructing a number of barracks, including a reconstruction of the old Ujazdów Palace into the Barracks of the Foot Lithuanian Guards, rebuilding the Saxon barracks of the Mounted Guards of the Crown and the erection of a new edifice for the Artillery of the Crown in Dzika Street. This was a monumental building, on a quadrilateral plan, with an internal courtyard. The dominating effects of this simple architecture were corner projections and a strongly projected pillared portico in the east elevation. Analysis of the layout of the building, confirmed by the original reports of commissions which supervised the architect's work, indicates the functional values of the edifice. In view of the scale of the design and the rich utilitarian programme, Zawadzki's barracks were among the major achievements of Polish architecture in the second half of the 18th century.

*Bibliography:* Malinowska, *S. Zawadzki*, pp. 10–14, 25–29

## Domenico Merlini(?)

**107** [91] Dęblin (Lublin District), palace and garden pavilion, of the 18th century
Z. Vogel, View of the Palace at Dęblin, water colour, 40.3×52.1; signed "S. Vogel dit Ptaszek en 1796", "Z. Vogel" on the back and "Vue du palais de Demblin" in the margin; National Museum in Warsaw, inv. no 46939

The palace and the garden pavilion were built for Michał Jerzy Mniszech in a landscape park laid out in 1779 to Jan Chrystian Schuch's design. Merlini has been recognized as the author of the palace and the pavilion. Regarding the palace, this attribution may raise objections, since its architecture is greatly different from that of his known works. It is above all interesting to note the austere composition and expressive detail, which were not typical of Merlini. There is, however, no doubt that Merlini designed the garden pavilion called the Temple of Memories. The architectural elaboration and the use of a bucranium frieze as the decorative element were analogous to those in Merlini's other designs: the kitchen at the palace at Królikarnia and the water-tower in the Łazienki Park.

Bibliography: W. Tatarkiewicz, *Wiadomości o życiu i pracach Dominika Merliniego* (*On the Life and Work of Domenico Merlini* – in Polish), "Rocznik Historii Sztuki", I, 1956, p. 399; *Katalog zabytków sztuki w Polsce* (*A Catalogue of Art Monuments in Poland*), vol. X, *woj. warszawskie* (*Warsaw District*), no 21, *pow. rycki* (*Ryki County* – in Polish), edited by I. Galicka, H. Sygietyńska, D. Kaczmarzyk, Warsaw 1967, pp. 6–7

## Chrystian Piotr Aigner (1756–1841)

**108** [88] Olesin (Lublin District), house of Stanisław Kostka Potocki, 1785

Z. Vogel, View of the Façade of the House of Stanisław Potocki, water colour, 30×42.7; signed "SV 1789"; with the inscription: "Façade de la maison de Ct: Sta: Potocki"; National Library in Warsaw, Graphic Art Collection, AFR 18 no 7

Olesin was the summer residence of Stanisław Kostka Potocki and his wife, Aleksandra, née Lubomirska. It took its name after her and their son Aleksander. The residence, which consisted of a large landscape park, a number of pavilions and garden buildings, was constructed in 1776–1793. Aigner, in close collaboration with the owner of the residence, S.K. Potocki, contributed essentially to its shape. Potocki's house, a building with an irregular overall shape, was the major part of the complex. The austere elevation facing the pond and the side elevation were in contrast to the other elevations imitative of ruins. This type of architectural composition was characteristic of most park buildings.

## Chrystian Piotr Aigner

**109** [89] Olesin, Orangery, 1788–1789

Z. Vogel, View of the Orangery, water colour, 28.3×42.6; signed "S.V. 1789"; with the inscription: "Vue de l'orangerie"; National Library in Warsaw, Graphic Art Collection, AFR 18 no 8

The pavilion of the Orangery was situated within dense vegetation on a small river. It had a well-designed, four-pillar recessed Ionic portico. Its composition was characteristic of Aigner's work. He gave similar shape to the front façade of the Orangery at Puławy and repeated the same layout in 1817, in the façade of St. Andrew's Church in Warsaw.

Bibliography: Jaroszewski, *Ch.P. Aigner*, pp. 61–71

## Domenico Merlini

**110** [86] Racot (Leszno District), palace of the Jabłonowski family, front elevation, c. 1785

The palace was built for Duke Antoni Barnaba Jabłonowski. There is no written evidence of the designer's name, but Jabłonowski's contacts, and above all analysis of the form of the palace, suggest as the author the King's architect, Merlini. The palace at Racot has a lucid layout, dominated by the four-pillar Tuscan portico in the front and a short three-sided projection on the side of the garden. Despite evident coincidences with the palace type represented by Sierniki, the palace at Racot has a less compact shape and a different arrangement of the interiors (lacking, for example, a two-storey salon on the axis). The sources of the conception of the palace at Racot should instead be sought in the pattern-books of French architects, whereas in turn the arrangement of the interiors suggests the influence of English architecture. The plan of the palace at Racot was echoed to some extent in later designs, notably by J. Kubicki (see Białaczów, Bejsce).

Bibliography: Ostrowska-Kębłowska, *Palace Architecture*, pp. 166–171

## Karl Gothard Langhans

**111** [87] Syców (Kalisz District), Evangelical Church, façade, 1785–1789

In Silesia Langhans built several Evangelical churches (Syców, Wałbrzych, Rawicz) on similar principles of composition. They were on an elliptic plan, with a characteristic cylindrical, two-storey recess between columns. Langhans's churches were distinct in the Silesian architecture of the end of the 18th century, because of their simple, lucid composition of the shape and economical architectural decoration.

Bibliography: Pilchowie, *Monuments in Lower Silesia*, p. 148

## Chrystian Piotr Aigner and Stanisław Kostka Potocki

**112** [92, 93] Warsaw, Krakowskie Przedmieście Street, façade of St. Anne's (Bernardine) Church, 1786–1788

The gothic Church of St. Anne was reconstructed in the 16th and 17th centuries. At the initiative of S.K. Potocki, in 1786 work was begun to rebuild the façade of the church in the neoclassical style. In addition to Potocki, the sponsors of the enterprise included King Stanislas Augustus (who donated the statues of the Four Evangelists), the Duchess Lubomirska, wife of the Marshal, and Józef Kwieciński, a burgher. The façade was designed by Aigner, who was inspired by S.K. Potocki. The conception of the design was influenced by the façades of the Venetian churches San Giorgio Maggiore and Il Redentore, built by A. Palladio at the end of the 16th century. The façade of St. Anne's Church has been recognized as the most outstanding example of Palladianism in the neoclassical architecture in Poland. Also, the composition principle of the Bernardine façade provided the basis for reduced versions of standard façades, elaborated by Aigner in his *Construction of Churches*... which was published in 1825.

Bibliography: Miłobędzki, *Concise History*, pp. 258–259; Jaroszewski, *Ch.P. Aigner*, pp. 77–82

## Unknown architect

**113** [95] Poznań, palace of the Działyński family, front elevation, 1773–1781; 1786–1788

The palace was built in 1773–1781, reconstructed and

finished in 1786–1788 for Władysław Roch Gurowski. The designer of the palace is unknown; in the second stage the work was supervised by the architect Antoni Hoene. It was then that the arrangement of the interiors was determined and their decoration and the sculpted decoration of the façade carried out. In 1808 the palace passed to the Działyński family and was partly reconstructed, including the attic reliefs, kerchief decoration below the third-floor windows and in the attic. It was burnt down in 1945 and rebuilt after 1953.

The composition of the façade of the palace, which was articulated by pilasters over the two upper storeys and crowned with a tympanum, was characteristic of baroque architecture. Some formal neoclassicism can be seen above all in the rejection of dynamic baroque forms and rich decoration and their replacement by the restrained, subtle outline of architectural divisions. The palace of the Działyński family was one of the earliest neoclassical designs in Great Poland.

### 114 [96] Poznań, palace of the Działyński family, Red Chamber, 1786–1788

This reception chamber of the palace, on the first floor, in the suite on the side of the street, runs along the whole width of the palace. It was composed on a square plan, with the central part separated by columns and with two niches contained between pilasters and columns. The red marbled walls wre articulated by green marbled pilasters. In the niches were set statues of Casimir the Great and Władysław Łokietek (the Short), and in the opposite wall those of Mieszko I and Boleslas Chrobry (the Bold). They may have been the work of the sculptor Augustyn Szeps (Schöps). Reliefs o Stephen Báthory, Ladislas IV and John III Sobieski were placed over the doors. This introduction into the interior decoration of the representations of these wise and just Polish rulers gave the room an unambiguous character, propounding the political idea of a powerful and united Poland. Gurowski took over the conception of an interior with patriotic and political meaning which Stanislas Augustus had repeatedly employed (see the unrealized Senatorial Chamber at the Royal Castle in Warsaw, also the Marble Chamber and the Knights' Hall there, and the Rotunda at Łazienki in Warsaw).

*Bibliography:* Z. Ostrowska-Kębłowska, *Pałac Działyńskich w Poznaniu* (*The Palace of the Działyński Family in Poznań* – in Polish), Poznań 1958; Ostrowska-Kębłowska, *Palace Architecture*, pp. 230–232

## Stanisław Zawadzki

### 115 [94] Krzyżanowice (Kielce District), Parish Church of St. Tekla, façade, 1786–1789

The Church was founded by Hugo Kołłątaj, the priest of the Krzyżanowice parish. The façade of the Church was articulated by four Great order columns which supported the entablature, while a simple block of attic wall closed this whole of compact composition. This facade design

employed by Zawadzki at the Krzyżanowice church frequently occurred in his works (the outbuildings at Lubostroń or at Śmiełów).

*Bibliography:* Malinowska, *S. Zawadzki*, p. 14; *Katalog zabytków sztuki W Polsce* (*A Catalogue of Art Monuments in Poland*), vol. III, *woj kieleckie* (*Kielce District*), no 9, *pow. pińczowski* (*Pińczów County* – in Polish), Warsaw 1961, pp. 38–40

## Unknown architect

### 116 [97] Czerniejewo (Poznań District), palace of the Lipski family, front elevation, c. 1771–1775, portico, c. 1789–1791

The palace was built for Jan Lipski. Its authors are unknown. The spatial design and the elements of its architecture were still baroque. The four-pillar portico finished in 1789–1791 provided a neoclassical motif.  t the same time the interiors were also rebuilt. The portico at Czerniejewo was one of the most monumental in neoclassical architecture in Great Poland.

*Bibliography:* Ostrowska-Kębłowska, *Palace Architecture*, pp. 84–87, 186–191

## Unknown architect

### 117 [100, 101] Cracow, 11 Św. Jana Street, palace of the Wodzicki (Przebendowski) family, front elevation, 1787

Cracow neoclassicism was not of primary importance in the history of Polish architecture, since no truly monumental neoclassical edifice arose there. Work was limited to the reconstruction, specifically mostly new decoration, of a dozen-odd buildings, mainly palaces and houses. The palace which used to belong to the Potocki family and the one which was the property of the Wodzicki family were among the earliest. The palace of the Wodzicki family, was a conversion of two houses made in about 1780, and in 1787 was provided with a new decoration of the front elevation and the interiors on the first floor. As a result of the elements of the Doric order used to divide the elevation, the composition of the whole appears more austere and more disciplined compared to the elevations of other early neoclassical palaces in Cracow (see the palace of the Potocki family). Similar restraint can be seen in the interior decoration of the palace, where the decorative motifs of the wainscoting, stucco work and polychromy were drawn from classical ornamentation and where gold and white dominate.

*Bibliography:* T. Dobrowolski, *Sztuka krakowa* (*The Arts in Cracow* – in Polish), Cracow 1959, p. 456; J. Łoziński, A. Miłobędzki, *Atlas zabytków architektury w Polsce* (*An Atlas of Architectural Monuments in Poland* – in Polish), Warsaw 1967, p. 107

## Jan Chrystian Kamsetzer

### 118 [99] Poznań, Guardhouse, Market Place, finished in 1787

The Guardhouse was built at the initiative of Kazimierz Raczyński. There is no written evidence of Kamsetzer's authorship; however, the fact that he was working for Raczyński at that time (the palace in Długa Street in Warsaw and the work on the palace at Rogalin), and above all the presence of distinct formal analogies with Kamsetzer's New Guardhouse at Łazienki Park in Warsaw make his authorship quite probable.

The Guardhouse, one of the earliest works with features of mature neoclassicism in Great Poland, was highly appreciated by contemporaries. It attracts attention by its lucid composition of the overall shape, austere colonnade and the simple crowning attic, on which sculpted trophy decoration was set, indicating the function of the building.

Bibliography: Z. Ostrowska-Kębłowska, Pałac Działyńskich w Poznaniu (The Palace of the Działyński Family in Poznań – in Polish), Poznań 1958, p. 60

## Jan Chrystian Kamsetzer
**119** [104, 105] Warsaw, 32 Krakowskie Przedmieście Street, palace of the Tyszkiewicz family, general view, 1785–1792

The palace was built for Grand Marshal of Lithuania, Ludwik Tyszkiewicz, in several stages: the first in 1785–1786, to Stanisław Zawadzki's design (basements, part of the ground floor); the second in 1786–1792, to Jan Chrystian Kamsetzer's design. The four sculpted atlases supporting the balcony were the work of André Le Brun (1787). In 1840–1932 it was the property of the Potocki family. It was damaged in 1939 and burnt down in 1944. The palace of the Tyszkiewicz family represented the street palace type, without a courtyard and lateral wings. It was thus essentially different from the more popular types of Warsaw palaces, such as Blank's palace or the Primate's Palace. The modest elevations of the building had richer motifs in the elaboration of the balcony supported by the atlases and the four-pillar wall portico facing the square in front of the Church of the Nuns of the Visitation.

**120** [106, 107, 108] Palace of the Tyszkiewicz family, Ballroom, view of the wall and details of decoration, 1788–1789

In the palace of the Tyszkiewicz family there is one of the richest neoclassical suites of palace chambers, which were reconstructed with the greatest care following damage in World War II (vestibule, staircase, billiards room, dining, chamber and ballroom).

The principle of the composition of the interiors designed by Kamsetzer was very different from that of the interiors designed by Merlini (see the Royal Castle, Łazienki). Kamsetzer used only architectural and plastic means of decoration, giving up the rich, illusionistic painted effects and wall hangings. Stucco decoration dominated, but mostly ungilded. His only effects of colour were marbled walls and columns. A good example of Kamsetzer's style is the Ballroom, with its rich combination of decorative elements, including the particularly beautiful eagles with spread wings. The Ballroom was decorated in 1788–1789

by the stucco workers Giuseppe Amadio and Paolo Casasopra.

Bibliography: Z. Batowski, Pałac Tyszkiewiczów w Warszawie, dzieje budowy i dekoracji w XVIII wieku (The Palace of the Tyszkiewicz Family in Warsaw, A History of its Construction and Decoration in the 18th Century – in Polish), "Rocznik Historii Sztuki", I, 1956, pp. 305–368

## Unknown architect
**121** [102, 103] Lewków (Kalisz District), palace of the Lipski family, front elevation, c. 1788–1791

The palace was built for Wojciech Lipski. Its designer is unknown, but comparison with the palace at Sierniki indicates that the draft designs of the palace at Sierniki made by Kamsetzer were strictly followed at Lewków. Some differences were the result of changes introduced by the executors and by a different conception of the elaboration of the elevation. The elevations of the palace at Lewków were covered with stucco, painted and sculpted decoration. As a result of the introduction into it of heraldic motifs, monograms and portraits (?), a delibrate heraldic and genealogical programme referring to the founders' family could be read from the elevations of the palace. The interiors were also finished with rich stucco and painted decoration (now only partly preserved).

Bibliography: Z. Ostrowska-Kębłowska, Pałac gen. Lipskiego w Lewkowie (The Palace of General Lipski at Lewków), (in:) Studia i materiały do dziejów Wielkopolski i Pomorza (Studies and Materials on the History of Great Poland and Pomerania – in Polish), (13), vol. VII, no 1, Poznań 1962, pp. 115–168

## Chrystian Piotr Aigner
**122** [109] Puławy (Lublin District), palace called "Marynki", front elevation, 1790–1794

The palace is situated in the south part of the park. It was built for a daughter of Adam Kazimierz and Izabela Czartoryski, Maria, Duchess of Wittenberg, and was named after her.

The palace was designed on a rectangular plan, with a rotunda salon facing the garden, in the form of a multi-sided projection. The front elevation contains a four-pillar Corinthian portico. The architectural composition of the palace was typical of the early, more decorative stage of neoclassicism (pilasters over two storeys, attic) and was slightly out of date compared to the works by Zug or Kamsetzer dating from the same period.

Bibliography: Jaroszewski, Ch.P. Aigner, pp. 115–120

## Chrystian Piotr Aigner
**123** [110] Puławy, Sybil's Temple, 1798–1801

The Temple was built as one of the park buildings for Duchess Izabela Czartoryska, née Fleming. It was finished in 1804. The stucco interior decoration was the work of Fryderyk Baumann. The building was patterned after the ancient Sybil's Temple at Tivoli near Rome. The Sybil's

Temple was one of the most highly appreciated works of Aigner's. This was the combined result of its extremely picturesque situation on a precipitous escarpment and the use of the beautiful classical pattern, from which, apart from the characteristic Corinthian colonnade, the architect also drew decorative elements, such as the bucranium frieze on the entablature running round the Temple at Puławy. Its purpose was to house precious relics of the national past, which was emphasized by the inscription over the entrance to the upper room: The Past for the Future.

*Bibliography:* Jaroszewski, *Ch.P. Aigner,* pp. 120–124; Z. Żygulski Jr., *Dzieje zbiorów puławskich (The History of the Puławy Collections),* (in:) *Rozprawy i sprawozdania Muzeum Narodowego w Krakowie (Dissertations and Reports of the National Museum in Cracow – in Polish),* VII, 1962

## Unknown architect

**124** [111, 112] Chocz (Kalisz County), palace of the Mitred Prelates, portrait chamber, 1790

The palace, founded by the mitred prelate Kazimierz Lipski, was built in about 1785–1790, partly using the walls of the previous building. The interior stucco decoration carried out in 1790–1793 came from the same workshop which decorated the palace at Lewków the next year. The portrait chamber was situated on the first floor, in the west suite. The walls and the ceiling were decorated with stucco: with the eight medallions in ornate frames over the fireplaces, showing the representations of the mitred prelates of the Chocz Collegiate Church from the Lipski family with the Grabie coat of arms. Emblems were set in the panels and the motifs of pontificals, KL monograms and the Grabie coat of arms were woven into vegetal decoration. On the ceiling there was the Polish Eagle and the date of 1790. The purpose of the iconographic content of the chamber was to emphasize the standing and merits of the Lipski family. The composition and decorative elements of the chamber were different from other neoclassical decorations in Great Poland. Despite the neoclassical repertory of motifs, the workshop at Chocz was related to the baroque tradition in its manner of composition.

*Bibliography: Katalog zabytków sztuki w Polsce (A Catalogue of Art Monuments in Poland),* vol. V, *woj. poznańskie(Poznań District),* no 19, *pow. pleszewski (Pleszew Country – in Polish),* edited by A. Kodurowa, Warsaw 1959, pp. 4–5; Ostrowska-Kębłowska, *Palace Architecture,* pp. 192, 226–228

## Unknown architect

**125** [113] Jarogniewice (Poznań District), palace of the Sokolnicki family, front elevation, c. 1790–1792

The palace was built for Celestyn and Urszula (née Golińska) Sokolnicki; it was partly rebuilt in the 19th century (including new front decoration, the attics of the projection on the side of the garden and new capitals of columns and pilasters). The mass and the interior arrangement of the palace was related to the composition of the palace at Racot, from which the unknown designer of the palace at Jarog-

niewice must have taken his pattern. However, the portico of the palace was composed in an individual way, consisting of two pairs of columns against the background of a wider pseudo-projection with Great order pilasters.

*Bibliography:* Ostrowska-Kębłowska, *Palace Architecture,* pp. 171–173

## Karl Gothard Langhans (?)

**126** [114, 115] Pakosław (Leszno District), palace of the Krzyżanowski family, detail of the rotunda and relief "Boleslas the Bold (Chrobry) Sticks Frontier Poles in the Schaale and the Elbe", after 1791

The palace was built for Michał Krzyżanowski, probably to K.G. Langhans's design. It was fully rebuilt in the early 19th century; the colonnade of the rotunda was destroyed in 1954.

The reception interior of the palace was a two-storey rotunda with a free-standing colonnade round it, which supported a gallery. On the walls, among the columns, four reliefs were set (one of which has since been destroyed).

The reliefs in the rotunda at the palace at Pakosław were based on the graphic compositions of Franciszek Smuglewicz, from his series of illustrations for "The History of Poland". Nine of them were published in 1791. For the interior decoration Krzyżanowski chose four illustrations, which were related in theme to the rule of Mieszko I, Boleslas the Bold (Chrobry) and Mieszko II. They were: "Mieszko I Destroys the Statues of Pagan Gods", "Wichman Lays Arms Before Mieszko I", "Boleslas the Bold (Chrobry) Sticks Frontier Poles" and "Mieszko II Receives the Homage of Rebellious Pomeranians".

The ideological content of the scences was related to the postulates for strong royal power, topical during the sessions of the Four-Year Parliament, which were caused by the danger to the borders of the Commonwealth and by anxiety about the loss of independence. Whereas the architecture of the palace was related to the community of Berlin architects, the ideological programme of the rotunda must have come from the Warsaw community.

*Bibliography:* Ostrowska-Kębłowska, *Palace Architecture,* pp. 173–178, 239–244

## Jan Chrystian Kamsetzer

**127** [116] Petrykozy (Piotrków District), St. Dorothy's Church, façade, 1791–1795

The Church was built at the initiative of Stanisław Nałęcz Małachowski, Speaker of the Four-Year Parliament, and may have been intended to celebrate the passing of the Third of May Constitution, the most important event in Małachowski's political career.

The avant-garde façade of the church was composed from simple, massive geometrical forms, without any columns or pilasters. The architect enlivened the cubic block of the façade by rusticating the walls, by set-offs between the overall shape and the decided outline of the windows in the upper storey. The composition of the facade of the church at Petrykozy was one of the most outstanding works of the mature phase of Polish neoclassicism, reflecting the purist tendencies of the architecture in the nineties of the 18th century.

*Bibliography:* Jaroszewski, *Architecture in the Age of Enlightenment,* pp. 135–138

## Zygmunt Vogel (1764–1826)

**128** [117] Siedlce, Sepulchral Chapel of the Holy Cross, 1791

Z. Vogel, View of the Sepulchral Chapel, water colour, 39.8×59; with the inscriptions "Dessiné d'apres nature par S. Ptaszek en 1791" and, in the margin, "Widok Kaplicy Grobowej w Siedlcach" (View of the Sepulchral Chapel at Siedlce); Cabinet of Drawings, Warsaw Univ. Lib. Royal Collection, T. 175 no 226

The Sepulchral Chapel of Aleksandra Ogińska, née Czartoryska, is the only known work by Vogel in architecture. He had sufficient knowledge in this art, but in practice he never did more than a few occasional architecture decorations. The Chapel was on an octagonal plan and was covered by a dome. From the wall there projected three two-pillar Tuscan porticoes and an annexe housing the sacristy. The composition of the plan and mass of this small chapel was an example of the tendency to simplify architectural forms, which was common at that time.

*Bibliography:* Sroczyńska, *Z. Vogel,* pp. 102, 158, 204

## Szymon Bogumił Zug

**129** [118] Łańcut, Castle, Column Room, interior, early nineties of the 18th century

This interior in the southeast part of the Castle, on the first floor, was probably rebuilt to neoclassical forms in the early nineties of the 18th century, to, as T. Sulerzyska has shown, a slightly modified design by Zug. As a result of its restrained decoration and the separation of the interior by a double Ionic colonnade, despite its relatively small size, this chamber has acquired a solemn, monumental character, becoming one of the outstanding interiors of the mature stage of Polish neoclassicism.

*Bibliography:* T. Sulerzyska, *Nowe określenia kilku rysunków S.B. Zuga* (*New Determinations of Some Drawings by S.B. Zug* – in Polish), BAH, XXVIII, 1965, no 4, pp. 338–340; Kossakowska-Szanajca, Majewska-Maszkowska, *Łańcut Castle,* pp. 211–215; Kwiatkowski, *S.B. Zug,* pp. 296–197

## Jan Chrystian Kamsetzer

**130** [119] Warsaw, Łazienki, New Guardhouse, elevation facing the pond, 1793

In keeping with its character, this building, situated on the east bank of the north pond, was given austere Tuscan architectural decoration. The colonnade was in pronounced projections, with arcaded passageways of simple cut. Here, Kamsetzer repeated the essential principle of the composition of the Guardhouse in Poznań, which he

had built 6 years before. As a result of rejecting some and simplifying other elements, the structure of this building at Łazienki was, however, more lucid and clearly indicated the constant working of this architect towards the simplest designs.

*Bibliography:* W. Tatarkiewicz, *Łazienki warszawskie* (*Łazienki in Warsaw* – in Polish), Warsaw 1957, pp. 113–114; M. Kwiatkowski, *Łazienki* (in Polish), Warsaw 1972, pp. 228–231

## Stanisław Zawadzki

**131** [120] Lubostroń (Bydgoszcz District), palace of the Skórzewski family, view from the front, 1795–1800

The palace was built for Fryderyk Skórzewski. The work on the interior decoration continued until 1806. The painted decoration was carried out by Antoni Smuglewicz, the stucco work by Michał Ceptowicz. The palace at Lubostroń was an example of the use of a composition making reference to the principle of the famous work of Andrea Palladio, the Villa Rotonda near Vicenza. The essential elements of this palace type included: a square or nearly square plan, pillared porticoes, cupola crowning the building and a rotunda in the central part. It has been traditionally believed that the construction of the Lubostroń palace used the capitals and bases which had been prepared for the unbuilt Temple of Divine Providence in Warsaw.

**132** [121] Lubostroń, palace of the Skórzewski family, detail of the rotunda with the relief "Queen Jadwiga Receives the Teutonic Knights at Inowrocław", c. 1800–1806

This is one of the most magnificent neoclassical interiors in Poland, whose main virtues are a skilful composition of

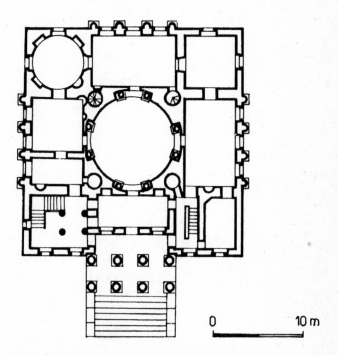

The palace at Lubostroń, ground plan

architectural and decorative elements and a subtle colour design. Despite its distinct richness, it is monumental and austere in character. It is interesting to note the good, artistic and technical, workmanship of the stucco reliefs, which are the most essential motifs in the decoration of the rotunda. The subject matter of the reliefs was drawn from the history of Great Poland. They represent: "The Battle of Płowce", "The Battle of Koronowo", "Queen Jadwiga Receives the Teutonic Knights at Inowrocław", "Frederic the Great Confirms the Plans for the Construction of the Noteć Canal". The emblems of Poland and Lithuania were set in the floor of the room. The ideological expression of the decoration was concentrated on the problems of Polish--German relations, indicating Polish superiority, both on the battle field and in the introduction of civilization.

Bibliography: Ostrowska-Kęblowska, *Palace Architecture*, pp. 271–290; Malinowska, *S. Zawadzki*, pp. 34–36

## Stanisław Zawadzki

**133** [124] Dobrzyca (Kalisz District), Gorzeński's palace, view from the front, c. 1795–1799

The palace was built for Augustyn Gorzeński. The work on the painted interior decoration was probably carried out after 1799, and the paintings were by Antoni Smuglewicz. The spatial design of the palace and park complex and the architecture of the palace at Dobrzyca were different from the type of country residence, characterized above all by strict symmetry and regular layout, which had been popular previously. The mass of the palace at Dobrzyca was composed of two wings, of different length and set at right angle to each other. The palace, which was placed amidst greenery, in a spacious park, made the impression of one of the garden pavilions. Such a treatment of the main building was not in keeping with the classical ideal residence and was an example of the nonclassical tendencies in the art of the second half of the 18th century. This uncommon design of the palace on the plan of a T-square was also affected by the wish of the founder, a member of a freemasons' lodge, as the T-square was for the freemasons a symbol for law and duty. Thus, Gorzeński emphasized his ties with freemasonry and the fact that sessions of a lodge were held in the palace.

**134** [125] Dobrzyca, Gorzeński's palace, Ballroom with painted decoration, after 1800

The walls and ceilings of this interior on the first floor in the west wing were painted by A. Smuglewicz. The walls had illusionistic painted architectural divisions among which views of Italian ports and trophies were set. On the ceiling were illusionistic painted balustrades and skies. The type of painted decoration was related to the baroque tradition of illusionistic painting.

**135** [122] Dobrzyca, garden pavilion called Pantheon, c. 1795–1799

This pavilion, situated on the edge of the park, in the south part, was related to the Roman Pantheon. This building frequently inspired neoclassical architects, becoming, as a result of its functional values, a pattern for church buildings. As a garden pavilion it was meant to inspire longing for antiquity.

The Pantheon in the Dobrzyca park had a strictly defined function: it was to house sessions of a freemasons' lodge.

**136** [123] Dobrzyca, outbuilding called the Gardener's Lodge, c. 1795–1799

This pavilion was situated in the park, not far from the palace. It was built on a plan close to a square and covered by a Polish mansard roof of the Cracow type. This type of roof occurred several times in Zawadzki's work (see "U-stronie" in Warsaw and the outbuildings at Śmiełów). The Gardener's Lodge was conceived of by the owner as a retreat where "in seclusion and loneliness vices must be eradicated". Garden pavilions with clearly specified functions, related to specific virtues, ideas or memories, were important elements of a rich subject matter programme which residences were usually expected to reflect.

Bibliography: Malinowska, *S. Zawadzki*, pp. 31–37; *Katalog zabytków w Polsce* (*A Catalogue of Art Monuments in Poland*), vol. V, *woj. poznańskie* (*Poznań District*), no 19, *pow. pleszewski* (*Pleszew County* – in Polish), edited by A. Kodurowa, Warsaw 1959, pp. 7–11; Ostrowska--Kłębowska, *Palace Architecture*, pp. 247–271

## Stanisław Zawadzki

**137** [126] Śmiełów (Kalisz District), Gorzeński's palace, view of the palace from the front, 1797

The palace at Śmiełów is a typical example of a Polish country residence, a great number of which were built in Poland at the end of the 18th and in the first half of the 19th century. In general, the layout of the whole was related to the traditional Palladian type. The architect treated the pavilions of the outbuildings in an individual way, covering them with Polish mansard roof of the so-called Cracow type. Adam Mickiewicz stayed at the palace in 1831 (plaque in a room on the first floor).

**138** [127] Śmiełów, Gorzeński's palace, salon with painted decoration, c. 1800

This eight-sided salon, projecting in the garden suite, is the most imposing interior of the palace. The surfaces of the walls and the ceiling were finished by painted decoration carried out by Antoni Smuglewicz. The walls have illusionistic painted architectural divisions, which frame views of ancient ruins. On the south wall there is a large oval composition "Hector Takes His Leave of Andromacha", based on a painting by Angelika Kaufmann. The principle of the composition of the elements of decoration was here different than that in the earlier complexes (see Łańcut, Mała Wieś). The figurative compositions were separated from grotesque-arabesque decoration and constituted autonomous works of art.

Bibliography: Malinowska, S. Zawadzki, pp. 33–34; Ostrowska-
-Kębłowska, Palace Architecture, pp. 204, 251–255; Katalog zabytków
sztuki w Polsce (A Catalogue of Art Monuments in Poland), vol. V, woj.
poznańskie (Poznań District), no 25, pow. śremski (Śrem County – in
Polish), edited by Z. Białłowicz-Krygierowa, Warsaw 1959, pp. 18–21

## Jakub Kubicki

**139** [128] Białaczów (Piotrków District), Małachowski's
palace, view of the palace from the front, 1797–1800

The palace was built for Stanisław Małachowski. The
ground-floor interiors had stucco and painted decoration,
mainly in the eight-sided salon and the so-called Etruscan
Cabinet. The west pavilion was burnt down in World War
II.

Like the palace at Śmiełów (see 137), the palace at
Białaczów was a typical example of a Polish neoclassical
country residence. The design of the main body with
a pillared portico and a multi-sided salon on the side of the
garden, on the axis of the palace, was repeated in a variety
of versions by Polish architects at the turn of the 18th and
19th centuries.

Bibliography: T. Szydłowski, T. Stryjeński, O pałacach wiejskich
i dworach z epoki po Stanisławie Auguście i budowniczym królewskim
Jakubie Kubickim (On the Country Palaces and Manors in the Epoch
after Stanislas Augustus and the Royal Architect Jakub Kubicki – in
Polish), Cracow 1925; J. Obarski, Materiały do życia i twórczości Jakuba
Kubickiego (Materials on the Life and Work of Jakub Kubicki – in
Polish), BAH, XVI, 1954, no 3, pp. 332–334

## Jakub Kubicki

**140** [129] Mokobody (Siedlce District), St. Hedviga's
parish church, 1798–1818

The church was founded by Jan Onufry Ossoliński.
According to tradition, Kubicki made reference to the
competition design of the Temple of Divine Providence in
Warsaw. It is known that this competition brought some
dozens of interesting designs, which, however, only remained in the volumes of the architectural collection of
Stanislas Augustus. Thus, the church at Mokobody was
the only result of this great royal enterprise, albeit on
a reduced scale. It was on a plan close to a square, with
projecting annexes on the axis. The architect's achievement was the extremely lucid composition of the interior in
which four powerful pillars, which supported the central
dome, divided its space into the nave, transept and four
domed chapels in the corners. The individual parts were
linked by arcaded passages.

Bibliography: Katalog zabytków w Polsce (A Catalogue of Art Monuments in Poland), vol. X, woj. warszawskie (Warsaw District), no 22,
pow. siedlecki (Siedlce County – in Polish), edited by I. Galicka,
H. Sygietyńska, D. Kaczmarzyk, Warsaw 1965, pp. 7–11

## Karl Gottfried Geissler (1755–1823)

**141** [130] Milicz (Wrocław District), palace, view from the
front, c. 1800

The residence at Milicz, which was built for the Maltzan
family, was the largest neoclassical palace design in Silesia.

The palace, on a very elongated rectangular plan, contained on both sides by pronounced projections, attracts
attention with a two-storey chamber on the axis, accentuated externally by a tower. The general spatial layout was
related to the well-known 17th century French design at
Vaux-Le-Vicomte.

Bibliography: Pilchowie, Zabytki Dolnego Śląska (Monuments in Lower
Silesia – in Polish), p. 98

## Chrystian Piotr Aigner

**142** [131] Łańcut, Orangery, front elevation, 1799–1802

The building of the Orangery is situated to the right of the
castle courtyard. The architect articulated the longer elevations of the building with Corinthian pilasters running over
two storeys and emphasized the front elevation with
a four-pillar Ionic portico (the capitals of the pilasters and
columns were executed by F. Baumann; only the pilasters
of the north elevation have survived). The cubic mass of the
Orangery and its pillared portico are important neoclassical
elements in the environment of the Łańcut Castle.

Bibliography: Kossakowska-Szanajca, Majewska-Maszkowska, Łańcut
Castle, pp. 275–278; Jaroszewski, Ch. P. Aigner, pp. 157–161

## Chrystian Piotr Aigner

**143** [132] Igołomia (Cracow District), palace of the Wodzicki family, after 1800

Lack of archival records has to date prevented a definite
solution of the authorship and the date of building of the
palace. T. Szydłowski and T. Stryjeński have attributed
the palace to Domenico Merlini or Jakub Kubicki, whereas
J. Piotrowski and S. Lorentz regard the building as a work
of Ch.P. Aigner and F. Baumann (stucco work). This
attribution seems the most probable and has been accepted
by the monographer of Ch.P. Aigner, T.S. Jaroszewski.
He believes that the palace was built in the early years of the
19th century and connects it with Franciszek Wodzicki,
who died in 1804. The palace at Igołomia represents
a palace type on a rectangular plan, with a four-pillar Ionic
portico and a three-sided projection on the side of the
garden, which was popular at the end of the 18th and the
beginning of the 19th century.

**144** [133] Igołomia, palace of the Wodzicki family, Round
Salon

A round or multi-sided salon, which mostly took two
storeys, was the most imposing interior of country palaces
at the end of the 18th century and the beginning of the 19th
century. It was situated on the axis of a palace, on the side
of the garden, and projected partly from the plane of the
wall. The interior of the salon was usually finished with
painted or stucco decoration. The Salon at Igołomia is
distinguished by the subtle colour and high-quality workmanship of the stucco work (griffin frieze, coffer decoration of the dome). The relief over the fireplace represents

an offering to Aesculapius. The stucco work was carried out by Fryderyk Baumann.

Bibliography: T. Szydłowski, T. Stryjeński, *O pałacach wiejskich i dworach z epoki po Stanisławie Auguście i budowniczym królewskim Jakubie Kubickim* (*On the Country Palaces and Manors from the Epoch after Stanislas Augustus and the Royal Architect Jakub Kubicki* – in Polish), Cracow 1925, pp. 26–30; J. Piotrowski, *Fryderyk Baumann: architekt i rzeźbiarz polski w okresie klasycyzmu i romantyzmu* (*Fryderyk Baumann: Polish Architect and Sculptor in the Period of Neoclassicism and Romanticism* – in Polish), "Sprawozdania Towarzystwa Naukowego we Lwowie", XVI (1936), no 1, p. 32; Lorentz, *Natolin*, p. 122; Jaroszewski, *Ch.P. Aigner*, pp. 175–182

## Jakub Kubicki

**145** [134, 135] Bejsce (Kielce District), palace, front and garden elevations, 1802

The palace at Bejsce, built for Marcin Badeni, represents a type of palace building which was very popular in Polish architecture in 1780–1830 (see Sierniki, Igołomia). However, Kubicki managed to give the individual hallmark of his style to the commonplace principles. He monumentalized the modest mass of the building by austere walls and the compact block of a unified chimney on top of it.

Bibliography: *Katalog zabytków sztuki w Polsce* (*A Catalogue of Art Monuments in Poland*), vol. III, *woj. kieleckie* (*Kielce District*), no 9, *pow. pińczowski* (*Pińczów County* – in Polish), edited by K. Kutrzebianka, J.Z. Łoziński, B. Wolff, Warsaw 1961, pp. 5–6

## Chrystian Piotr Aigner

**146** [136] Puławy, parish church of the Assumption of the Blessed Virgin Mary, 1800–1803
Ch.P. Aigner, view of the church, drawing-pen, India ink; with the inscription: "Eglise batie par Aigner a Puławy Dessiné par lui"; National Library in Warsaw, Graphic Art Collection, AR 39 no 10

It is situated on the Lublin road, on the north edge of a hill, near the residence. It was founded by Duke Adam Czartoryski as a palace chapel dedicated to the memory of Maria Zofia Czartoryska, née Sieniawska (his mother). The church was designed on a circular plan, covered by a dome and with a Corinthian portico in the front. Buildings of this type were patterned on the Roman Pantheon; the Puławy church was a reduced version of the classical building.

Bibliography: Jaroszewski, *Ch.P. Aigner*, pp. 128–133; Miłobędzki, *Concise History*, p. 264

## Chrystian Piotr Aigner, Fryderyk Baumann

**147** [137, 138, 139] Łańcut, Castle, Ballroom, general view and details of the interior, 1802

The Łańcut Castle, built in 1624–1641, was repeatedly rebuilt in the course of the 17th, 18th and 19th centuries. The neoclassical interiors, which were built as part of the reconstruction carried out by Aigner at the very beginning of the 19th century, are among the best examples of Polish neoclassicism. The most magnificent of them is the Ballroom which was built in the west wing, in place of the previous reception hall on the first floor of the Castle. The architectural decoration was designed by Aigner, the stucco work carried out by Baumann. In the Ballroom it is particularly interesting to note the high level of stucco decoration, whose motifs the architect drew in a very individual way from ancient Roman buildings. The type of the stucco fireplace in the Ballroom with its simple composition was often carried out by Aigner in his designs (see Igołomia). Aigner's layout of the frieze with griffins, vases and candelabra was based on the ancient friezes at the Palazzo della Valle and the temple of Antonius and Faustina in Rome, but composed with some modifications into a new whole.

In the stucco decoration in the Ballroom of the Łańcut Castle it is interesting to note the high precision and exactitude of the stucco work, combined with faithful rendering of classical motifs. In the corbel cornice round the walls of the room there are bands of ox eyes, cymation, astragal, palmettoes and the motifs of acanthus leaves. On the ceiling a row of coffers runs round the room.

Bibliography: Kossakowska-Szanajca, Maszkowska-Majewska, *Łańcut Castle*, pp. 224–230; Jaroszewski, *Ch.P. Aigner*, pp. 165–171

## Chrystian Piotr Aigner, Fryderyk Baumann

**148** [141] Łańcut, Castle, State Dining Room, fireplace and arcade with an eagle, 1800–1805

The Room is situated in a part of the castle which was added from the south in about 1800. The architectural decoration was designed by Aigner, the stucco work carried out by Baumann. The decoration of the Room consists of fluted composite pilasters and bands and cornices with the motifs of acanthus leaves, which divide the walls. In the semi-circular parts of the arcades there is decoration composed of wreaths with bands and with an eagle, a frequent motif of neoclassical decorations.

Bibliography: Kossakowska-Szanajca, Majewska-Maszkowska, *Łańcut Castle*, pp. 230–236; Jaroszewski, *Ch.P. Aigner*, pp. 168–170

## Chrystian Piotr Aigner, Fryderyk Baumann

**149** [140] Łańcut, Zameczek (Romantic Castle) in the palace park, decoration of the dome in the Round Salon on the second floor, 1807

Opinion is divided on the stages of its construction and its authorship. Jaroszewski, Kossakowska and Maszkowska believe that it was built about 1805, whereas the work on stucco decoration continued until 1807. They regard Aigner as the designer and Baumann as the author of the stucco work. J. Teodorowicz-Czerepińska has proposed, on the basis of architectural studies, that the Zameczek was built in two stages: the first between 1795 and 1802, to J. Griesmeyer's design (?), the other in 1806, to Aigner's design, with the exception of the form of the tower which has been attributed to Lubomirska, wife of the Marshal. Both parties agree as to the authorship and the date of the interior stucco decoration, distinguished particularly by the "whirling" dome in the Round Salon, covered by rhomboid coffers. This decoration is an example of the creative inventiveness and high worksmanship of the Aigner-Baumann team.

*Bibliography*: Kossakowska-Szanajca, Majewska-Maszkowska, *Łańcut Castle*, pp. 278–280; Jaroszewski, *Ch.P. Aigner*, pp. 171–174; Teodorowicz-Czerepińska, *Zameczek romantyczny w Łańcucie* (*The Romantic Castle at Łańcut* – in Polish), Łańcut 1970

## Chrystian Piotr Aigner

**150** [142, 143] Warsaw-Natolin, palace, Parlour, 1808

The interior is situated on the ground floor, next door to an open salon. The interior decoration consists of smooth, white-marbled walls crowned with a cornice and a stucco frieze round the room. The stucco work was carried out by Wirgiliusz Baumann. The composition of the frieze, whose subject matter is the celebration of the Dionysian Feast, was drawn from ancient patterns. On the whole, the interior is distinguished by the extreme purity of detail and good workmanship.

**151** [144] Warsaw-Natolin, palace, Mosaic Cabinet, 1808

Ground-floor interior, linked by an arcaded passageway with the Parlour. The interior decoration consists of grey, white-spotted marbled walls, crowned with a facet, and an all-round stucco frieze. The stucco work was carried out by Wirgiliusz Baumann. Over the frieze stucco frames contain four paintings *en grisaille*, painted on canvas, which represent allegories of architecture, sculpture, painting and music. The Cabinet, with its harmonized subtle colour, was combined with the Parlour, an outstanding achievement of late neoclassical interior decoration.

*Bibliography*: Lorentz, *Natolin*, pp. 125–166

## Fryderyk Albert Lessel (1767–1820)

**152** [145] Warsaw, 35/37 Senatorska Street, Blue Palace, front elevation and detail of the wing, 1812–1815

The original palace was built at the turn of the 17th and 18th centuries and subsequently was fully reconstructed in 1726 and 1776–1781. From 1811 it belonged to the Zamoyski family, for whom it was rebuilt by Lessel in late neoclassical forms. It was burnt down in 1944 and rebuilt in 1949–1950 under the supervision of Bruno Zborowski.
Lessel's reconstruction of the palace consisted in complete changes both in the external architecture and in the interior. This architecture was characterized by compositions of austere cubic solids, puristically reduced decoration and resignation from the traditional Great order portico in favour of an austere pillared portico in the front elevation of the main body. It is also necessary to point out the bold combination of austere, late neoclassical forms with "newly discovered" Renaissance forms (wide tripartite windows and hermas instead of the traditional capitals).
The form of the architecture of the Blue Palace reflected the tendencies towards economy and utilitarianism which became distinct in European architecture about 1800. The main representatives of this trend were the theoretician J.-N.-L. Durand and architects, mainly David and Friedrich Gilly, Heinrich Gentz and Peter J. Krahe.

*Bibliography*: T.S. Jaroszewski, A. Rottermund, *J. Hempel, F.A. Lessel, M. Ittar, W.H. Minter* (in Polish), Warsaw 1974, pp. 102–113

## Jakub Kubicki

**153** [146] Warsaw, view of one of the Grochów toll-houses, 36 Zamoyskiego Street, 1816–1818

The large-scale city planning reforms at the time of the Kingdom of Poland involved the erection of small toll-houses on the main routes out of Warsaw. Several pairs of buildings of this type were erected, of which only those at Mokotów and at Grochów have survived. In both cases, they are two symmetrically spaced pavilions, with recessed columnar porticoes and modest wall decoration.

## Chrystian Piotr Aigner

**154** [147] Warsaw, 48 Krakowskie Przedmieście Street, Governor's palace (of the Radziwiłł family, now of the Council of Ministers), elevation facing the street, 1818–1819

The palace, built in 1643–1645 for Stanisław Koniecpolski, Commander-in-Chief of the Army, was rebuilt in the first half of the 18th century. The later neoclassical reconstruction involved the old palace, the extension of the wings to the street, a new staircase and new apartments on the first and second floors. In his composition of the new elevation of the main body, Aigner treated the ground floor as a plinth for the upper two floors which he articulated with half-columns and pilasters. Over the cornice he set an attic wall with statues. With its elegance, this composition was fit for an imposing public edifice; however, it was not individual in its design, repeating a principle which was frequently followed by 18th-century architects. Despite the strong academic traditions which can be found in it, the Governor's palace is considered to have been one of the most outstanding works by Aigner.

*Bibliography*: Jaroszewski, *Ch.P. Aigner*, pp. 228–235

## Chrystian Piotr Aigner

**155** [148] Warsaw, Trzech Krzyży Square, St. Alexander's Church, elevation facing Nowy Świat Street, 1818–1825

The church was fully rebuilt in 1886–1894, destroyed in 1944 and reconstructed after 1945, when the form of 1818–1825 was restored. Apart from S.B. Zug's Evangelical Church, it was the most outstanding work built of Polish neoclassicism which was based on the pattern of the Roman Pantheon; the situation of the church in the centre of a square required, however, the introduction of two porticoes. Aigner's design responded to the situation and the function of a Catholic church. Among his works St. Alexander's church is distinguished by restraint in decoration and purist architecture. These features were chracteristic of late neoclassical buildings at the time of the Kingdom of Poland.

*Bibliography:* Jaroszewski, *Ch.P. Aigner*, pp. 236–243; Miłobędzki, *Concise History*, p. 264

## Jakub Kubicki

**156** [149, 151] Warsaw, Belwederska Street, Belweder palace, front and park elevations, 1818–1822

The original palace was built in the middle of the 17th century and was later rebuilt in the first half of the 18th century. From 1764 it belonged to King Stanislas Augustus, who founded here a pottery factory. At the request of Duke Konstanty Pavlovich, Kubicki carried out its full reconstruction. Kubicki is known mainly as the author of country palaces, which he built at the turn of the 18th and 19th centuries (see Białaczów, Bejsce). They represented the type of a small palace on a rectangular plan, with a pillared portico in the front. The architect employed this traditional type in designing Belweder, but he added to the main body on a rectangular plan lateral wings which refracted at right angles. Thus, the Belweder palace was a direct continuation of an architectural type which had taken shape as early as the reign of Stanislas Augustus.

## Jakub Kubicki

**157** [150] Warsaw, Belwederska Street, Sybil's (Diana's) Temple, general view, c. 1820

The park adjacent to the Belweder palace was separated from the Łazienki Park in 1818, and several park buildings, including the Sybil's Temple, the Egyptian Bridge and a well, were constructed here to Jakub Kubicki's design. The small building of the Sybil's Temple was designed according to the traditional pattern of an ancient temple: on a rectangular plan, with a four-pillar portico. This type of building was most frequently introduced into the "furnishings" of landscape parks in the second half of the 18th and the beginning of the 19th centuries.

## Antonio Corazzi (1792–1877)

**158** [152] Warsaw, 35 Nowy Świat Street, Hołowczyc's house, front elevation, 1820

This was built for Archbishop Szczepan Hołowczyc, destroyed in 1944 and reconstructed in 1949 under the supervision of Piotr Biegański.
As well as some dozens of public edifices, 419 dwelling tenements were built in Warsaw in 1817–1829. Most of them had modest architectural decoration, but a few multi-axis houses with monumental, palace-like façades were built in the more fashionable parts of the city, such as Nowy Świat Street and Teatralny Square. Hołowczyc's house, with its six-pillar Doric portico over two storeys was one of the best late neoclassical examples of this type of building in Poland.

## Hilary Szpilowski

**159** [153] Warsaw, 49 Nowy Świat Street, Bentkowski's house, front elevation, 1819–1822

This house was built for Feliks Bentkowski, professor of Warsaw University, destroyed in World War II and rebuilt in 1949 under the supervision of Zygmunt Stępiński and Mieczysław Kuźma.
In the times of the Kingdom of Poland, Hilary Szpilowski, mainly known as the author of country palaces (see Mała Wieś, Walewice), worked in the developing capital. As a result of the formally disciplined composition of the façade, Bentkowski's house was distinct among his late designs. The architect managed to avoid monotony by introducing into the modest architecture some accentuated motifs in the form of a Doric wall portico and a triglyph entablature frieze.

## Chrystian Piotr Aigner

**160** [155] Warsaw, 66 Krakowskie Przedmieście Street, Bernardine Guardhouse, front elevation, 1820–1821

The interior for the main city guardhouse was the result of the addition of an architectural structure to the Bernardine monastery which stood slightly back from the main building line. This building, which was burnt down in 1944, was restored to its original appearance in 1949. The Bernardine belfry was also fitted with new decoration in 1820–1821. The new architectural elements, combined with the façade of St. Anne's Church built thirty years before, constituted an imposing complex, generally recognized as one of the most interesting neoclassical designs in Warsaw. The architectural composition of the Bernardine guardhouse, particularly the slender first-floor arcading, was related to a famous classical building: Marcellus' theatre in Rome.

## Antonio Corazzi

**161** [154] Warsaw, 72 Nowy Świat Street, edifice of the Society of the Friends of Science (Staszic Palace), front elevation, 1820–1823

The edifice was built on the initiative of Stanisław Staszic, in the place of the late baroque church of Dominican Observants, to house the Warsaw Society of the Friends of Science. In 1892–1893 the palace was fully reconstructed; the new architectural decoration was related to Byzantine architecture. The architect M. Lalewicz restored the palace to its Corazzian form in 1924–1926. After the palace had been burnt down in World War II, Piotr Biegański reconstructed its original appearance in 1946–1950. The palace is situated at a focal point: it stands at the end of Krakowskie Przedmieście Street. The ground floor was treated as a plinth for the upper two storeys linked by the Great order. This type of composition was widely used in baroque architecture. Corazzi's design was, however, full of neoclassical restraint and simplicity, while the decoration was limited to sculpted griffins and Fames.

*Bibliography*: P. Biegański, *Pałac Staszica* (*Staszic Palace* – in Polish), Warsaw 1951

## Sylwester Szpilowski (d. 1832)

**162** [156] Kalisz, former edifice of the Court of Justice, front elevation, 1820–1824

Apart from Warsaw, the great project of town planning and architecture in the Kingdom of Poland in 1815–1830 covered a large number of urban centres, including Kalisz, Radom, Łowicz, Sochaczew and Łódź. At Kalisz, Św. Józefa Square and Babicza Street were laid out at that time and a large number of public edifices constructed or reconstructed. The work of the architect Sylwester Szpilowski, who transferred to Kalisz the monumental Warsaw patterns created by eminent Warsaw architects, such as Ch.P. Aigner and A. Corazzi, was very notable here. An example of the monumental architectural composition is the edifice of the former Court of Justice, which was built by Szpilowski.

*Bibliography*: *Katalog zabytków w Polsce* (*A Catalogue of Art Monuments in Poland*), vol. V, *woj. poznańskie* (*Poznań District*), no 6, *pow. kaliski* (*Kalisz County* – in Polish), edited by T. Ruszczyńska, A. Sławska, Z. Winiarz, Warsaw 1960, pp. 39–40

## Antonio Corazzi

**163** [157] Radom, former edifice of the Commission for Sandomierz District, front elevation, 1822–1827

Corazzi, the leading representative of late Warsaw neoclassicism and the author of the most outstanding edifices in the capital from 1818–1830, also designed buildings in the large towns of the Kingdom of Poland. There were buildings designed by Corazzi at Siedlce, Radom, Radzymin, Suwałki and Lublin. Thus, the monumental style of Corazzian architecture affected the work of provincial architects, which in turn was one of the reasons why neoclassical forms were preserved in the country until the middle of the 19th century.

*Bibliography*: *Katalog zabytków sztuki w Polsce* (*A Catalogue of Art Monuments in Poland*), vol. III, *woj. kieleckie* (*Kielce District*), no 10, *pow. radomski* (*Radom County* – in Polish), edited by K. Szczepkowski, E. Krygier, J.Z. Łoziński, Warsaw, pp. 33–34

## Karl Ferdinand Langhans (1781–1869)

**164** [158] Wrocław, 16 Solny Square, former stock exchange, detail of the elevation, 1822–1824

The edifice of the former stock exchange is one of the most imposing buildings in Wrocław. It was built by Langhans and it was related in composition to the façade of Hatzfeld's palace which had been built almost 60 years before; however, some elements of this composition, such as the tripartite windows on the central axis of the palace and the strongly rusticated surface of the ground-floor walls, augured neo-Renaissance designs. The most characteristic motif of the façade decoration – garlands with eagles – was drawn from the formal repertory of the Empire style. The former stock exchange should be recognized as a late neoclassical work in which a number of the elements of composition indicated the approach of new tendencies in architecture.

*Bibliography*: Pilchowie, *Monuments in Lower Silesia*, p. 190; *Sztuka Wrocławia* (*The Arts in Wrocław* – in Polish), Wrocław–Warsaw–Cracow 1967, pp. 398–399

## Antonio Corazzi

**165** [160, 163, 164] Warsaw, Dzierżyńskiego Square, general view of the design; 5 Dzierżyńskiego Square, palace of the Government Commission on Revenue and Treasury, general view and detail of the frieze, 1823–1825

Corazzi rebuilt the palace of the Government Commission on Revenue and Treasury from the former palace of the Leszczyński family. The sculptures in the tympanum, representing the allegories of Wisdom, Commerce and Industry and of the Vistula and Bug Rivers, were carried out by P. Maliński; the frieze which runs round the edifice and consists of cupids supporting garlands, was by M. Vincenti. The monumental architecture of the palace is very characteristic of Corazzi's style. He used here Ionic colonnades on the side of the square and as many as three Corinthian porticoes in the courtyard. The architect's design included the opening of a street on the opposite side of the square, and the central portico of the palace inside the courtyard was to become the central point of an axial planning composition. The palace, with the whole building complex, was destroyed in 1944. It was reconstructed in 1950–1954 under the supervision of Piotr Biegański.

*Bibliography*: P. Biegański, *Pałac Staszica* (*Staszic Palace* – in Polish), Warsaw 1951, pp. 50, 56; S. Łoza, *Szkice warszawskie* (*Warsaw Sketches* – in Polish), Warsaw 1958, pp. 51–67

## Antonio Corazzi

**166** [161] Warsaw, 3 Dzierżyńskiego Square, palace of the Minister of the Treasury, front elevation, 1825–1830

Together with the palace of the Government Commission on Revenue and Treasury and the edifice of the Bank, the palace of the Minister of the Treasury was part of the former complex of government buildings, constituting one of the best specimens of architecture in the capital. In building the palace of the Minister of the Treasury, Corazzi reemployed the walls of the old baroque palace of the Ogiński family. In contrast to the almost archaeological forms of porticoes and colonnades in the palace of the Government Commission on Revenue and Treasury, in the palace of the Minister of the Treasury, where the private character of the building allowed freer composition, the architect was able to design the elevation on a few planes and introduce terraces on two levels. In doing this, he achieved a picturesque effect, enhanced further by the impressive interplay of light on the highly differentiated elevation.

## Antonio Corazzi

**167** [162] Warsaw, 1 Dzierżyńskiego Square, edifice of the Polish Bank and Stock Exchange, front elevation, 1825–1828

The edifice of the Polish Bank and Stock Exchange closed from the south the monumental west frontage of the old Bankowy Square which, once wider at the junctions with Senatorska and Elektoralna Streets (the edifice of the Bank used to stand on this corner), became narrower to the north. The external architecture of the Bank was reduced to the simple arcading over two storeys, which ran round the circular transaction room situated in the rounded corner on Elektoralna Street. This room rose over the arcading with its simple, dome-covered drum. The perfection in architectural design lay in the use of extremely economical means, making the function of the building completely clear. In 1828–1830 the edifice was expanded, to J.J. Gay's design, on the side of Elektoralna Street.

## Antonio Corazzi

**168** [165] Warsaw, Grand Theatre of Opera and Ballet, view from the square, 1826–1833

The Theatre was built in the place of Marywil, a big city residential and commercial centre from the end of the 17th century. The so-called Fair House, designed by Ch.P. Aigner, had been added to Marywil in 1819. In 1826 Marywil was pulled down and the Fair House was integrated by Corazzi within the Grand Theatre to his design, which was under construction in 1826–1833. A. Schuch and L. Kozubowski collaborated with Corazzi in this work, the sculpted decoration of the tympanum was carried out by T. Acciardi and the remaining decoration by K. Hegel, L. Kaufmann and P. Maliński. In 1893, a portico was added on the side of the drive. The Theatre was badly damaged in 1939 and burnt out in 1944. The present-day edifice (with only the façade remaining from the old Theatre) was built in 1951–1965 to Bohdan Pniewski's design.

The monumental composition of the edifice of the Grand Theatre is the best work of neoclassical architecture in Poland, its scale and the size of design put it in the ranks of the most outstanding European designs of the early 19th century. Before beginning to work on its construction, Corazzi had devoted some years to studying abroad.

*Bibliography:* P. Biegański, *Teatr Wielki w Warszawie* (*The Grand Theatre in Warsaw* – in Polish), Warsaw 1961

## Józef Lessel (1802–1844)

**169** [159] Warsaw, 40 Nowy Świat Street, house, detail of the front elevation, 1827

This was built for the architect himself, destroyed in World War II and reconstructed in 1949 under the supervision of Teodor Bursze.

Among the 419 houses built in Warsaw in 1817–1829, most had two or three storeys, most frequently with five or seven axes, and modest elevations. The appearance was to a large extent determined by contemporary construction regulations. Several burgher's houses of this type have survived until the present day; the house at 40 Nowy Świat Street is the most typical of them. It was discretely decorated with pairs of pilasters and panels with griffin motifs.

## Henryk Marconi (1792–1863)

**170** [166] Warsaw, 15 Miodowa Street, Pac's palace, front elevation, 1824–1828

The palace, which was built in 1681–1697 to a design by Tylman of Gameren, was fully rebuilt by Marconi in 1824–1828 for Ludwik Pac. Partly destroyed in 1944, it was rebuilt in 1948–1951, under the supervision of Henryk Białobrzeski and Czesław Konopka. Marconi's reconstruction essentially changed the previous baroque architecture of the palace, including not only the main body of the building itself, but also the interiors and ancillary buildings. Marconi's artistic stance was distinctly different from that of his predecessors. Zug, Kamsetzer or Aigner had been inspired above all by the antiquity and the neoclassicism of the 16th and 18th centuries. For Marconi, in keeping with the theory of equality of all historical styles, which was popular at that time, the classical or Palladian forms provided only one of the possible solutions. His reconstruction of Pac's palace in Warsaw was the best demonstration of this stance. In the composition of the façade the architect made reference to Palladian patterns, but he introduced in the interiors elements from Moorish, gothic, Renaissance, ancient Greek and Roman architecture.

*Bibliography:* A. Bartczakowa, *Pałac Paca* (*Pac's Palace* – in Polish), Warsaw 1973

## Bonifacy Witkowski (d. 1840)

**171** [168, 169] Łowicz, town hall, front elevation and detail, 1825–1828

Among the buildings designed for towns and settlements in the first half of the 19th century, particular attention was paid to town halls. Their strictly observed programme, which emphasized economy and functionality, brought about the standardization of all new town halls. The building at Łowicz is a typical large town hall design with a simple outline shape and modest decoration, with a pillared portico and a characteristic tower on the axis.

*Bibliography:* *Katalog zabytków sztuki w Polsce* (*A Catalogue of Art Monuments in Poland*), vol. II, *woj. łódzkie* (*Łódź District*), no 5, pow. *łowicki* (*Łowicz County* – in Polish), edited by S. Kozakiewicz, J.A. Miłobędzki, Warsaw 1953, p. 45

## Unknown architect

**172** [167] Łowicz, post office, 1829

The demand for architecture which was utilitarian and at the same time entailed low construction costs brought in the twenties of the 19th century typical designs of the few most necessary kinds of urban building: inns, post offices, schools, butcher's shops, town halls, administration edifices, breweries, guardhouses, prisons, town toll-houses and bridges. Their architecture was austere, with decorative motifs of classical origin. The post office at Łowicz is a very characteristic example of the use of a typical design, one that was propagated by publications and the elaborations of typical designs which we know from the archives of the Government Commission on Internal Affairs.

*Bibliography: Katalog zabytków sztuki w Polsce (A Catalogue of Art Monuments in Poland), vol. II, woj. łódzkie (Łódź District), no 5, pow. łowicki (Łowicz County – in Polish), edited by S. Kozakiewicz, J.A. Miłobędzki, Warsaw 1953, p. 46*

## Unknown architect

**173** [173] Płock, one of the toll-houses on the Dobrzyń road, c. 1830

The broad-scale planning project at the time of the Kingdom of Poland involved about 140 towns. Its results included the regulation of the points at which roads entered towns and the correct situation of toll-houses. Apart from Warsaw, the toll-houses at Płock and Kalisz were most noteworthy. Those small buildings were always given interesting architectural forms.

## Unknown architect

**174** [172] Radziejowice (Skierniewice District), manor, front elevation, c. 1830

The pillared portico in the front, the essential element of composition in neoclassical architecture, was employed in hundreds of country mansions built in the first half of the 19th century. These small single-storey mansions were usually designed in austere, very restrained form, whereas the pillared portico or porch gave them a presentable character, distinguishing them from the other manor buildings. The manor at Radziejowice was such a typical design of a small mansion.

*Bibliography: Katalog zabytków sztuki w Polsce (A Catalogue of Art Monuments in Poland), vol. X, woj. warszawskie (Warsaw District), no 4, pow. grodzisko-mazowiecki (Grodzisk Mazowiecki County – in Polish), edited by I. Galicka, H. Sygietyńska, Warsaw 1967, p. 14*

## Unknown architect

**175** [171] Kaleń (Skierniewice District), granary and stables, general view, c. 1830

The out-buildings, such as granaries, stables, coach-houses etc., were a major part of all large palace or mansion complexes. Since they were in the direct vicinity of the main building, they had to be in harmony with the latter, whereas their modest, austere architectural form indicated their secondary status in the complex. Quite frequently, this architecture had serious artistic value. It seems necessary to point particularly to the complexes of neoclassical out-buildings at Kaleń, Babsk, Wrząca and Łęgonice, all from the first half of the 19th century.

## Alfons Kropiwnicki (1803–1881)

**176** [171] Warsaw, 2/4 Bednarska Street, Bath-house, front elevation, 1831

The building was erected to house the Chamber of Water Management, since it was on the road to a bridge over the Vistula River. From 1839 in turn it housed "Majewski's Bath-house".

Kropiwnicki's design is an example of a late neoclassical, simple composition of the overall shape. Its sculpted decoration was reduced to a relief filling the fronton of the building, "The Abduction of Proserpine by Poseidon" by P. Maliński.

## Peter von Nobile (1774–1854)

**177** [174] Cracow, Wawel Cathedral, chapel of the Potocki family (also of the Różyc family and Padniewski), of the Exculpation of the Most Blessed Mary, view of the dome, 1830–1840

The old Renaissance chapel of Bishop Padniewski was fully reconstructed by Peter von Nobile (a Swiss architect working in Vienna and Trieste), at the request of Zofia Potocka, wife of Artur Potocki. The walls of the chapel were given new facing in which were set tall, semi-circular niches. The old Renaissance decoration was replaced by neoclassical motifs in stucco and bronze. Essential changes were also introduced to the composition of Padniewski's Renaissance tombstone itself. In his designs von Nobile drew on his excellent knowledge of the history of architecture, particularly ancient architecture, both Greek and Roman.

*Bibliography: J. Szablowski (ed.), Katalog zabytków sztuki w Polsce (Catalogue of Art Monuments in Poland), vol. IV, miasto Kraków (Cracow Town), part I, Wawel (in Polish), Warsaw 1965, p. 79; A. Rottermund, Nowe przekazy ikonograficzne do kaplicy Potockich (d. Padniewskiego) w katedrze na Wawelu (New Iconographic Sources for the Chapel of the Potocki Family, Previously Padniewski's, at Wawel Cathedral – in Polish), BAH, XXXII, 1970, no 2, pp. 199–201*

## Henryk Marconi

**178** [176] Warsaw-Natolin, Doric Temple in the park, 1834–1838

Situated in the north part of the park, not far from the side entrance from Wilanów, amidst densely spaced trees. It was a typical pavilion in the disguise of an ancient temple. The distant pattern for the Natolin building was the Doric Temple of Poseidon at Paestum, which the then owner of Wilanów, Aleksander Potocki, and Marconi may have known from numerous graphic publications. The choice of Doric forms was a reflection of a movement in the architecture of the end of the 18th century which made reference to Doric architecture in its Greek form. This movement, termed the Greek Revival, had supporters in England. In Poland, the temple at Natolin was one of the few, very late, examples of this trend.

*Bibliography: Lorentz, Natolin, pp. 268–274*

## Adam Idźkowski (1798–1879), Wacław Ritschel (1794–1872)

**179** [175] Warsaw, Saski (Saxon) Palace, view from the square (state before 1939), 1838–1842

At the turn of the 18th and 19th centuries the bad condition and the outdated architecture of the Saxon Palace made its reconstruction necessary. The authors of designs included Fryderyk Albert Lessel, Hilary Szpilowski and Wilhelm Henryk Minter. In 1836 a competition was held for the design of the reconstruction of the palace, in which H. Marconi's works were most highly placed. The competitors also included Józef Lessel, Alfons Kropiwnicki, Wac-ław Ritschel and Antonio Corazzi. The design finally accepted was the work of Wacław Ritschel; however, the reconstruction followed Adam Idźkowski's design, strictly based on Ritschel's conception. The latter's ideas included the monumental central colonnade on the arcading, which linked the two parts of the palace and determined its artistic value. Ritschel and Idźkowski's work concluded the almost eighty-year-long period of the supremacy of neoclassical architecture in Warsaw.

*Bibliography:* A Rottermund, *Zwycięstwo i porażka historyczna, konkurs a przebudowa pałacu Saskiego w Warszawie* (*Victory and Historical Defeat, Competition and Reconstruction of the Saxon Palace in Warsaw*), (in:) *Muzeum i Twórca* (*Museum and Creator* – in Polish), Warsaw 1969, pp. 433–441

# Painting

## Franciszek Smuglewicz (1745–1807)

**180** [177] Ariadna and Bacchus, plate from the album "Vestigia delle Terme di Tito e loro interne pitture", Rome 1776; copperplate, 56×66.5, engraved by Marco Carloni; National Museum in Warsaw, inv. no 145031

F. Smuglewicz studied in Rome under the supervision of A. Maron and later, on a fellowship granted him by King Stanislas Augustus, in St. Luke's Academy. Over his twenty-year stay in Rome he collaborated, for instance, on a publication which contained reproductions of the paintings of Nero's Domus Aurea (which in the 18th century were thought to refer to Titus' Hot Baths) in Rome and designs of this building; he also prepared drawings for an engraved album of ancient monuments at the Vatican Museo Pio Clementino. The album "Vestigia delle Terme di Tito..." played a particularly important role in the history of decorative painting in Europe. Published in a black and white edition and a in dozen-odd series of engravings with added colour, it became a sort of pattern--book for painted wall decoration (e. g. the decoration of the gallery at Packington or a pavilion at Tsarskoe Selo, USSR). From Smuglewicz's engravings the French graphic artist N. Ponce edited the album "Descriptions des Bains de Titus ou collection des Peintures trouvées dans les Ruines de Thermes de cet Empereur", Paris 1786.

*Bibliography:* Lorentz, *Nero's Domus Aurea and Villa Laurentina,* pp. 314–324; D. Fitz-Gerald, *A gallery after the antique,* "The Connoisseur", vol. 181, no 727, September 1972, pp. 3–13

## Franciszek Smuglewicz

**181** [XXVII] The Prozor Family, 1789, oil on canvas, 182×144; National Museum in Warsaw, inv. no 130885

The painting was made in 1789, commissioned by Karol Prozor, Lithuanian Camp Superintendent, one of the eminent patriots of the times of Stanislas Augustus. Prozor himself took part in establishing the composition and conception of the portrait. The painting was to be a sort of glorification of the Witebsk Voivode Józef Prozor, Karol's father, who had died in 1788. The members of the Prozor family, except the children, were painted from life. The centre of the composition is taken by the medallion with Józef Prozor. Karol Prozor stands on the left, pointing at an inscription on the tree trunk, which was composed by Franciszek Karpiński and dedicated to the late father. On the right sits Ludwika, wife of Karol. Ignacy Prozor, brother of Karol, stands behind her, and beside Karol stand his two brothers-in-law, Franciszek Bukaty and Stanisław Jelski. In the foreground there are the children of Karol and Ludwika, Józef and Marianna. The artist consciously used the fully expressive means of traditional Sarmatian painting, in order to emphasize the memorial--like character of the work. Smuglewicz's painting provides an excellent example of the individuality of the Polish portraiture tradition against the background of the mainstream of European portrait painting in the second half of the 18th century and also constitutes an outstanding example of neoclassicism in Polish painting.

*Bibliography:* Ryszkiewicz, *Polish Group Portrait,* pp. 101–103; *Portraits of Polish Personages,* item 186, pp. 173–174.

## Franciszek Smuglewicz

**182** [178] Peasants by the Candle, c. 1794, oil on canvas, 47×59.5; National Museum in Cracow, inv. no 102304

One of themes which Smuglewicz repeatedly painted were scenes of folk life in the area of Cracow and in Lithuania. This was related to the political situation and the peasant problem which was topical in the nineties of the 18th century. His best known composition, which he repeated several times, was the "Peasants by the Candle". Smuglewicz painted it during his stay at Bronowice near Cracow. Apart from the subject matter, it is interesting to note the painting values, particularly conspicuous in the figures of the peasants, above all the skilful use of the effect of artificial lighting.

*Bibliography:* V. Drema, *Franciškus Smuglevičius*, Vilna 1973, pp. 166–167

## Franciszek Smuglewicz

**183** [179] The Oath of Kościuszko in the Cracow Market Place; oil on canvas, 104×118.5, signed "Franciscus Smuglewicz Pinxit Anno 1797. Varsovie"; National Museum in Warsaw, inv. no 189047 (deposit of the National Museum in Poznań, inv. no Mp 339)

Smuglewicz painted religious themes, genre scenes, portraits, landscapes and wall decoration. Apart from historical motifs, he had a predilection for contemporary themes, representing, for example, "The Death of Jakub Jasiński" or "The Oath of Kościuszko". In the latter work he shows us the appearance of those who participated in this historic event. In the foreground it is possible to recognize General Kościuszko, A. Madaliński, S. Wodzicki, Canon W. Sierakowski, and the painter himself is seen on the left. The individually characterized personages are contrasted with the schematically painted figures of the soldiers. Smuglewicz's painting enjoyed great popularity; it was copied and also became the pattern for Stachowicz's later composition on the same subject.

*Bibliography:* V. Drema, *Franciškus Smuglevičius*, Vilna 1973, p. 155; Ryszkiewicz, *Polish Group Portrait*, pp. 95-98

## Józef Peszka (1767–1831)

**184** [XXII] Adam Kazimierz Czartoryski, 1791; oil on canvas, 154×109.5; National Museum in Warsaw, inv. no 2690

Adam Kazimierz Czartoryski was a son of August Aleksander Czartoryski and Maria Zofia Czartoryska, née Sieniawska. He was, among other things, one of the founders and commander of the Cadet Corps, fellow of the Warsaw Society of the Friends of Science and an outstanding patron of science, literature and the arts. In the portrait he is shown in a golden dress coat, with an ermine-lined overcoat thrown over his shoulders, with the band and star of the White Eagle Order on his chest. This portrait of Czartoryski was one of a series of portraits of eminent political personages from the period of the Four-Year Parliament, which Józef Peszka painted at the order of the Warsaw town authorities for the Town Hall. Apart from the portrait of Stanisław Kubicki, that of A.K. Czartoryski is one of the best in this series. In the composition and the treatment of the model an attempt can be discerned to combine the rules of official court painting and the strong tradition of the native portrait painting, frequently called Sarmatian.

*Bibliography:* J. Kąkolewska, *Twórczość Józefa Peszki* (*The Work of Józef Peszka* – in Polish), BAH, XVI, 1954, no 1, pp.135–145; *Portraits of Polish Personages*, item 37, p. 50

## Aleksander Kucharski (1741–1819)

**185** [XXIII] Portrait of the Dauphin (Louis XVII), 1794; oil on canvas, 45×37.5; signed "Kucharsky fecit en 1794"; Royal Castle in Warsaw, inv. no ZKW/296

Aleksander Kucharski was a Polish painter who worked in France throughout his life. His historical significance is mainly due to his authorship of the last two portraits of Marie Antoinette. In addition to the latter, his portraits of the Dauphin enjoyed the greatest fame. They are striking with the representiveness of approach and the atmosphere of internal calm. Batowski has determined that Kucharski's first task on the subject was a miniature portrait. He repeated the arrangement from the miniature several times. Collections in France include two small portraits signed and dated 1792. The portrait, dated 1794, one of the gifts for the collections of the Royal Castle, was a repetition of his own earlier representation of the Dauphin.

*Bibliography:* Z. Batowski, *Aleksander Kucharski*, (in:) *Prace z Historii Sztuki wydawane przez Towarzystwo Naukowe Warszawskie* (*Art History Papers Published by the Warsaw Scientific Society* – in Polish), vol. III, no 1, Warsaw 1948, pp.22–25

## Jean Pierre Norblin de la Gourdaine (1745–1830)

**186** [180] Arkadia, Diana's Temple, Aurora, ceiling painting, 1783–1785; fresco

Jean Pierre Norblin, a French painter, was brought to Poland in 1774 by the ducal Czartoryski family. In about 1790 he settled in Warsaw. In 1804 he returned to Paris. He left an extremely rich artistic output. Apart from idealized paintings in the rococo taste, he painted and drew realistic scenes inspired by Polish political events, Polish customs and social reality. He also plied decorative painting, and his most outstanding achievement in this field was the decoration of the ceiling at the Diana's Temple at Arkadia by a fresco representing Aurora. In this work he came closest to the ideals of classical painting. This composition makes a monumental impression, an effect which was usually sought in neoclassical art.

*Bibliography:* Z. Batowski, *Norblin* (in Polish), Lvov 1911, pp. 84–86

## Jean Pierre Norblin de la Gourdaine

**187** [181] Polish Marionettes, c. 1780; oil on wood, 29×24; National Museum in Warsaw, inv. no 179330

The painting shows a Nativity play taking place in a rather indefinite interior; perhaps at one of the pavilions at Powązki, the sentimental park of the Czartoryski family. The most important painter's problem in this composition was the introduction of the effects of an interplay of light and shadow. Throughout his artistic career Norblin studied the work of Rembrandt and Dutch masters of light. The Marionettes was probably an effect of this fascination by the art of the masters. Wierzbicki has attempted to define the personae of the painting: they include Maria Czartoryska and Izabela Czartoryska, who are seated on the bench, and Teresa Czartoryska, who stands behind the latter.

*Bibliography:* Z. Batowski, *Norblin* (in Polish), Lvov 1911, p. 95; R. Wierzbicki, *Co przedstawia obraz Jana Piotra Norblina "Les Marionettes Polonaises"* (*What Does the Painting "Les Marionettes Polonaises" by Jean Pierre Norblin Represent?* – in Polish), "Pamiętnik Teatralny", XVII, no 2 (66), Warsaw 1968, pp. 203–242

## Jean Pierre Norblin de la Gourdaine

**188** [182] Sarcophagus of August and Zofia Czartoryski Erected at the Wild Promenade of the Puławy Park, 1800–1801, sepia, 31.3×41.5; National Museum in Cracow, Czartoryski Collections, inv. no MNK XV R.r. 21

Norblin probably made the drawing after 1800, when he was staying at Puławy and working on a series of several score drawings on Puławy subjects for Izabela Czartoryska. This series shows us the image and atmosphere of the residence, in which progressive and patriotic ideas were cultivated and the national culture maintained. In addition to picturesque buildings and freely composed trees and shrubs, in the park there were a few monuments which were inspired by classical patterns. One of them was a monument in memory of August and Zofia Czartoryski, made in Rome and set up in the park in late 1800 or in 1801. The pattern for the Puławy monument was the ancient sarcophagus of Lucius Cornelius Scipio. The present drawing represents the neoclassical trend in Norblin's work. Here, the artist gave up the whimsical, free line and theatrical composition in favour of distinct outline and static representation.

*Bibliography:* Z. Batowski, *Norblin* (in Polish), Lvov 1911; M. Suchodolska, *Ikonografia Puław w twórczości Jana Piotra Norblina* (*The Iconography of Puławy in Jean Pierre Norblin's Work*), (in:) *Puławy. Teka konserwatorska* (*Puławy. Conservator's File – in Polish*), no 5, pp. 87-106; T.S. Jaroszewski, *Puławy w okresie klasycyzmu* (*Puławy in the Period of Neoclassicism – in Polish*), ibidem, pp. 64–86

## Kazimierz Wojniakowski (1772–1812)

**189** [XXX] Portrait of General Józef Kossakowski, 1794; oil on canvas, 57×48; National Museum in Cracow, inv. no II. 280

Wojniakowski's painting was very diversified in theme. In addition to history compositions he painted allegorical scenses, but above all he worked on partraits. He represented General Józef Kossakowski, Grand Duke of Lithuania, commander of the 3rd Brigade of National Cavalry, against a background of a romantic rocky landscape. He characterized his model in an excellent manner, in a heroic pose. Wojniakowski's type of portrait painting for a national hero, became very popular at the turn of the 18th and 19th centuries, being most frequently employed in representations of the Polish national hero, Tadeusz Kościuszko. In this portrait by Wojniakowski it is interesting to note the correctly worked out composition of colour and the free, slightly rough texture of the painting. These values

permit the portrait to be included among the outstanding achievements of Polish neoclassical painting.

*Bibliography:* Dobrowolski, *Modern Polish Painting*, pp. 112–114

## Kazimierz Wojniakowski

**190** [183] Portrait of Izabela Czartoryska, née Fleming; oil on canvas, 64×53 (oval); signed "C.W. pinx 1796"; National Museum in Cracow, Czartoryski Collections, inv. no XII–427

Working on a variety of themes, Wojniakowski's best achievements were portraits. His models included Stanislas Augustus, Stanisław Sołtyk, Tadeusz Kościuszko, Józef Kossakowski (see item 189 in the present catalogue) and a number of other Polish personages. In Wojniakowski's portraits it seems necessary to emphasize his realism in the treatment of a model, which made his work different from the idealized images executed by the circle of painters connected with the court. Some scholars even believe that he made reference to the native tradition of Sarmatian painting. This feature is conspicuous, for example, in the portrait of Izabela Czartoryska, née Fleming, where the painter quite objectively characterized the face of this Polish aristocrat.

*Bibliography:* Dobrowolski, *Modern Polish Painting*, pp. 111–112

## Kazimierz Wojniakowski

**191** [184] Party at Łazienki Park (?); oil on canvas, 82×116.5; signed "C.W. 1797 p"; National Museum in Warsaw, inv. no 21038

Kazimierz Wojniakowski, like his contemporaries: Smuglewicz, Bacciarelli or Peszka, often painted group portraits. The most famous work of this type is the painting showing a party imaged against the background of a park (attempts have been made to identify it as the Łazienki Park). Here, Wojniakowski made a portrait of two families of Warsaw burghers: the Lafontaines and the Haukes, whereas the person farthest to the right is reputedly the painter himself. There is a party of 27 persons gathered round the memorial statue which was to be set to glorify King Stanislas Augustus Poniatowski. The statue, which symbolizes victorious freedom, closely resembles the allegory on the headpiece of the 1785 Parliament Diary, engraved after a drawing by Franciszek Smuglewicz.

As a result of such a clear introduction of the allegory of freedom, the Party acquired the meaning of a political declaration and, apart from the role of a family portrait, it also had propaganda functions.

*Bibliography:* J. Ruszczycówna, *Konstytucja 3 Maja 1791 r. w grafice XVIII w.* (*The Third of May Constitution of 1791 in 18th-Century Graphic Arts* – in Polish), BAH, 1955, no 2, p. 239; Ryszkiewicz, *Polish Group Portrait*, pp. 128–129

## Konstanty Aleksandrowicz (working in the last quarter of the 18th century)

**192** [XXVIII] Portrait of Duke Karol Radziwiłł "My Dear Sir"; oil on canvas, 81×63.8; signed on the back "in Varsovia Alexandrowicz pinxit 1786"; National Museum in Cracow, inv. no 101619

Aleksandrowicz studied painting in Warsaw under the supervision of Łukasz Smuglewicz. In 1777 he was staying at Poryck, the property of T. Czacki, for whom he made a series of portraits of "famous Poles". In the seventies he was working in Lithuania. From 1782 he stayed permanently in Warsaw. Like J. Faworski, he represented portrait painting derived from the Polish tradition of the "Sarmatian" portrait.

The portrait of Radziwiłł was one of the best works in this field by Aleksandrowicz; it strikes with its strong and very adequate characterization of the model and with its extreme accuracy, which verges on meticulousness, in the treatment of the realia. The characteristic features of Aleksandrowicz's portraits are the geometrization and evenness of composition, which derived from Sarmatian painting.

*Bibliography: Sztuka warszawska od średniowiecza do połowy XX wieku. Katalog wystawy w Muzeum Narodowym w Warszawie (The Arts in Warsaw from the Middle Ages to the Middle of the 20th Century. The Catalogue of the Exhibition at the National Museum in Warsaw – in Polish)*, Warsaw 1962, item 47, pp. 47–48

## Maciej Topolski (1766–1812)

**193** [185] Unknown Dignitary; oil on canvas, 62.2×49.5; signed "Topolski pinxit Var. A. 1804"; National Museum in Warsaw, inv. no 681

Maciej Topolski, a student of Franciszek Smuglewicz, was a representative of late neoclassicism in Polish painting. He painted quite conventional works, which, however, employed a great deal of technical skill and well characterized their models. Among the several know portraits by Topolski, the portrait of an unknown dignitary is one of the best. Until recently, this painting has been thought to be the portrait of Józef Sierakowski, a well-known politician, who was also active in culture, from the turn of the 18th and 19th centuries. The authors of the catalogue *Portraits of Polish Personages* have, however, determined that this portrait depicts another person of high status, since J. Sierakowski was never granted the White Eagle Order, nor that of St. Stanislas, which the man in the portrait has.

*Bibliography: Portraits of Polish Personages*, item 296, p. 260

## Józef Faworski (working 1790–1805)

**194** [186] Portrait of Jan Piędzicki, Łęczyca Burgrave; oil on canvas, 75×60.5; signed on the back "Topacz Jan Piędzicki Burgrabia Grodzki Łęczycki. Malował Józef Faworski Roku 1790" (Topacz Jan Piędzicki, Burgrave of Łęczyca Town. Painted by Józef Faworski in 1790); National Museum in Poznań, inv. no Mp. 706

This portrait is part of a larger series of portraits of the Piędzicki family from Łęczyca, which Faworski painted in 1790–1793. The portrait of Jan represents best the "style" of Faworski's portraits, with their simplified shapes and linear and flat treatment of solids. These means indicate the presence of the Sarmatian tradition in Faworski's painting, distinctly different from the mainstream of European portraiture.

*Bibliography: Sztuka warszawska od średniowiecza do połowy XX wieku. Katalog wystawy w Muzeum Narodowym w Warszawie (The Arts in Warsaw from the Middle Ages to the Middle of the 20th Century. The Catalogue of the Exhibition at the National Museum in Warsaw – in Polish)*, Warsaw 1962, item 48, p. 48

## Bernardo Bellotto called Canaletto (1721–1780)

**195** [IX] Miodowa Street; oil on canvas, 84×197.5; National Museum in Warsaw, inv. no 128654

This is one of a series of 22 *vedute* of Warsaw which were painted at the request of Stanislas Augustus for the Canaletto Room at the Royal Castle in Warsaw. The series used to be at the Castle; in 1832 it was taken away to Russia and returned by the USSR in 1922. In September 1939 this set was moved to the National Museum in Warsaw, it was taken away to Germany during World War II, regained in 1945, and is now at the Royal Castle in Warsaw. The view of Miodowa Street is seen from the corner of Senatorska Street. On the left there are the palace of Cracow bishops and Tepper's palace, the latter no longer standing, and on the other side of the street the palace of the Branicki family can be seen. In the background there is the Palace of the Commonwealth (of the Krasiński family). In this painting the author employed a large number of accessories, quite characteristic of his works. In addition to an elegant carriage, he represented groups of passersby in conversation, street spectators, pedlars of engravings, beggars. The diversity of human types and the representatives of different walks of life give an excellent image of the 18th-century Warsaw street. One of the greatest values of the whole series of Warsaw *vedute* is the documentary faithfulness. After the damage caused by World War II Canaletto's works provided valuable information, which was used in reconstructing large parts of town architecture. Bernardo Bellotto, an Italian painter, worked for Stanislas Augustus in 1767–1780. His paintings are characterized by precise outline, fautless perspective, colour based on local hues and free texture. Bellotto played an important role at the court of Stanislas Augustus; he not only painted *vedute* and documented the life of the capital, but above all he was one of the first artists at the Warsaw court to start giving up the baroque tradition in favour of neoclassicism, and in some of his magnificent paintings even pre-romanticist features can be seen.

*Bibliography: S. Kozakiewicz, Bernardo Bellotto genannt Canaletto*, Recklinghausen 1972

## Marcello Bacciarelli (1731–1818)

**196** [XIII] Portrait of Stanislas Augustus in a Plumed Hat, c. 1790; oil on canvas, 71×57; National Museum in Warsaw, inv. no 22468

Bacciarelli was born in Rome and began to study painting there. He visited Warsaw as early as 1756–1763, and in 1766 he came here to stay until his death, in 1818. Bacciarelli's painting, despite some of its neoclassical features, was based on baroque and rococo traditions. Among the many portraits of King Stanislas Augustus painted by Bacciarelli (the coronation portrait, the portrait in armour, that with a sand-glass or that in general's uniform) the King's portrait in a tall, plumed hat seems to be the most interesting artistically. With its small size, in warm golden colours, emphasized further by the red of the King's cloak, it shows much of the author's fresh inventiveness. The magnificent frame was specially composed for this portrait.

*Bibliography: Chyczewska, M. Bacciarelli, pp. 87–88*

## Marcello Bacciarelli

**197** [187] Helena Radziwiłł, née Przeździecka, c. 1784; oil on canvas, 69×55, oval; Art Museum in Łódź, inv. no 797

Bacciarelli painted a whole series of portraits of members of the Polish aristocracy. It would as a rule be difficult to find in these portraits any features of neoclassical painting. Particularly in women's portraits, the atmosphere of rococo painting can be discerned in the treatment of the model and in the delicate, pastel gamut of colours. An example of such a portrait from the eighties of the 18th century is the portrait of Helena Radziwiłł, née Przeździecka, who founded Arkadia. Chyczewska supposes that the portrait was painted about 1784 and was probably a portrait study for a historical painting meant for the Knights' Hall at the Royal Castle in Warsaw: *The Conferment of Rights on Cracow University.*

*Bibliography: Chyczewska, M. Bacciarelli, p. 93* ,

## Marcello Bacciarelli

**198** [XIV] Sketch for ceiling painting in the Ballroom at the Royal Castle in Warsaw, c. 1778; oil on canvas, 76.7× 109.5; National Museum in Warsaw, inv. no 120 969

The ceiling painting in the Ballroom, alternatively called "The Division of the Four Elements" or "Jove Brings the World Out of Chaos", was the largest work by Bacciarelli (18×7m). The painting was destroyed in 1939; only two oil sketches have survived, to serve as the basis for its reconstruction. The present, so-called second sketch, was more mature artistically in terms of composition. In its composition Bacciarelli drew upon the engravings of French 18th-century masters from the King's collection. Neither did Bacciarelli's work deviate in terms of its colour gamut from the baroque tradition of ceiling painting.

*Bibliography: Chyczewska, M. Bacciarelli, pp. 74–76*

## Marcello Bacciarelli

**199** [188] Casimir the Great Listening to Peasants'Pleas, c. 1785–1786; oil on canvas, 332×300; National Museum in Warsaw inv. no 164030

This painting is one of the series of history paintings meant for the Knights' Hall at the Royal Castle in Warsaw. The themes of the six compositions included great events and scenes from the history of Poland: "The Battle of Vienna", "The Peace of Chocim", "The Conferment of a Charter on the Cracow Academy", "The Prussian Homage", "The Union of Lublin" and "Casimir the Great Listening to Peasants' Pleas". They were painted in succession, in 1782–1786. With this cycle Bacciarelli initiated modern history painting in Poland. In those paintings the protagonists are the Polish kings whom Stanislas Augustus appreciated in particular. Combined with a painted and sculpted series of portraits of famous Poles, these paintings glorifying royal virtues constituted the patriotic expression of the Hall, referring to the glorious past.

*Bibliography: Chyczewska, M. Bacciarelli, pp. 79–86*

## Per Krafft the Elder (1724-1793)

**200** [XXIV] Portrait of Izabela (Elżbieta) Lubomirska, née Czartoryska; oil on canvas, 67.2×53.5; signed "Krafft 1767"; National Museum in Warsaw, inv. no 129124

The model was the daughter of August Aleksander Czartoryski and Maria Zofia Czartoryska, née Sieniawska, and from 1753 was the wife of Stanisław Lubomirski, the Grand Marshal of the Crown. Izabela Lubomirska was one of the best known patrons of the arts in Poland in the second half of the 18th century. Her estates included Mokotów and Wilanów, Łańcut and Krzeszowice. Her portraits were the work of outstanding artists who were working in Poland, including Per Krafft the Elder, a Swedish painter who was active in Poland in 1767–1768. He was an outstanding painter of the second half of the 18th century, irrespective of the fact that his work was related to baroque rather than neoclassicism. He demonstrated his skilful technique and evident talent in the portrait of Izabela Lubomirska, which he painted after a painting by Alexander Rosslin rather than from life (since in 1767 Lubomirska was in Paris).

*Bibliography: Portraits of Polish Personages, p. 109*

## Jan Bogumił Plersch (1737–1817)

**201** [189] Detail of wall painting from the Conference Closet at the Royal Castle in Warsaw, 1783–1784; fresco

The walls of this small eight-sided salon were covered by arabesque decoration. It provided the background for the portraits of seven European monarchs who were ruling simultaneously with Stanislas Augustus. Below these representations Plersch set six small single-colour paintings (*en grisaille*), framed by arabesque work and showing important events related to the royal persons in the portraits. The type of arabesque or grotesque decoration, patterned after classical and Renaissance patterns, was popular in the age of general admiration for classical forms. Such decorations can frequently be encountered in interiors sponsored by King Stanislas Augustus (see Łazienki–Palace, Ballroom; Łazienki–White Pavilion, Dining Chamber). Details of the frescoes were cut off from the walls of the Closet in the winter of 1940. About 50 per cent was salvaged. They are now at the Royal Castle in Warsaw.

*Bibliography:* Król, *Royal Castle in Warsaw*, pp. 119–121, 201

## Giovanni Battista Lampi the Elder (1751–1830)

**202** [XXV] Portrait of Teresa Potocka, née Ossolińska, with Her Grandson Alfred, 1791–1792; oil on canvas, 141×120; National Museum in Warsaw, inv. no 128849

Ryszkiewicz considered this painting to be a copy by Bacciarelli of the original work by Lampi. In turn the authors of the catalogue of the collection of the National Museum: *European Painting* have attributed this work to Lampi. From the boy's age, the portrait was painted in 1791–1792. It has been recognized as the best woman's portrait to have been painted by Lampi over his stay in Poland. It is interesting to note the regular features and the calm of the figure, the realism of the representation and its simplicity.

*Bibliography:* Ryszkiewicz, *Polish Group Portrait*, pp. 86, 87; *Malarstwo europejskie. Katalog zbiorów* (*European Painting. The Catalogue of the Collection* – in Polish), I, National Museum in Warsaw, Warsaw 1967, item 630, p. 215

## Josef Grassi (1758–1838)

**203** [XXI] Portrait of Stanisław Kostka Potocki, 1792; oil on canvas, 156×111; National Museum in Warsaw, inv. no 2684

Stanisław Kostka Potocki, the owner of Wilanów, was a well-known politician, writer, theoretician, historian and patron of the arts. He also carried out archaeological excavations, was an amateur architect and collector of works of art. Grassi shows Potocki against the background of a mountain landscape, by a gun, in the uniform of an artillery general of the Polish Army, which rank Potocki was granted in 1792. The portrait of Potocki is one of those works by Grassi in which the influence of English portrait painting is particularly distinct.

*Bibliography:* J. Ruszczycówna, *Portrety polskie Józefa Grassiego* (*The Polish Portraits of Josef Grassi* – in Polish), BAH, XVI, 1954, no 2, pp. 262-269; *Portraits of Polish Personages*, item 181, pp. 168–169

## Józef Wall (1754–1798)

**204** [190] Fryderyk Skórzewski with the Plenipotentiary Maciej Grabowski; oil on canvas, 135×97; signed "J. Wall, pinx (illegible) 1787"; National Museum in Poznań, inv. no Mp. 323

This interesting portrait, which A. Ryszkiewicz has defined as "coldly elegant" and "awkwardly rigid", preceded with its neoclassical features the Polish portraits which were painted during the reign of Stanislas Augustus. Z. Kębłowska has attributed to it the "English" character and given an exhaustive analysis of its subject matter. This portrait by Wall probably shows the moment of taking over his estates by Fryderyk Skórzewski who has just come of age. The scene is patronized by the sculpted bust of Marianna Skórzewska, mother of Fryderyk. Both the map which Grabowski is depicted showing to Skórzewski and the landscape in the background relate to the Łabiszyn estate, where Skórzewski built the palace at Lubostroń in 1795–1800

*Bibliography:* Ostrowska-Kębłowska, *Palace Architecture*, pp. 272–274; Ryszkiewicz, *Polish Group Portrait*, p. 138

## Jan Gładysz (c. 1762–1830)

**205** [193] Portrait of Stanisław Staszic, c. 1820; oil on canvas, 69×57.5; National Museum in Poznań, inv. no Mp. 372

Jan Gładysz, a Poznań painter, gained popularity outside of the Warsaw community. His work began at the turn of the 18th and 19th centuries, whereas the last of his paintings were made in the twenties of the 19th century. He mainly painted portraits, which were characterized by a predilection for realistic treatment of models. His most outstanding works include the portrait of Stanisław Staszic, where the painter has managed, using quite simple means, to characterize suggestively the face of the great scholar.

*Bibliography:* Dobrowolski, *Modern Polish Painting*, pp. 196–197

## Aleksander Orłowski (1777–1832)

**206** [191] Kościuszko's Soldiers Dance at an Inn; pencil, sepia-washed, 44.7×60.2; signed and dated, bottom left, "Orłowski f. 1797"; National Museum in Warsaw, inv. no Rys. Pol. (Polish Drawings) 4300

Aleksander Orłowski was one of the most outstanding personalities in Polish painting at the turn of the 18th and 19th centuries. A student of J.P. Norblin, he took over from his master the skilful use of outline and great sensitivity to an interplay of light and shadow. His spontaneous temper and the extraordinary passion for drawing made him give up very soon the formal principles which Norblin had taught him. Orłowski replaced a certain charm and elegance of Norblin's drawing by temperament combined with inquisitive observation and honest expression. The artist gave up the current neoclassical principles, to bring into Polish art a new, refreshing look into the future. "Kościuszko's Soldiers Dance" is an excellent example of the verve of Orłowski's work and shows the formal values of his works mentioned above.

*Bibliography:* *Aleksander Orłowski* (1777–1832). *Katalog wystawy w Muzeum Narodowym w Warszawie, grudzień 1957–luty 1958* (*Aleksander Orłowski, 1777–1832. Catalogue of the Exhibition at the National Museum in Warsaw, December 1957–February 1958* – in Polish), item 58, p. 97

## Aleksander Orłowski

**207** [192] Battle of Racławice, 1798; India ink, washed, 30.3×49; National Museum in Cracow, Czartoryski Collection, inv. no R.r 1920

The events of the Kościuszko Insurrection must have greatly affected young Aleksander Orłowski. He returned to them in dozens of water colours and drawings throughout his artistic career. He drew portraits of Tadeusz Kościuszko himself and types of his soldiers, camp scenes, skirmishes and battles of the insurgent troops. Particularly in those very dynamic scenes, he could give full rein his spontaneity, sensitive observation and his extraordinary gift of drawing. In the "Battle of Racławice" he managed superbly to recreate the extraordinary, heroic atmosphere of Kościuszko's victorious battle.

*Bibliography: Aleksander Orłowski (1777–1832). Katalog wystawy w Muzeum Narodowym w Warszawie, grudzień 1957 – luty 1958 (Aleksander Orłowski, 1777–1832. Catalogue of the Exhibition at the National Museum in Warsaw, December 1957 – February 1958 – in Polish), item 66, p. 99*

## Jan Rustem (1762–1835)

**208** [XXXI] Maria Mirska, Adam Napoleon Mirski and Barbara Szumską, c. 1808; oil on canvas, 159×124.5; National Museum in Warsaw, inv. no 231803

This group portrait shows Maria Mirska as Terpsychore, Adam Napoleon Mirski as Amor and Barbara Szumska as Polyhymnia. The former two were children of Stanisław Wojciech Mirski and Stanisława Mirska, née Koszczyc, whereas Barbara Szumska was the daughter of Wawrzyniec Szumski and Ludwika Szumska, née Koszczyc. From the age of Adam Napoleon Mirski and the style of the painting, the authors of the catalogue *Portraits of Polish Personages* have dated the portrait at about 1808, correcting the earlier date of 1822. Among the preserved works by Rustem, this portrait is the most neoclassical in character. The composition and outline are governed by neoclassical discipline, whereas Mirska's figure and dress resemble the dancers from Herculaneum.

*Bibliography: Ryszkiewicz, Polish Group Portrait, pp. 222–223; Portraits of Polish Personages, item 133, p. 126*

## Antoni Brodowski (1784–1832)

**209** [XXIX] Portrait of the Artist's Brother, Karol Brodowski, 1815; oil on canvas, 59×44; National Museum in Warsaw, inv. no 180814

This portrait is one of the most typical and most beautiful works by Brodowski. In keeping with the principles of neoclassical painting, the artist emphasized the outline and correctly modelled the head. Despite the unattractive colour, it deserves attention, in view of the use of a unified gamut, quiet and harmonious. The personal attitude of the painter towards his model and the greater interest in the

colour of the painting cause the viewer to discern some note of romanticist atmosphere in the portrait.

*Bibliography: Ryszkiewicz, Polish Group Portrait, pp. 133–137*

## Antoni Brodowski

**210** [195] Saul's Anger with David, 1812–1819; oil on canvas, 265×317; National Museum in Warsaw, inv. no 150

Both in form and subject matter, this work is the best example in Polish painting of the implementation of the neoclassical doctrine of David's circle. Outline dominates here over colour, which is reduced to local tones. The sculpture-like modelled figures of the protagonists are petrified in the rigid, deliberately balanced composition. At the Warsaw Exhibition of 1819, Brodowski got a Gold Medal for this work.

*Bibliography: Malarstwo polskie od XVI do początku XX wieku. Katalog Galerii w Muzeum Narodowym w Warszawie (Polish Painting from the 16th to the Early 20th Century. The Catalogue of the Gallery of the National Museum in Warsaw – in Polish), Warsaw 1962, item 119*

## Antoni Brodowski

**211** [XXXIII] Portrait of Archbishop Szczepan Hołowczyc, 1828; oil on canvas, 128×104; signed "AB 1828"; National Museum in Poznań, inv. no Mp. 373

Brodowski achieved best the effect of monumentalism, so greatly sought by the artists of late neoclassicism, in the portrait of Archbishop Szczepan Hołowczyc. He achieved it as a result of the spatial isolation of the model, the ideally harmonized composition and the undoubted power to attract attention, contained in the realistically represented face and hands of the protagonist. Brodowski painted the portrait after Archbishop Szczepan Hołowczyc (1741–1823) had died. Apart from his office of archbishop of Warsaw, Hołowczyc was the Primate of the Kingdom of Poland and a fellow of the Warsaw Society of the Friends of Science.

*Bibliography: S. Kozakiewicz, Malarstwo polskie, oświecenie-klasycyzm-romantyzm (Polish Painting, Enlightenment-Neoclassicism-Romanticism – in Polish), Warsaw 1976, pp. 50–53*

## Antoni Blank (1785–1844)

**212** [194] Self-portrait with Wife and Two Daughters, 1825; oil on canvas, 206×147; National Museum in Warsaw, inv. no 126360

This group portrait shows the painter Antoni Blank, his wife, Amelia, née Pechwell, and their daughters, Aniela and Ludwika. This work is one of the most outstanding in the rich output of the artist. He frequently painted family portraits, undoubtedly under the influence of late German neoclassical painting where this subject was favoured. According to A. Ryszkiewicz, "From the Germans he took, among other things, the predilection to showing the domestic retreat, in an atmosphere of family prosperity and order". In terms of form, Blank's works are different from those of other Polish neoclassicists: they are more rigid, harder in modelling and more disciplined in colour, which when combined gives them a more austere character.

*Bibliography: Ryszkiewicz, Polish Group Portrait, pp. 137–139; Portraits of Polish Personages, item 10, pp. 30-31*

## Aleksander Kokular (1793–1846)

**213** [XXXII] Oedipus and Antigone; oil on canvas, 261×199; signed "ALEX: KOKULAR POL pinx. ROMAE MDCCCXXV"; National Museum in Warsaw, inv. no 157

Apart from Antoni Brodowski, Kokular was the most outstanding painter of mature neoclassicism in Poland. In "Oedipus and Antigone" he strictly implemented the ideals of neoclassical painting. He achieved here a harmonious compactness of figures treated as statues, while precise outline and correct proportions became the dominating means in a static composition. The canvas, painted for the competition on the theme of "Oedipus and Antigone", was sent by Kokular from Rome in 1825. The other competitors included A. Brodowski and A. Blank. At the 1828 exhibition Kokular's work was awarded the first prize.

*Bibliography: Sztuka warszawska od średniowiecza do połowy XX wieku. Katalog wystawy w Muzeum Narodowym w Warszawie (The Arts in Warsaw from the Middle Ages to the Middle of the 20th Century. Catalogue of the Exhibition at the National Museum in Warsaw – in Polish), Warsaw 1962, item 516, pp. 191–192*

# Sculpture

## André Le Brun (1737–1811)

**214** [198] Medallion with a bust of Stanislas Augustus Poniatowski, 1780; white marble, 70×55; National Museum in Warsaw, inv. no 191 542

André Le Burn, a French sculptor, came to Warsaw in 1768, at request of King Stanislas Augustus. The medallion was made in about 1780 for the Ballroom at the Royal Castle in Warsaw. Together with the allegorical statues of Justice and Peace (by J. Monaldi), it formed the overdoor above the main doorway. At the court of Stanislas Augustus Le Brun was the chief sculptor, producing, with collaboration of J. Monaldi and Franciszek Pinck, sculptures for the decoration of the Royal Castle, the Ujazdów Castle and Łazienki. Among the many compositions with mythological, historical, allegorical and religious themes, an important part in his creative work was taken by portrait sculpture. In the low-relief medallion with an image of the King, it is interesting to note the realistic treatment of the model's face.

*Bibliography: Król, Royal Castle in Warsaw, p. 134; Kaczmarzyk, Polish Sculpture, item 56, p. 33*

## André Le Brun

**215, 216** [196, 197] Busts of Jan Zamoyski and Jerzy Ossoliński from the series of famous Poles from the Knights' Hall at the Royal Castle in Warsaw

The clay models were made after 1770, and in 1782–1786 the moulder Johann Ehrenfried Dietrich cast them in bronze. The cycle consisted of 4 large and 18 small busts (5 by Monaldi and 17 by Le Brun). The artistic and ideological values of the series made it popular in Poland and numerous plaster-of-Paris casts were made. The cycle from the Knights' Hall was taken away to Russia in 1833, to return to Warsaw in 1921. It was salvaged in September 1939.

Bust of Jan Zamoyski:
bronze, 72 cm high; with the inscriptions: "IOHANN EHRENFRIED DIETRICH GOSS. MICH IN WARSCHAU 1782" and, on the base, "IOANNES: ZAMOYSKI+MDCV"; National Museum in Warsaw, inv. no 158 401

Bust of Jerzy Ossoliński:
bronze, 47 cm high; with the inscriptions: "Ossoliński" and, on the base, "GEO: OSSOLIŃSKI+MDCL"; National Museum in Warsaw, inv. no 131 697

*Bibliography: T. Mańkowski, Rzeźby portretowe w brązie na Zamku Królewskim w Warszawie (The Bronze Portrait Sculptures at the Royal Castle in Warsaw – in Polish), Warsaw, p. 125; Kaczmarzyk, Polish Sculpture, pp. 36–40*

## Jacoppo Monaldi (1730–1798)

**217** [199] Statue of Chronos, 1784–1786; white marble; globe with a mobile clock face, metal; scythe (refitted), 254 cm high, gilded bronze; National Museum in Warsaw, inv. no 156 113

The statue, intended for the Knights' Hall at the Royal Castle in Warsaw, was placed there in 1786. On the plinth there was the inscription S.A.R.F.F. ANNO MDCCLXXXVI. In September 1939 it was moved to the underground stores of the National Museum in Warsaw, and in 1940 was taken by the Germans to Wawel. It returned to the Museum in 1946.

The statue of Chronos was the most important motif of the Knights' Hall. It was set in the centre, on the wall facing the windows. Its counterpart between the windows was a statue of Fame, by Le Brun. These two monumental sculptures emphasized the ideological meaning of the interior, glorifying those who had rendered service to the national cause. The statue of a woman blowing a trumpet declared their glory to the world; Chronos, a personification of time, was an expressive symbol of the everlasting memory of the great accomplishments of famous Poles.

Bibliography: Król, *Royal Castle in Warsaw*, p. 123; Kaczmarzyk, *Polish Sculpture*, item 95, pp. 42–43

## Jan Regulski (c. 1760–1807)

**218** [200] Cameo with a bust of Tadeusz Kościuszko, c. 1794; 4.7×3.4; National Museum in Cracow, inv. no EW-IV-ZŁ-1607

Jan Regulski, sculptor and medallist, studied in Italy. When he returned to Poland in 1783 he began working for King Stanislas Augustus. He also made intaglios, cameos and small reliefs with images of the outstanding persons of his times. His art was particularly appreciated in that epoch of a return to antiquity. Regulski frequently stylized his models on ancient leaders and heroes. An example of such stylization is this small portrait of Tadeusz Kościuszko, in the pose of an ancient leader; with only the revolutionary symbols on the shield relating the representation to contemporary times.

Bibliography: *Historia sztuki polskiej* (*A History of Polish Art* – in Polish), vol. III, Cracow 1962, p. 77

## Antonio Canova (1757–1822)

**219** [201] Memorial statue of Henryk Lubomirski, 1787, marble, about 140 cm; Łańcut Museum, inv. no S 2232 MŁ

Canova was the most outstanding European sculptor of the turn of the 18th and 19th centuries and, apart from Thorvaldsen, exerted the greates influence on the development of neoclassical sculpture. He had only one Polish commission, a statue of Henryk Lubomirski, although King Stanislas Augustus tried to win his interest for a group representing Venus and Adonis. The statue in question was made at request of Duchess Elżbieta Lubomirska, née Czartoryska, wife of the Marshal. The artist represented Henryk Lubomirski as Amor standing, leaning on a bow. This iconographic type was, like other works by Canova, inspired by classical sculpture. In creating the famous statues of Venus, Three Graces, Perseus or the recumbent one of Paulina Borghese, Canova worked in an analogous way. The artist repeated the statue of Lubomirski, replacing the head of the model by one with ideal features and calling the new composition "Amor".

Bibliography: Lorentz, *On the Sculpture Acquisitions*, p. 289; Kossakowska-Szanajca, Majewska-Maszkowska, *Łańcut Castle*, pp. 111, 160, 212, 213, 393

## Bertel Thorvaldsen (1768–1844)

**220** [202] Memorial statue of Nicolaus Copernicus, 1830; bronze; situated against the background of Staszic Palace in Warsaw

The work of Thorvaldsen, a Danish sculptor, included some Polish commissions. For his Polish customers he executed a dozen or so sculptures, including the statues of Nicolaus Copernicus, Włodzimierz Potocki, Ganimedes and Prince Józef Poniatowski. Thorvaldsen signed the contract for the statue of Nicolaus Copernicus in 1820; he made drafts in 1822–1828. The model was brought to Warsaw in 1828 and was cast in bronze by A.J. Norblin and J. Gregoire (the latter finished the casting). It was unveiled in 1830. After the damage of 1944 the statue was reset on July 22, 1945. It was renovated in 1949, under the supervision of S. Jagmin, and unveiled again on July 22, 1949.

In the statue of Copernicus the artist solved the difficult sculptural problem of the monumental representation of a seated figure. He achieved the desired effect, primarily as a result of the use of a toga as the astronomer's dress, which provided the compact composition sought for by the sculptor. It is interesting to note the high artistic value of the realistically treated head of the scholar. Thorvaldsen managed in an excellent way to fit the memorial into the neoclassical architectural setting of the Staszic Palace in the background.

Bibliography: Lorentz, *On the Sculpture Acquisitions*, pp. 294–295

## Bertel Thorvaldsen

**221** [203] Memorial statue of Prince Józef Poniatowski, 1832; bronze; situated against the background of the palace of the Presidium of the Council of Ministers in Warsaw

Thorvaldsen signed the contract for the statue of Prince Józef Poniatowski in 1818, and added to it in 1818 and 1820. He made draft designs in 1822–1827. The model was brought to Warsaw in 1829. The statue was cast in bronze by J. Gregoire and finished in 1832. During the period following the Uprising of 1830 it was impossible to set it up in Warsaw. It was moved to Modlin in 1834 and later Homel, a residence of Paskewich. After the Soviet government had returned it in 1923, it was set up in front of the Saski (Saxon) Palace in Warsaw, where it was destroyed in 1944. A new cast was made from the original model in Copenhagen an subsequently brought to Warsaw as a gift from the city of Copenhagen. In 1952 the statue was set up in front of the Orangery at Łazienki and moved in 1965 to the courtyard of the Presidium of the Council of Ministers, whose neoclassical architecture provided a good setting for this work by Thorvaldsen. The statue of Poniatowski illustrates well the creative method of this sculptor; it consists in the reduction of a national hero to the classical pattern of an equestrian monument (in this case, that of Marcus Aurelius at the Roman Capitol). Prince Józef poses as a Roman leader, with only the features of his face treated realistically. The Warsaw monument is considered one of the best works by Thorvaldsen.

Bibliography: Lorentz, *On the Sculpture Acquisitions*, p. 294

## Bertel Thorvaldsen
**222** [204] Statue of Włodzimierz Potocki, 1820–1830; marble; Cracow, Wawel Cathedral, Chapel of the Holy Trinity

Włodzimierz Potocki, son of Szczęsny Potocki and Józefa Amalia, née Mniszech, died in 1812. His monument was the most outstanding sepulchral sculpture that Thorvaldsen made for Poland. Negotiations on the commission of the sculpture had continued since 1816, and Thorvaldsen signed the contract with Tekla Potocka, née Sanguszko, widow of Włodzimierz, in 1820. Eventually the statue was sculpted in 1830 and set up in the Cathedral in 1831. The conception of the work was directly derived from the ancient statue of Apollo Belvedere, of which Thorvaldsen's sculpture was a recreation. On the plinth of the monument there is a relief representing a winged genius of death, which was sculpted in 1829.

*Bibliography:* Lorentz, *On the Sculpture Acquisitions*, pp. 298–306

## Jakub Tatarkiewicz (1798–1854)
**223** [205] Maternal Love, c. 1828; marble, 60×64; Tatarkiewicz family, Warsaw

In the first quarter of the 19th century, in the representational arts, particularly in neoclassical sculpture, an ideal artistic work was one that did not copy Nature, but imitated it instead. This imitation was to be effected by the simplest means, bereft of any illusion. In order to implement this ideal, artists would study both Nature and antiquity. In his "Maternal Love" Tatarkiewicz drew upon ancient masterpieces; but there was in his work a good deal of warmth, the charm of gesture and delicacy, alien to ancient imagination. This gave the sculpture a specific impress of the epoch when the dignity of the antiquity combined with good-natured sentimentalism.

*Bibliography:* W. Tatarkiewicz, *Rzeźbiarz polskiego klasycyzmu* (*The Sculptor of Polish Neoclassicism*), (in:) *O sztuce polskiej XVII i XVIII wieku* (*On the Polish Art of the 18th and 19th Centuries* – in Polish), Warsaw 1966, pp. 484–485

## Jakub Tatarkiewicz
**224** [206] Dying Psyche; marble, 68×106; signed "Tatarkiewicz f. 1830"; National Museum in Warsaw, inv. no 46

The model for this composition was executed in Rome before 1828, and the sculpture itself in 1830, when the artist had returned from Italy. In Rome Tatarkiewicz had worked under the influence of his great master, Thorvaldsen, strictly observing the classical patterns and canons. The sculpture "Dying Psyche" is the best work by Tatarkiewicz.

*Bibliography:* W. Tatarkiewicz, D. Kaczmarzyk, *Klasycyzm i romantyzm w rzeźbie polskiej* (*Neoclassicism and Romanticism in Polish Sculpture* – in Polish), "Sztuka i Krytyka", VII, 1956, nos 1–2, pp. 57–59; W. Tatarkiewicz, *Rzeźbiarz polskiego klasycyzmu* (*The Sculptor of Polish Neoclassicism*), (in:) *O sztuce polskiej XVII i XVIII*

*wieku* (*On the Polish Art of the 17th and 18th Centuries* – in Polish), Warsaw 1966, p. 481

## Ludwik Kaufmann (1801–1855)
**225** [207] Natolin, park, the statue of Natalia Sanguszko, née Potocka, 1836; grey sandstone, with the inscription on the wall of the tomb: "Alexander hrabia Potocki pamięci jedyney córki Natalji xiężnej Sanguszkowey zgasłey w kwiecie wieku 1830 roku ten pomnik poświęcił" (Alexander Count Potocki has dedicated this monument to the memory of his only daughter Natalia, Duchess Sanguszko, who died in her prime in 1830)

The architectural setting of the memorial statue of Natalia Sanguszko, née Potocka, is provided by a semi-circular niche contained on either side by screening walls. In this niche, on a double foundation and a plinth, there is a sarcophagus with a half-recumbent figure of Natalia. The sarcophagus was patterned on the classical one of Scipio; the statue itself was indirectly modelled on Etruscan sarcophagi and directly on some works by Antonio Canova, particularly the sculptures representing Paulina Borghese and Dirce. In 1818–1828 Kaufmann studied under the supervision of A. Canova; therefore his relationship with the works of his master seems self-evident.

*Bibliography:* Lorentz, *Natolin*, pp. 260–261

## Ludwik Kaufmann
**226** [208, 209] Warsaw, 15 Miodowa Street, Pac's palace, relief on the frieze of the gate, 1826

The subject of the frieze adorning the gate was a scene from the history of ancient Rome, representing the declaration by Consul Titus Quintus Flaminius, at the Corinthian games, of freedom for the Greek towns. In the centre the Consul is shown surrounded by his soldiers; on the left, two chariots stopping and, on the right, civilians and soldiers can be seen. The choice of the subject of a declaration of freedom was a distinct allusion to the political situation in the Kingdom of Poland. The saturation of subject matter drawn from the history of the ancient world by contemporary ideas was one of the essential features of neoclassical art. The form of the frieze, the closest among munumental Warsaw sculptures to the ancient prototypes, is also in accord with the subject matter.

*Bibliography:* A. Bartczakowa, *Pałac Paca* (*Pac's Palace* – in Polish), Warsaw 1973, pp. 68–69

## Paweł Maliński (1790–1853)
**227** [211] Workers Building a Road, model for the Monument of Labour, relief, plaster-of-Paris, 86×68; National Museum in Warsaw, inv. no 158314/4

In 1825, at the initiative of Stanisław Staszic, a memorial was set up on the present Grochowska Street in Warsaw to commemorate the construction of the Brześć road. It was in the form of an obelisk, on which were set nine reliefs representing the work on the construction of the road and panoramas of three towns: Warsaw, Siedlce and Brześć. Paweł Maliński had prepared plaster-of-Paris models in 1823, and they were cast in iron in 1825: one for the monument in Warsaw, the other for that at Terespol. The series of reliefs for the Monument of Labour was important both for Maliński's work and the development of Polish sculpture in the 19th century. The artist introduced here realistic motifs related to the everyday labour of the workers; the latter appearing for the first time in Polish art as an autonomous theme.

Bibliography: D. Kaczmarzyk, *Realistyczne rzeźby Pawła Malińskiego na Pomniku Pracy* (*The Realistic Sculptures by Paweł Maliński on the Monument of Labour* – in Polish), "Rocznik MNW", II, 1956, pp. 381–410; Kaczmarzyk, *Polish Sculpture*, item 369, p. 106

## Paweł Maliński

**228** [210] Figures of old men, detail of the frieze on the façade of the Grand Theatre in Warsaw, 1830; stucco in relief, 50×78; Historical Museum of Warsaw, inv. no 2176

The theme of the frieze adorning the façade of the theatre was a scene from Greek mythology representing the return of Oedipus and the common people from the Olympic Games. Only two fragments have survived from this relief, which was very badly damaged in 1939. As in his other works related to architecture (e.g. in the tympanum of the Kazimierzowski Palace or the fieze in the salon of Blue palace), so here Maliński strictly observed the classical patterns. He tended to emphasize the neoclassical forms of monumental edifices by sculpted compositions in the same style. In his other works, particularly in portraits and religious sculptures, he revealed his ties with the tradition of baroque sculpture, and in his last work some preromanticist forms could be detected.

Bibliography: W. Tatarkiewicz, D. Kaczmarzyk, *Klasycyzm i romantyzm w rzeźbie polskiej* (*Neoclassicism and Romanticism in Polish Sculpture* – in Polish), "Sztuka i Krytyka", VII, 1956, nos 1–2, pp. 48–50; *Dary i nabytki. Katalog Muzeum Historycznego m.st. Warszawy* (*Gifts and Purchases. A Catalogue of the Historical Museum of Warsaw* – in Polish), Warsaw 1970, item 128

# Artistic Handicrafts

## Unknown author

**229** [XII] Coronation sword of King Stanislas Augustus, 1764; oxidized steel pommel, gilded inscriptions; gilded and enamelled silver hilt; silk-covered wooden sheath, 91.3×15.5; on one side of the blade can be found the emblem of the Commonwealth, the Ciołek coat of arms (Stanislas Augustus') and the inscription "Stanislaus Augustus Rex Dedit ANNO 1764", on the other side there is the same inscription and the initials SAR (Stanislaus Augustus Rex) with a crown; National Museum in Warsaw, inv. no SZM 6752

The sword was specially made on the occasion of the coronation of King Stanislas Augustus. It was one of the earliest examples of introducing a neoclassical set of motifs into works of decorative crafts. Research has so far failed to identify the author of this outstanding work of art. It is presumed that the sword was made by a Warsaw goldsmith carrying out the King's orders. The sword, and other regalia, can be seen in the well-known portrait of King Stanislas Augustus in coronation dress, painted by Marcello Bacciarelli in 1768–1771.

Bibliography: *The Catalogue of the Exhibition "Polonia: arte e cultura"*, item 146, p. 155

## Philippe Caffieri the Younger (1714–1774)

**230** [212] Candelabrum from the Ballroom at the Royal Castle in Warsaw, 1766–1768; gilded bronze, 93×65×44; signed "fait par Caffiery en 1766"; National Museum in Warsaw, inv. no MŁ 529

Philippe Caffieri the Younger was one of the most outstanding French bronze-founders in the second half of

the 18th century. For Stanislas Augustus he made, among other things, six candelabra for the decoration of the Ballroom. These candelabra were among the earliest neoclassical examples in artistic handicrafts in Europe. Their composition was derived from the ancient tripod, whereas the decorative motifs, such as meander, garlands, cornucopias etc., were drawn from the classical repertory.

Bibliography: Iskierski, *Bronze Works*, item 1, p. 7

## Jean Louis Prieur (18th century)

**231** [214] Candelabrum from the Throne Room at the Royal Castle in Warsaw, 1766; gilded bronze, 62×36×36; National Museum in Warsaw, inv. no MŁ 531

The two candelabra which were designed in 1766 for the King's Bedchamber can be seen in a drawing made by Victor Louis the same year. The idea of the candelabra was conceived of by Prieur, whose candelabrum design has survived in the royal archives. They were made in Paris and sent to Warsaw in 1777. D. Merlini used them to furnish the Throne Room, which he was decorating in 1781–1786. Apart from the candelabra from the Ballroom, they were among the best of French bronze works which were used to furnish the Stanislas Augustus interiors at the Royal Castle. The candelabra were composed from typically neoclassical decorative motifs: eagles, ram's heads and garlands.

Bibliography: Iskierski *Bronze Works*, item 7, p. 8; *Catalogue of Drawings*, part 1, *Varsaviana*, item 306, p. 90 and item 333, p. 95

## Jan Chrystian Kamsetzer

**232** [213] Sconces from the Knights' Hall at the Royal Castle in Warsaw, 1786; gilded bronze, 62×45×26; National Museum in Warsaw, inv. no MŁ 847

Kamsetzer designed the sconces as part of his work with Merlini in the elaboration of the decoration and furnishings for the Knights' Hall. 14 works made in Dresden to Kamsetzer's design. 3 pieces have been salvaged from this set, now providing the pattern for the reconstruction of the lost eleven. Kamsetzer's sconces were distinguished by their highly individual elaboration, whereas their form of laurels was strictly related to the decorative motifs in the interior, devoted to the glory of eminent Poles, where the motifs of laurels was fully justified.

*Bibliography: Iskierski, Bronze Works, item 4, p. 8; Catalogue of Drawings, part 1, Varsaviana, items 492 and 493, p. 116*

## Jan Jerzy Bandau (d. before 1817)

**233** [215] Soup tureen with base, 1785–1787; silver, gilded parts, height 51.5 cm, tureen diameter 29, base diameter 52.5; signed "IGB" in an oval, "12"; on the base the engraved Wczele coat of arms; National Museum in Warsaw, inv. no SZM 5496

Jan Jerzy Bandau came to Warsaw from Hungary before 1768. He was one of the most eminent Polish goldsmiths in the second part of the 18th century and the early 19th century. The soup tureen in the collections of the National Museum in Warsaw is an example of neoclassical goldsmith's work in Warsaw. This took shape under the influence of French neoclassicism, drawing upon its decorative motifs, which were combined with naturalistic ones, such as the boar's legs which support the tureen or the snail on the top of its cover. The tureen used to belong to Władysław Roch Gurowski (1717–1790), Grand Marshal of the Crown, whose cort of arms, Wczele, was engraved on the base of the vessel.

*Bibliography: The Catalogue of the Exhibition "Polonia: arte e cultura", item 140, p. 151*

## Teodor Pawłowicz (working 1784–1794)

**234** [217] Champagne cooler, 1789; silver, height 19.5, diameter 18; signed "TP" in a double oval, a small eagle in an oval, "12" in an oval and a mermaid with the date "1789", engraved coats of arms Leliwa and Korczak; National Museum in Warsaw, inv. no 1977

Apart from J.J. Bandau and J. Skalski, Teodor Pawłowicz was the most outstanding goldsmith working in Warsaw in the last years of the 18th century. His works were characterized by their simple, neoclassical form and restrained use of decorative motifs, mainly from the repertory of neoclassical ornamentation.

*Bibliography: The Catalogue of the Exhibition "Polonia: arte e cultura", item 138, p. 151*

## Józef Skalski (working 1790–1820)

**235** [216] Wine jug, c. 1800; silver, gilded inside, height 33, diameter 13.9; signed "I.S" in a rectangle, "12"; National Museum in Warsaw, inv. no SZM 5455

Works by Józef Skalski were representative of the period of

mature neoclassicism. They were characterized by geometrized forms and conspicuous restraint in using decorative elements. The artistic values of those works were constituted above all by the balanced proportions of the particular parts.

*Bibliography: The Catalogue of the Exhibition "Polonia: arte e cultura", item 139, p. 151*

**236** [XX] Vase, produced by the King's manufactory at Belweder, 1770–1780; faience, height 44.5, diameter 24; National Museum in Warsaw, inv. no 52C 1293/1

The King's manufactory of pottery called Belweder began production in 1770, directly sponsored by King Stanislas Augustus. The Belweder pottery was patterned on Far Eastern ceramics. The greatest popularity was gained by decorative sets, as a rule of three vases, with decoration of the Far Eastern, most often Chinese, type painted in rich, vivid colours. The vase shown here repeats the Far Eastern pattern in shape, whereas distinctly neoclassical moderation and order can be felt in the decoration.

*Bibliography: T. Mańkowski, Królewska fabryka farfurowa w Belwederze (The King's Factory of Pottery at Belweder – in Polish), "Sztuki Piękne", 1932, no 3, pp. 73–90*

**237** [XVIII] Set of three vases, Warsaw, produced by Karol Wolff's manufactory, 1780–c. 1794; faience, height of the larger vase 42, height of the smaller ones 37; National Museum in Warsaw, inv. nos 128987, 128988, 128757

The pottery manufactory founded by Karol Wolff at Bielin in Warsaw was in production in 1779–1800. Wolff's pottery, like that from the Belweder manufactory, was derived from Chinese ceramics. A characteristic feature of these vases was gilded flower decoration against a chocolate brown background. Sets of such vases, when placed on mantlepieces or console-tables, were fairly characteristic element of Polish neoclassical interior decoration.

*Bibliography: Sztuka zdobnicza, dary i nabytki 1945–1964. Katalog (Decorative Arts, Gifts and Purchases 1945–1964. Catalogue – in Polish), National Museum in Warsaw, Warsaw 1964, item 478, p. 113*

**238** [XIX] Soup tureen, Korzec, 1790–1796, porcelain, 24×23×19; National Museum in Warsaw, inv. no 130196

The manufactory founded by Józef Klemens Czartoryski at Korzec was the first manufactory in Poland to produce porcelain. The earliest porcelain objects were made in 1790, and the manufactory was closed down in 1832. In the first years it took its patterns from renowned manufactories, mainly at Meissen and in Vienna. In painted decoration, however, very individually treated flower motifs – roses, pansies, bluebottles, forget-me-nots etc. – were introduced. The shapes of the Korzec products, a typical example of which is the tureen in the collections of the National Museum in Warsaw, were still strongly rooted in the baroque tradition.

*Bibliography: Ryszard Stanisław Ryszard, Porcelana od baroku do* empiru (*Porcelain from the Baroque to the Empire Style* – in Polish), Warsaw 1964, pp. 90–97

**239** [218] Cup with a view of the castle ruins at Łobzów, Baranówka, c. 1820; porcelain, cup height 11.5, saucer diameter 15.4; National Museum in Warsaw, inv. no 76621

The manufactory at Baranówka was founded in 1804 and produced throughout the 19th century. Despite its strong ties, particularly initially, with the manufactory at Korzec, the Baranówka products were characterized by definitely neoclassical form. They were unique with their painted miniature landscape and architectural views, in distinctly documentarily exact representation. In this they were different from the Korzec products with their more freely selected landscape motifs. This new approach to architectural views was a reflection of the broad interest in antiquarianism. On the one hand, outstanding monuments of Polish architecture, on the other, classical architectural themes were shown. For this purpose the manufactory drew upon graphic publications, above all, in the case of Polish architecture, upon Z. Vogel's album of views. For instance, the cup with a view of the castle at Łobzów was decorated on the basic of an etching by J.Z. Frey after Z. Vogel. Patterns were also provided by Domenico Pronti's album with views of Rome.

*Bibliography:* S. Gebethner, H. Chojnacka, *Krajobraz z architekturą na ceramice polskiej* (*The Architectural Landscape on Polish Ceramics*), (in:) *Treści dzieła sztuki* (*The Subject Matter of Works of Art* – in Polish), Warsaw 1969, pp. 251–276

**240** [220] Malmsey bottle, Urzecze, c. 1785; cut glass, height 20; National Museum in Warsaw, inv. no 19454

The bottle is adorned with the Odrowąż coat of arms of Michał Straszewicz, Upita Castellan, and the Murdelio coat of arms of Maria Straszewicz, née Oskierko. The highest prosperity of the Urzecze manufactory came in the middle of the 18th century when its products became an important part of the furniture of baroque interiors (mirrors, chandeliers). A change in taste, followed by a change in style, brought about in the eighties of the 18th century a simplification in forms and the introduction of neoclassical ornamentation in glassware. Patterns, as in the case of the malmsey bottle with the Odrowąż and Murdelio coats of arms, were drawn from English glassware.

*Bibliography:* *Polskie szkło do połowy 19 wieku* (*Polish Glassware until the Middle of the 19th Century* – in Polish), Wrocław 1974, p. 139

**241** [219] Tankard and wine glass, Urzecze, c. 1810; cut glass, tankard height 17, wine glass height 12; National Museum in Warsaw, inv. nos 30034 and 19791

The tankard is adorned by the initials "DXR" of Duke Dominik Radziwiłł. These objects are representative of the late neoclassical products of the Urzecze manufactory. Characteristic features of this stage of the development of glassware were the strongly geometrized shapes and the so-called diamond cut. This cut, which consisted in carving out in the walls a compact system of diamond-shaped prisms, was then popular in all the centres of European glassware production.

*Bibliography:* *Polskie szkło do połowy 19 wieku* (*Polish Glassware until the Middle of the 19th Century* – in Polish), Wrocław 1974, p. 139

**242** [221] Console-table from the Throne Room at the Royal Castle in Warsaw, c. 1780; gilded wood, mosaic table-top, 85×160×63; National Museum in Warsaw, inv. no MŁ 909

Two console-tables from the Throne Room are among the most valuable pieces of furniture from the Stanislas Augustus interiors of the Royal Castle in Warsaw. It is particularly interesting to note the mosaic panels of these console-tables. The multi-coloured mosaic was probably the work of an Italian, Pompeo, Savini. Scenes with representations of doves and ducks and ornamental motifs were based, quite strictly, on classical prototypes. The borders of the tables contain the motif of meander, characteristic of the early stage of neoclassicism.

*Bibliography:* M. Kwiatkowska, *Hebanowa konsola z Zamku Królewskiego w Warszawie i zagadnienia stylu "à la grecque"* (*The Ebony Console-Table from the Royal Castle and the Problems of the Style "à la grecque"* – in Polish), BAH, 1969, no 1, p. 87

**243** [XV] Table, France, 1777–1780; mahogany, bronze, Sèvres porcelain panels, 84×82×82; signed (on the porcelain) "Dodin 1777" and (on the wood) "Carlin"; National Museum in Warsaw, inv. no SZMb 1962

The table, as Pierre Verlet has recently determined, was bought in Sèvres in 1780 by the Duke d'Artois and as early as 1782 it was in Warsaw. King Stanislas Augustus intended it for the Closet of European Monarchs, or Conference Closet, at the Royal Castle in Warsaw, furnished in 1783–1784. The central scene, referring to a painting of 1772 by J. Raoux, was the work of Ch.-N. Dodin, the table itself that of M. Carlin. The central colour scene and six other scenes painted *en grisaille* represent episodes from the life of Telemachus, the protagonist of the well-known novel *Les Aventures de Télémaque* by François de Salignac de Mothe-Fénelon. The subject matter of this work includes, for example, the presentation of an ideal form of government, with its essential principles of avoiding wars, being supported by a strong gentry stratum and providing conditions for development in commerce and agriculture. The ideas contained in the scenes adorning the table must have greatly impressed the King, for he had this table set in a room dedicated to European monarchs.

*Bibliography:* P. Verlet, *Objects prestigieux retrouvés*, "Revue de l'art", no 314, 1976, pp. 64–66; A. Rottermund, *Stolik z Gabinetu Monarchów Europejskich* (*The Table from the Closet of European Monarchs*), (in:) *Ars Auro Prior* (in Polish), Warsaw 1981, pp. 567–574

**244** [222] Chair, Kolbuszowa, c. 1790, walnut, leather upholstery (new), 87×42×38.5; National Museum in Warsaw, inv. no MŁ 482

Kolbuszowa, a small town in the area of Rzeszów, was one of the most important centres of Polish furniture-making in the 18th century. The furniture from Kolbuszowa and other centres nearby was characterized by veneered surfaces, mainly from walnut, less frequently from yew and a kind of birch-wood, and by rich inlaid work mostly from ash, sycamore, cherry-tree, pear-tree, plum-tree, and black oak. Geometrical and vegetal motifs were most frequent. Patterns from West European furniture were used, but adapted to the native traditions. An example of this can be a set of chairs made under the influence of English patterns from the end of the 18th century, with geometrized form, motifs of meander and garlands, characteristic of products dating from that period.

*Bibliography:* Maszkowska, *History of Polish Furniture-Making*, pp. 14–19, 87

**245** [223] Armchair, Polish make, end of the 18th century; oak, 88×123×47.5; National Museum in Warsaw, Nieborów Branch, inv. no NB 627 MNW

The armchair was made at the request of Duchess Helena Radziwiłł, née Przeździecka, for the Diana's Temple in the park of Arkadia. It used to stand on a stone plinth in the central room of the Temple. Its shape was patterned after the Italian type of Renaissance armchairs; its back was adorned by a Roman eagle in relief.

*Bibliography:* Maszkowska, *History of Polish Furniture-Making*, p. 88

**246** [224] Escritoire, Polish make, c. 1780; oak, rosewood veneer, inlaid work, waxed and painted cloth, bronze, 106.5×76×53; National Museum in Warsaw, Nieborów Branch, inv. no NB 233 MNW

A lady's escritoire, composed of a table and a case-like top, called a bonheur-du-jour, was a characteristic piece of French furniture in the epoch of Louis XVI. This type spread to Poland; we know of pieces of furniture produced by Polish cabinet-makers. A feature which made them distinct from West European furniture was the covering of large surfaces by waxed cloth on which symmetrically composed flower decoration would be painted.

*Bibliography:* Maszkowska, *History of Polish Furniture-Making*, p. 91

**247** [225] Chest of drawers, Warsaw make, c. 1780; oak, rosewood veneer, inlaid work, waxed and painted cloth, bronze, 90×118×53; National Museum in Warsaw, Łazienki Branch, inv. MŁ 148

In her work on the Polish furniture of the Age of Enlightenment, Maszkowska has attributed the chest to the royal workshops, working for Stanislas Augustus. This furniture was characterized by a simple case form. It was mostly decorated by cut-out and applied geometrical openwork ornamentation and by flower decoration painted on cloth. Bronze fittings with commonplace neoclassical motifs formed major complements of the whole.

*Bibliography:* Maszkowska, *History of Polish Furniture-Making*, p. 92; item 77

The catalogue was prepared in 1974 by Andrzej Rottermund

# List of illustrations

Fleming, from 1771, drawing by an unknown author, last quarter of the 18th century; Cabinet of Drawings, Warsaw Univ. Lib. [cat. 41]

6. Warsaw, villa of Izabela Lubomirska at Mokotów, E. Szreger, 1772–74. J. Frey's etching after a drawing by Z. Vogel, 1806 [cat. 42]

7. Rogalin, garden elevation of the palace of the Raczyński family, unknown architect, 1768–73 [cat. 40]

8. Warsaw, Tepper's house, front elevation, E. Szreger, 1774, lithograph by L. Schmidtner [cat. 43]

9. Warsaw, Royal Castle, Old Reception Chamber, 1774–77, D. Merlini [cat. 45]

10. Warsaw, Royal Castle, Ballroom, D. Merlini with collaboration of J. Ch. Kamsetzer, 1777–81 [cat. 47]

11. Royal Castle, Ballroom, recessed doorway, D. Merlini, J. Monaldi, A. Le Brun [cat. 49]

12. Royal Castle, Ballroom, "Doors with banners", V. Louis, D. Merlini, 1766 and 1777–1781 [cat. 48]

13. Warsaw, Łazienki, Myślewice palace, front elevation, D. Merlini, 1775–76 [cat. 50]

14. Myślewice palace, Dining Chamber, paintings by J.B. Plersch, 1778 [cat. 51]

15. Warsaw-Wilanów, Guardhouse, S.B. Zug, 1775–76 [cat. 52]

16. Warsaw-Wilanów, Bath-house of Izabela Lubomirska, interior of the Bedchamber, S.B. Zug, 1775–76 [cat. 53]

17. Jabłonna, palace, garden elevation, D. Merlini, 1775–79 [cat. 55]

18. Jabłonna, palace, front elevation, D. Merlini, 1775–79 [cat. 55]

19. Jabłonna, palace, from the front. Drawing by F. Smuglewicz, c. 1784; Cabinet of Drawings, Warsaw Univ. Lib. [cat. 54]

20. Warsaw, Skalski's house, E. Szreger, 1775–80 [cat. 56]

21. Warsaw, garden of K. Poniatowski at Książęce, S.B. Zug, 1776–79. Water colour by Z. Vogel, lost [cat. 59]

22. Samotwór, palace, front elevation, K.G. Langhans, 1776–81 [cat. 60]

23. Siedlce, palace, front elevation, S. Zawadzki, 1776–82 [cat. 57]

24. Cracow, palace of the Potocki family, detail of the elevation [cat. 61]

25. Cracow, palace of the Potocki family, elevation from the Market Place, unknown architect, 1777–83 [cat. 61]

26. Warsaw, palace of Piotr Blank, staircase, Z.B. Zug, J.Ch. Kamsetzer, 1777 [cat. 63]

27. Warsaw, Evangelical-Augsburg Church, S.B. Zug, 1777–81 [cat. 62]

28. Evangelical-Augsburg Church, portico [cat. 62]

29. Warsaw, Primate's Palace, view from Miodowa Street, E. Szreger, 1777 [cat. 65]

30. Primate's Palace, view from Senatorska Street. Water colour by Z. Vogel, 1789; National Museum in Warsaw [cat. 64]

31. Primate's Palace, detail of the façade [cat. 65]

32. Primate's Palace, Ballroom, E. Szreger, J.Ch. Kamsetzer [cat. 66]

33. Pawłowice, Palace of the Mielżyński family, Columnar Chamber designed by J.Ch. Kamsetzer, stucco work by G. Amadio and G. Borghi, 1789–92 [cat. 68]

34. Palace of the Mielżyński family, detail of the stucco work [cat. 70]

35. Palace of the Mielżyński family, detail of the stucco work [cat. 70]

36. Palace of the Mielżyński family, detail of the stucco work [cat. 69]

37. Palace of the Mielżyński family, front elevation and right-hand outbuilding, K.G. Langhans, 1779–87 [cat. 67]

38. Palace of the Mielżyński family, detail of the stucco work [cat. 70]

39. Palace of the Mielżyński family, detail of the stucco work [cat. 70]

40. Palace of the Mielżyński family, detail of the stucco work [cat. 70]

41. Warsaw, Royal Castle, Library, D. Merlini with collaboration of J.Ch. Kamsetzer, medalions designed by J.B. Plersch and made by J. Monaldi, F. Pinck, G. Staggi, J.M. Graff, 1779–82 and after 1784 [cat. 72]

42. Warsaw, Royal Castle, Throne Room, D. Merlini, 1781–86 [cat. 71]

43. Throne Room, detail of the wall decoration [cat. 71]

44. Skierniewice, parish church, general view, E. Szreger, 1780 [cat. 75]

45. Kock, palace of A. Jabłonowska, S.B. Zug, c. 1780. Drawing by Z. Vogel, 1796; National Museum in Warsaw [cat. 73].

46. Skierniewice, parish church, interior [cat. 76]

47. Kock, parish church and town hall, S.B. Zug, 1779–82. Water colour by Z. Vogel, 1796; National Museum in Warsaw [cat. 74]

48. Warsaw-Natolin, palace, general view from the courtyard, S.B. Zug, 1780–1782, and S.K. Potocki and Ch.P. Aigner, 1806–1808 [cat. 78]

49. Warsaw-Natolin, palace, elevation from the courtyard [cat. 78]

50. Warsaw-Natolin, palace, elevation from the park, S.B. Zug, 1780–82 [cat. 77]

51. Warsaw-Natolin, view of the palace from the park [cat. 77]

52. Warsaw, palace at Królikarnia, D. Merlini, 1782–1786 [cat. 79]

53. Tulczyn, palace from the front, Lacroix, 1775–1782. Water colour by J. Richter, 1835; National Museum in Warsaw [cat. 80]

54. Walewice, palace of the Walewski family, front elevation, H. Szpilowski, 1783 [cat. 81]

55. Palace of the Walewski family, side view of the main body and an outbuilding [cat. 81]

56. Mała Wieś, palace of the Walicki family, front elevation, H. Szpilowski 1783–86 [cat. 82]

57. Palace of the Walicki family, detail of the portico [cat. 82]

168. Łowicz, town hall, detail of the griffin frieze [cat. 171]

169. Town hall, front elevation, B. Witkowski, 1825–28 [cat. 171]

170. Warsaw, Bath-house, front elevation, A. Kropiwnicki, 1831 [cat. 176]

171. Kaleń, granary and stables, general view, unknown architect, c. 1830 [cat. 175]

172. Radziejowice, manor, front elevation, unknown architect, c. 1830 [cat. 174]

173. Płock, toll-house on the Dobrzyń road, unknown architect, c. 1830 [cat. 173]

174. Cracow, Wawel Cathedral, chapel of the Potocki family, view of the dome, P. von Nobile, 1832–40 [cat. 177]

175. Warsaw, Saski Palace, view from the square (state before 1939), A. Idźkowski, W. Ritschel, 1838–42 [cat. 179]

176. Warsaw-Natolin, Doric Temple in the park, H. Marconi, 1834–38 [cat. 178]

177. F. Smuglewicz, *Ariadna and Bacchus*, 1776, copperplate; National Museum in Warsaw [cat. 180]

178. F. Smuglewicz, *Peasants by the Candle*, c. 1794, oil on canvas; National Museum in Warsaw [cat. 182]

179. F. Smuglewicz, *The Oath of Kościuszko in the Cracow Market Place*, 1797, oil on canvas; National Museum in Warsaw [cat. 183]

180. J.P. Norblin, *Aurora*, ceiling painting at the Diana's Temple at Arkadia, 1783–85, fresco [cat. 186]

181. J.P. Norblin, *Polish Marionettes*, c. 1780, oil on wood; National Museum in Warsaw [cat. 187]

182. J.P. Norblin, *Sarcophagus of August and Zofia Czartoryski Erected at the Wild Promenade of the Puławy Park*, 1800–1801, sepia; National Museum in Cracow [cat. 188]

183. K. Wojniakowski, *Portrait of Izabela Czartoryska, née Fleming*, 1796, oil on canvas; National Museum in Cracow [cat. 190]

184. K. Wojniakowski, *Party at Łazienki Park*(?), 1797, oil on canvas; National Museum in Warsaw [cat. 191]

185. M. Topolski, *Unknown Dignitary*, 1804, oil on canvas; National Museum in Warsaw [cat. 193]

186. J. Faworski, *Portrait of Jan Piędzicki*, 1790, oil on canvas; National Museum in Poznań [cat. 194]

187. M. Bacciarelli, *Helena Radziwiłł, née Przeździecka*, c. 1784, oil on canvas; Art Museum in Łódź [cat. 197]

188. M. Bacciarelli, *Casimir the Great Listening to Peasants' Pleas*, c. 1785–86, oil on canvas; National Museum in Warsaw [cat. 199]

189. J.B. Plersch, detail of wall painting from the Conference Closet at the Royal Castle in Warsaw, 1783–84, fresco, now at the Royal Castle in Warsaw [cat. 201]

190. J. Wall, *Fryderyk Skórzewski with the Plenipotentiary Maciej Grabowski*, 1787, oil on canvas; National Museum in Poznań [cat. 204]

191. A. Orłowski, *Kościuszko's Soldiers Dance at an Inn*, 1797, pencil, sepia; National Museum in Warsaw [cat. 206]

192. A. Orłowski, *Battle of Racławice*, 1798, India ink; National Museum in Cracow [cat. 207]

193. J. Gładysz, *Portrait of Stanisław Staszic*, c. 1820, oil on canvas; National Museum in Poznań [cat. 205]

194. A. Blank, *Self-portrait with Wife and Two Daughters*, 1825, oil on canvas; National Museum in Warsaw [cat. 212]

195. A. Brodowski, *Saul's Anger with David*, 1812–19, oil on canvas; National Museum in Warsaw [cat. 210]

196. A. Le Brun, *Bust of Jan Zamoyski*, cast, 1782–86, bronze; National Museum in Warsaw [cat. 215]

197. A. Le Brun, *Bust of Jerzy Ossoliński*, cast, 1782–86, bronze; National Museum in Warsaw [cat. 216]

198. A. Le Brun, medallion with bust of Stanislas Augustus Poniatowski, c. 1780, marble; National Museum in Warsaw [cat. 214]

199. J. Monaldi, statue of Chronos, 1784–86, marble and metals; National Museum in Warsaw [cat. 217]

200. J. Regulski, cameo with bust of Tadeusz Kościuszko, c. 1794; National Museum in Cracow [cat. 218]

201. A. Canova, statue of Henryk Lubomirski, 1787, marble; Łańcut Museum [cat. 219]

202. B. Thorvaldsen, statue of Nicolaus Copernicus, 1830, bronze, Warsaw [cat. 220]

203. B. Thorvaldsen, statue of Prince Józef Poniatowski, 1832, bronze, Warsaw [cat. 221]

204. B. Thorvaldsen, statue of Włodzimierz Potocki, 1820–30, marble, Cracow, Wawel Cathedral [cat. 222]

205. J. Tatarkiewicz, *Maternal Love*, c. 1828, marble; Tatarkiewicz family, Warsaw [cat. 223]

206. J. Tatarkiewicz, *Dying Psyche*, marble, 1830; National Museum in Cracow [cat. 224]

207. L. Kaufmann, statue of Natalia Sanguszko, née Potocka, 1836, sandstone, park at Natolin [cat. 225]

208. L. Kaufmann, detail of the relief on the frieze of the gate at Pac's palace in Warsaw [cat. 226]

209. L. Kaufmann, reliefs on the gate of Pac's palace in Warsaw, 1826 [cat. 226]

210. P. Maliński, figures of old men, detail of the frieze on the façade of the Grand Theatre in Warsaw, 1830, stucco in relief; National Museum in Warsaw [cat. 228]

211. P. Maliński, *Workers Building a Road*, model for the Monument of Labour, before 1825, relief in plaster-of-Paris; National Museum in Warsaw [cat. 227]

212. Candelabrum from the Ballroom at the Royal Castle in Warsaw, Ph. Caffieri the Younger, 1766–68, gilded bronze; National Museum in Warsaw [cat. 230]

213. Sconces from the Kinghts' Hall at the Royal Castle in Warsaw, J.Ch. Kamsetzer, 1786, gilded bronze; National Museum in Warsaw [cat. 232]

214. Candelabrum from the Throne Room at the Royal Castle in Warsaw, J.L. Prieur, 1766, gilded bronze; National Museum in Warsaw [cat. 231]

215. Soup tureen, J.J. Bandau, 1785–87, silver, gilded parts; National Museum in Warsaw [cat. 233]

216. Wine jug, J. Skalski, c. 1800, silver, gilded inside; National Museum in Warsaw [cat. 235]

217. Champagne cooler, T. Pawłowicz, 1789, silver;

National Museum in Warsaw [cat. 234]

Colour Plates

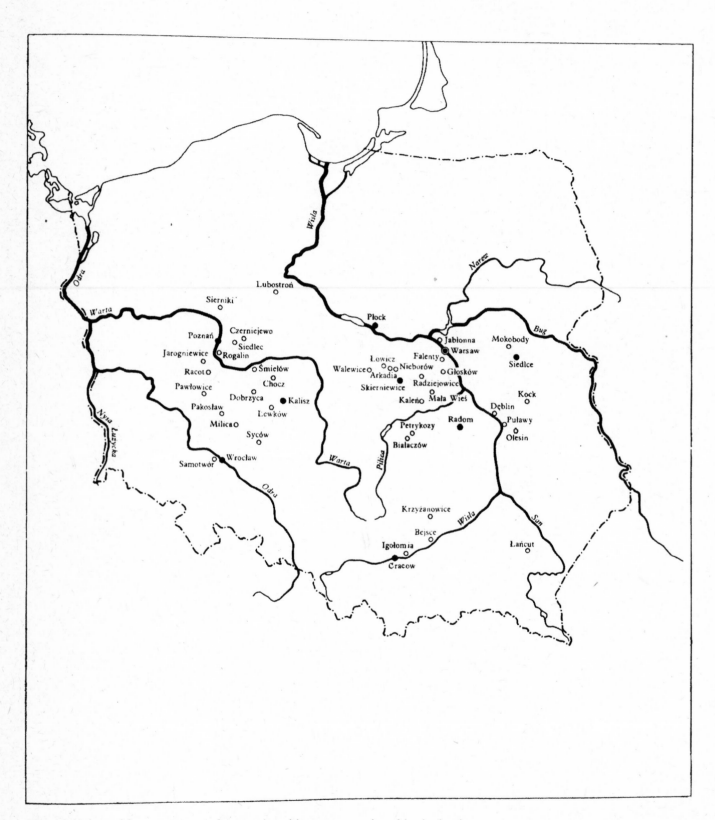

Map of places with monuments of art and architecture mentioned in the book

# Index of Localities and Monuments

(the names and monuments mentioned in the bibliography have not been included; numbers after semicolons refer to illustrations, numbers in italics are the numbers of illustrations)

Abbreviations of the names of districts:
Bg – Bydgoszcz, Bp – Biała Podlaska, K – Kalisz, Kl – Kielce, Kr – Kraków, Le – Leszno, Lb – Lublin, Ł – Łódź, P – Poznań, Pi – Piła, Pł – Płock, Pt – Piotrków, Ra – Radom, Rz – Rzeszów, Si – Siedlce, Sk – Skierniewice, Wa – Warszawa, Wł – Włocławek, Wr – Wrocław.

Aleksandria (Si) see Siedlce, Ogińska's garden called Aleksandria (water colour by Z. Vogel)
Arkadia (Sk) 12, 34, 280
– Aqueduct 258; *65*
– Diana's Temple 258; *67, 68*
– – J. P. Norblin, Aurora, ceiling painting 277; *180*
– Greek Arch 258; *66*
– Tomb of Illusions 44, 247
Athens (Greece) 12

Baalbek (Lebanon) 12, 27, 262
Babsk (Sk) 275
Baranówka (USSR), former porcelain manufactory
– cup with a view of the ruins at Łobzów (National Museum in Warsaw) 288; *218*
Bejsce (Kl), palace 43, 263, 272
– front elevation 270; *134*
– garden elevations 270; *135*
Białaczów (Pt), Małachowski's palace 14, 254, 255, 263, 272
– front elevation 269; *128*
Białystok 10, 40
Boremel (USSR) 36
Bronowice near Cracow 276
Brześć 47, 285, 286

Canton (China) 24
Chocim (USSR) 280
Chocz (K), palace of Mitred Prelates
– portrait chamber 266; *111, 112*
Copenhagen (Denmark) 284
Cracow (Kraków) 45, 49, 276, 277
  *churches*
    Wawel Cathedral
    – chapel of the Holy Trinity
    – – statue of Włodzimierz Potocki (B. Thorvaldsen)

48, 285; *204*
– chapel of the Potocki family 275; *174*
*palaces*
  palace of the Potocki family, general view 252; *24, 25*
  palace of the Wodzicki (Przebendowski) family, general view 264; *100*
– interior of the salon *101*
*public buildings*
  Jagiellonian (Cracow) University
  – Astronomical Observatory 29
  National Museum
  – K. Aleksandrowicz, Portrait of Duke Kazimierz Radziwiłł 279; *XXVIII*
  – M. Bacciarelli, Portrait of King Stanislas Augustus with an Hour-Glass 41
  – J.P. Norblin, Sarcophagus of August and Zofia Czartoryski at Puławy 278; *182*
  – A. Orłowski, Battle of Racławice 282; *192*
  – T. Regulski, cameo with bust of T. Kościuszko 284; *200*
  – F. Smuglewicz, Peasants by the Candle 276; *178*
  – J. Tatarkiewicz, Dying Psyche 285; *206*
  – K. Wojniakowski, Portrait of General Józef Kossakowski 278; *XXX*
  – K. Wojniakowski, Portrait of Izabela Czartoryska, née Fleming 278; *183*
Czerniejewo (P), palace of the Lipski family
– front elevation 264; *97*

Dęblin (Lb) 33
– Mniszech's palace and garden pavilion (water colour by Z. Vogel) 262; *91*
Dobrzyca (K), garden pavilions 268; *122, 123*
  Gorzeński's palace 43, 245
  – Ballroom 268; *125*
  front elevation 268; *124*
Dowspuda (USSR), Pac's palace 46
Dresden (GDR) 15, 16, 18, 33, 38, 40, 41, 287

Falenty (Wa), P. Fergusson Tepper's palace
– Ballroom, S.B. Zug's design 246; *43*
Fawory – see Warsaw-Fawory
Florence (Italy) 45

Głosków (Wa), P. Tepper's villa, S.B. Zug's design 241, 249; *16*
Gniezno 11
Grodzisk 10

299

town hall, W. Gucewicz's design 12, 29, 243; 30
Vilna Academy
– Astronomical Observatory 29

Walewice (Sk), palace of the Walewski family 14, 30, 272
– front elevation 257; *54*
– view towards right outbuilding *55*

Warsaw (Warszawa) 286
Cabinet of Drawings of Warsaw University Library 19, 21
– J.S. Becker, draft design of Theatre Room in the palace of the Sapieha family *see* Różana
– J. Fontana, draft design of the Marble Chamber at the Royal Castle *see* Warsaw, Royal Castle
– W. Gucewicz, draft design for reconstruction of Vilna Cathedral *see* Vilna, Cathedral
– W. Gucewicz, draft design of town hall in Vilna *see* Vilna, town hall
– J.Ch. Kamsetzer, draft design of the Bedchamber and Study at the Royal Castle *see* Warsaw, Royal Castle
– M. Knakfus, draft design of the parish teachers' college in Vilna, *see* Vilna, parish teachers' college
– J. Kubicki, draft design of the Ujazdów Church in Warsaw *see* Warsaw, churches
– J. Kubicki, draft design of the triumphal arch in the Castle Square in Warsaw 242; *22*
– V. Louis, draft design of the Dressing Room at the Royal Castle *see* Warsaw, Royal Castle
– V. Louis, draft design of the Ballroom at the Royal Castle *see* Warsaw, Royal Castle
– V. Louis, draft design of the Throne Room at the Royal Castle *see* Warsaw, Royal Castle
– V. Louis, draft design of the Bedchamber at the Royal Castle *see* Warsaw, Royal Castle
– D. Merlini, unrealized design of the edifice of the Academy of Sciences *see* Warsaw, palaces, Staszic Palace
– D. Merlini, so-called first design for reconstruction and expansion of the Royal Castle *see* Warsaw, Royal Castle
– D. Merlini, draft design of the Knights' Hall at the Royal Castle *see* Warsaw, Royal Castle
– W.H. Minter, draft design of the Main Warsaw Store *see* Warsaw, public buildings
– F. Smuglewicz, View of the Palace at Jabłonna *see* Jabłonna
– E. Szreger, draft design for reconstruction and new shaping of the Castle Square *see* Warsaw, Royal Castle
– Unknown author, garden of Izabela Czartoryska, née Fleming, at Powązki *see* Warsaw, parks and gardens
– Z. Vogel, View of the Sepulchral Chapel of Aleksandra Ogińska *see* Siedlce
– Z. Vogel, View of Part of the Garden at Siedlce *see* Siedlce
– S. Zawadzki and S.K. Potocki, design for reconstruc-

tion of the Piarist college in Warsaw *see* Warsaw, public buildings
– S.B. Zug, draft design of the inn at Raszyn *see* Raszyn
– S.B. Zug, draft design of the "White Eagle" Hotel *see* Warsaw, public buildings
– S.B. Zug, draft design of the edifice of National Theatre *see* Warsaw, public buildings
– S.B. Zug, draft design of W. Arndt's house *see* Warsaw, houses
– S.B. Zug, draft design of the palace of the Sanguszko family at Aleksandria *see* Warsaw, palaces
– S.B. Zug, draft design of the Ballroom at Tepper's palace at Falenty *see* Falenty
– S.B. Zug, draft design of the Ballroom at Tepper's "Four Winds" Palace *see* Warsaw, palaces
– S.B. Zug, draft design of an artificial ruin and a wooden mill in the garden at Solec *see* Warsaw, parks and gardens
– S.B. Zug, draft design of the villa at Głosków for Tepper the Elder *see* Głosków
*churches*
Bernardine Nuns 240
Carmelites 10, 247; *1*
Charles Boromeus' 47
Dominican Observants 272
Evangelical-Augsburg 12, 14, 43, 252, 253; *27*
– cross-section and ground plan 253
– portico *28*
Nuns of the Visitation 265
Piarist (former), Długa Street 47
St. Alexander's 44, 271; *148*
St. Andrew's 45, 263
St. Anne's (Bernardine Order) 13, 263, 272; *92, 93*
St. John's 241
Ujazdów – Temple of Divine Providence, J. Kubicki's design 12, 43, 245, 269; *36*
Historical Museum
– P. Maliński, figures of old men, detail of the frieze on the façade of the Grand Theatre in Warsaw 286; *210*
*houses*
Arndt's, S.B. Zug's design 244, 245; 33
Bentkowski's, 49 Nowy Świat Street 272; *153*
Hołowczyc's, 53 Nowy Świat Street 46, 272; *152*
40 Nowy Świat Street 274
Roeslers and Hurtig's, Krakowskie Przedmieście Street 28, 259; *69, 70*
Skalski's, 45 Krakowskie Przedmieście Street 251; *20*
Tepper's, E. Szreger's design (lithograph by L. Schmidtner) 28, 249; *8*
Łazienki 23, 24, 31, 39, 41, 257, 265, 278, 283
– Amphitheatre 12, 27, 262; *83, 84, 85*
– Ermitaż (Hermitage) 23
– monument to John III Sobieski 27
– Myślewice palace 17, 23, 24, 246
– – Dining Chamber 250; *14*
– – front elevation 250; *13*
– New Guardhouse 26, 265, 267; *119*

# Index of Names

306